Martin Klemm

Intraoperative Planning and Execution of Arbitrary Orthopedic Interventions Using Handheld Robotics and Augmented Reality

Karlsruhe Series on Intelligent Sensor-Actuator-Systems

Volume 20

ISAS | Karlsruhe Institute of Technology
Intelligent Sensor-Actuator-Systems Laboratory

Edited by Prof. Dr.-Ing. Uwe D. Hanebeck

Intraoperative Planning and Execution of Arbitrary Orthopedic Interventions Using Handheld Robotics and Augmented Reality

by
Martin Klemm

KIT Scientific Publishing

Dissertation, Karlsruher Institut für Technologie
KIT-Fakultät für Informatik

Tag der mündlichen Prüfung: 26. Januar 2018
Gutachter: Prof. Dr.-Ing. Uwe D. Hanebeck
Prof. Dr.-Ing. Harald Hoppe
Prof. Mag. Dr. Michael Nogler

Impressum

KIT Scientific Publishing

Karlsruher Institut für Technologie (KIT)
KIT Scientific Publishing
Straße am Forum 2
D-76131 Karlsruhe

KIT Scientific Publishing is a registered trademark
of Karlsruhe Institute of Technology.
Reprint using the book cover is not allowed.

www.ksp.kit.edu

Print on Demand 2018 – Gedruckt auf FSC-zertifiziertem Papier

ISSN 1867-3813
ISBN 978-3-7315-0800-7
DOI 10.5445/KSP/1000083234

Intraoperative Planning and Execution of Arbitrary Orthopedic Interventions Using Handheld Robotics and Augmented Reality

zur Erlangung des akademischen Grades eines

Doktors der Ingenieurwissenschaften

von der Fakultät für Informatik
des Karlsruher Instituts für Technologie (KIT)

genehmigte

Dissertation

von

Martin Klemm

aus Lörrach

Tag der mündlichen Prüfung:	26.01.2018
Erster Gutachter:	Prof. Dr.-Ing. Uwe D. Hanebeck
Zweiter Gutachter:	Prof. Dr.-Ing. Harald Hoppe
Dritter Gutachter:	Prof. Mag. Dr. Michael Nogler

Acknowledgments

This dissertation is the result of my research at the Laboratory for Computer-Assisted Medicine (CompAssMed) at Offenburg University, which was funded by Stryker IMT in Freiburg. For over four years I benefited from the support of many people, all of whom contributed to the success of my PhD.

First, I would like to thank my advisor Uwe D. Hanebeck from the Intelligent Sensor-Actuator-Systems Laboratory (ISAS) at the Karlsruhe Institute of Technology (KIT) for accepting me as a doctoral candidate and sharing his knowledge with me. Special thank goes to my co-advisor Harald Hoppe for giving me the opportunity to perform this research at the CompAssMed laboratory, for his guidance and his continuous support. Furthermore, I want to thank Michael Nogler for co-advising and sharing his medical knowledge with me.

I want to express my great gratitude to my working colleagues Fabian Seebacher, Simon Strzeletz und Simon Hazubski for the great programming support, the useful discussions and all the help I could count on when I was stuck.

I wish to thank José-Luis Moctezuma, Ingmar Wegner, Peter Zimmermann and all other staff of Stryker IMT in Freiburg that were supporting me with this research. I would also like to extend my thanks to David Putzer for advising me in medical questions.

My research stay in the department of Computer-Assisted Medical Interventions (CAMI) at the German Cancer Research Center (DKFZ) in Heidelberg was an unforgettable experience thanks to the collaboration with Alfred Franz and all members of the team.

Special thanks to Neus Planas Pàmies for proofreading this dissertation and the countless hours of supporting conversations.

Last but not least, I wish to thank my parents and my family for their support and encouragement throughout my studies.

Offenburg, April 2018 Martin Klemm

Zusammenfassung

Die Mehrheit aller orthopädischen Eingriffe wird heutzutage immer noch konventionell von Hand durchgeführt, obwohl computer-assistierte Systeme schon seit mindestens zwei Jahrzehnten verfügbar sind. Orthopädische Planungs- und Ausführungsanwendungen geben überwiegend einen festen Arbeitsablauf vor und sind auf spezifische Interventionen maßgeschneidert. Hierauf können einige Nachteile zurückgeführt werden, wie z. B. die hohen Anschaffungs- und Instandhaltungskosten oder die fehlende Möglichkeit, intraoperativ auf unvorhergesehene anatomische Gegebenheiten reagieren zu können. Diese Dissertation beschreibt eine generische, intraoperative und bildlose Planungs- und Ausführungsapplikation für beliebige orthopädische Interventionen unter der Verwendung eines handgehaltenen Roboters. Dieser Ansatz ermöglicht es, die zuvor angesprochenen Nachteile deutlich zu verbessern.

Um eine chirurgische CAD-Anwendung zu implementieren, wurden chirurgische Schritte analysiert und in technische Funktionen überführt. Neue Interaktions- und Visualisierungsparadigmen erlauben es, die Anwendung innerhalb des Operationssaales zu benutzen. Eine OpenIGTLink-Implementierung ermöglicht die Benutzung zusätzlicher Eingabegeräte und Simulationsumgebungen. Neben einem Monitor wird eine zusätzliche Visualisierung mittels Augmented-Reality-Durchsichtbrille angeboten. Diese erlaubt eine Visualisierung der Planung direkt am Knochen des Patienten. Hierfür wurde eine neuartige pixelweise Kalibrierung entwickelt, welche sich von bisherigen modellbasierten Kalibrierungen abhebt. Die Ausführung des intraoperativen Planes wird mit Hilfe eines in der Hand gehalten Fräsroboters mit drei Freiheitsgraden durchgeführt. Hierfür wurden angepasste Kontrollalgorithmen und Modi entwickelt. Mit Hilfe einer Methode basierend auf Lichtschnitten werden die austauschbaren Fräsköpfe des Roboters intraoperativ kalibriert.

Das Gesamtsystem erlaubt einen flexiblen Wechsel zwischen Planung und Ausführung während die Genauigkeit des Systems in der Größenordnung von stationären Robotern liegt. Aufgrund der generischen Arbeitsweise des vorgestellten Ansatzes, welches dem Vorgehen bei konventionellen Eingriffen ähnlicher ist als bisherige Systeme, kann ein Wechsel von konventioneller zu computer-assistierter Chirurgie vereinfacht werden. Obwohl diese Arbeit sich auf orthopädische Eingriffe konzentriert, können diese Ansätze auf die Gegebenheiten der Neuro-, Mund-, Kiefer- und Gesichtschirurgie angepasst werden.

Beitrag 1: OrthoCAD: Eine intraoperative CAD-Planungsanwendung für beliebige orthopädische Interventionen

Bei orthopädischen Interventionen kommt es oft vor, dass präoperative Planungen verworfen werden müssen, da die intraoperativ vorgefundenen anatomischen Gegebenheiten derart sind, dass die Planung nicht exakt umgesetzt werden kann. Darüber hinaus ist der Großteil der Planungs- und Ausführungsapplikationen im orthopädischen Bereich maßgeschneidert auf eine oder wenige Interventionen. Dies führt zu erhöhten Kosten und zusätzlicher Trainingszeit. Es besteht demnach der Wunsch nach einer flexiblen intraoperativen Planungsmöglichkeit, die nicht auf eine bestimmte Intervention beschränkt ist. Da orthopädische Interventionen aus einer Folge von wenigen elementaren Arbeitsschritten aufgebaut werden können, orientiert sich das Systemkonzept an einem CAD-System. Es können Primitive, bspw. Punkte, Linien oder Ebenen, intraoperativ direkt am Knochen des Patienten digitalisiert werden. Diese Primitive lassen sich anschließend zu komplexeren Objekten zusammensetzen. Punktwolken können digitalisiert werden, um somit beispielsweise den Knochen des Patienten abzutasten. Ein Bemaßungssystem erlaubt es, Objekte genau zu platzieren. Bereits digitalisierte Objekte können, wie bei CAD-Systemen gängig, nachträglich verschoben und rotiert werden. Objekte können relativ zu anderen platziert werden (bspw. eine Ebene senkrecht zu einer Achse). Der Chirurg bedient das Gesamtsystems mit Hilfe eines getrackten Zeigegerätes und eines Touchscreens. Die Planung wird sowohl auf dem Touchscreen als auch ortsgenau in einer Durchsichtbrille visualisiert.

Beitrag 2: Pixelweise kamerabasierte Kalibrierung einer optischen Durchsichtbrille

Bisherige Kalibrierungen von optischen Durchsichtbrillen basieren meist auf Punktkorrespondenzen, welche vom Benutzer aufgenommen werden. Da dieses Vorgehen nur eine geringe Anzahl an Korrespondenzen generiert, benutzen diese Kalibrierungen parameterbasierte Modelle. Diese weisen jedoch vor allem im Randbereich starke Fehler auf. Die entwickelte Kalibrierung ermöglicht es, jedes einzelne Pixel der Durchsichtbrille ohne Parametermodell individuell und vollautomatisch zu kalibrieren. Dabei kommen ein Monitor und präzis kalibrierte Kameras zum Einsatz. Darüber hinaus wird die Kalibrierung des Displays von der Kalibrierung der Augenposition getrennt. Der maximale Fehler der Displaykalibrierung liegt bei 0,04°, was einem Fehler von 0,33 mm in einer Distanz von 500 mm entspricht.

Beitrag 3: Erweiterbarkeit mittels OpenIGTLink

In der computer-assistierten Chirurgie ist die Auswahl verwendeter Eingabegeräte genauso groß, wie die Vielfalt an Eingriffen. Die Benutzung der Geräte hängt vom Chirurgen als auch von der Verfügbarkeit innerhalb der Klinik ab. OrthoCAD benötigt nur ein Zeigegerät und einen Touchscreen. In manchen Fällen ist es jedoch vorteilhaft, zusätzliche Eingabegeräte zu benutzen, zum Beispiel einen 3D-Scanner, welcher dabei hilft, größere Teile der Knochenoberfläche zu digitalisieren. Um in OrthoCAD beliebige Geräte benutzen zu können, wurde das Netzwerkprotokoll OpenIGTLink in das Toolkit MITK integriert, auf welchem OrthoCAD basiert. Eine Evaluation der Übertragungsraten und der Latenzen wurde durchgeführt. Die Ergebnisse zeigen, dass die Implementierung problemlos typische Anwendungsszenarien zulässt.

Beitrag 4: Eine intraoperative Kalibrierungsmethode für beliebige navigierte chirurgische Instrumente

In robotischen Anwendungen ist es essentiell die Position und die Größe des Endeffektors im Koordinatensystem des befestigten Trackers zu kennen. Beispielsweise lässt sich ein Fräskopf während einer Intervention austauschen bzw. seine Tiefe einstellen. Somit ist es wichtig, eine schnelle, einfache und intraoperative Kalibrierung bereitzustellen. Bisher werden kugelförmige Werkzeuge pivotiert und andere mittels individuell angepassten Vorrichtungen kalibriert. In der vorgestellten Arbeit wird das zu kalibrierende Instrument vor einer oder mehreren navigierten Kameras um seine eigene Achse gedreht, um somit die dreidimensionale Oberfläche mittels Lichtschnitten zu rekonstruieren. Hierbei partitioniert ein dreidimensionales Raster den Arbeitsbereich. Mit jedem zusätzlichen Bild werden mehr Elemente des Rasters als Hintergrund markiert. Am Ende bleiben nur noch die Elemente übrig, welche zum Instrument selbst gehören. Anschließend wird die Oberfläche generiert, an welche vereinfachte Geometrien (bspw. eine Kugel) angepasst werden, damit diese in der Planungs- und Ausführungssoftware zur Verfügung stehen. Die Genauigkeitsanalyse zeigt, dass dieses System für Fräsköpfe genauere Ergebnisse liefert als ein einfaches Pivotieren.

Beitrag 5: Kontrollalgorithmen für die Planungsausführung mittels in der Hand gehaltenem Fräsroboter

In orthopädischen Interventionen werden heutzutage verschieden Typen von Robotern eingesetzt. Stationäre Roboter, beispielsweise RIO (Stryker, USA) oder ROBODOC (Think Surgical, USA), verbessern die Genauigkeit, definieren allerdings einen neuen chirurgischen Ablauf. Im Gegensatz dazu lassen sich in der Hand gehaltene Roboter einfacher in bestehende Abläufe integrieren und stellen deswegen auch eine kostengünstigere Variante dar. Ihre eingeschränkte Bewegungsfreiheit wird durch die Geschicklichkeit des Chirurgen kompensiert. Der wissenschaftliche Beitrag liegt hier in der Entwicklung von Kontrollalgorithmen für einen in der Hand gehaltenen Fräsroboter mit drei Freiheitsgraden. Die Algorithmen stellen sicher, dass der Roboter prä- und intraoperativ definierte Begrenzungen nicht durchdringen kann. Ein ausweichender Modus sorgt dafür, dass der Roboter, so lange dies möglich ist, ausweicht, ohne die Geschwindigkeit zu drosseln. Dies ermöglicht es dem Chirurgen, den Plan präzise umzusetzen, ohne den Patienten dabei zu verletzen. Ein halbautomatischer Modus regelt aktiv die Position des Fräskopfes, um somit die notwendigen Bewegungen des Chirurgen zu minimieren. Die Algorithmen wurden an einem stationären Prototyp mit drei Freiheitsgraden getestet. Die Analyse zeigte dabei, dass die entwickelten Algorithmen Genauigkeiten erzielen, welche in der Größenordnung von stationären Robotern liegen (maximale Abweichung $\pm 0{,}8\,\mathrm{mm}$).

Abstract

Most orthopedic interventions are still performed in a conventional manual way, although computer-assisted systems have been available for at least two decades. Several possible reasons explaining this fact are identified, which are mainly attributed to dedicated workflows in orthopedic planning and execution applications. The focus of this dissertation is a generic, intraoperative and image-free planning and execution application for arbitrary orthopedic interventions using a novel handheld robotic device (HHRD) aiming to facilitate the transition from conventional to computer-assisted surgery.

Surgical steps are analyzed and transformed into technical functions in order to implement a surgical CAD application. New interaction and visualization paradigms enable the use of this application inside the OR. An OpenIGTLink implementation allows the usage of additional input devices and simulation environments. The surgeon can plan directly on the patient's bone by means of an augmented in-situ visualization based on optical see-through glasses (OSTG). A robot control system (RCS) is described, which allows the execution of the intraoperative plan with an HHRD. The RCS implements different control modi considering the fact that the surgeon holds the device. In order to calibrate the interchangeable tool tips of the HHRD as well as other surgical instruments, an intraoperative reconstruction and calibration method is presented.

Several planned and executed interventions show the effectiveness of OrthoCAD and the developed interaction and visualization approaches. The pixel-wise OSTG calibration works well and produces higher accuracy than previous works. The maximal deviations are less than 0.04°, which are 0.33 mm at a distance of 500 mm. Accuracy tests on hard-foam blocks with a self-developed table-top robot and the presented RCS show maximal deviations of ± 0.8 mm, which is comparable to accuracies of stationary robots. With the presented intraoperative calibration method, the center of instrument tips used for HHRD can be calibrated with an RMS deviation of 0.18 mm, which is more accurate than pivoting.

An intraoperative, generic and image-free planning and execution application, which is applicable to arbitrary orthopedic interventions, improves many disadvantages of existing applications that are based on dedicated workflows. Since the generic nature of the presented approach is closer to conventional orthopedic surgeries, the presented approach can simplify the transition from conventional to computer-assisted surgery. Although this environment is presented in the field of orthopedics, it can be adapted to neurological, oral and maxillofacial surgery.

Contents

CHAPTER
1

Introduction

Contents

1.1 Motivation

Despite extensive research and miscellaneous innovations in the field of orthopedic surgery, the basic surgical procedure is still the same as at the end of the last century. Since bones adapt themselves to the new situation, the surgical accuracy is less relevant. Many surgeons consider the outcomes of conventional techniques generally successful [1]. The basic procedure can be split into three phases:

1. The diagnosis and planning
2. The surgery
3. The evaluation and aftercare

In conventional orthopedic surgery, the diagnosis, the planning and the evaluation are based on X-ray images and the surgery is carried out without computer assistance. Since CT scans increase the radioactive exposure of the patient, they are only used in more complex scenarios (fractures, revisions, tumors). The surgeon transfers the X-ray-based plan onto the patient using conventional tools such as rulers for measurement and saws for resection.

Computer-assisted orthopedic surgery (CAOS) utilizes the advantages of computers to increase the accuracy and the reproducibility of interventions, which in turn should further improve the outcome. Computer assistance is given in all three phases of a surgical treatment. The planning is often based on computer tomography (CT) or magnetic resonance (MR) images, the surgery is performed using robots and special evaluation software allows comparing the actual outcome with the planned intervention.

Most CAOS applications are dedicated to one or few surgical interventions, which entails a predefined workflow. In case of a robotic execution, a detailed plan is required, which results in a preoperative planning based on CT or MRT images. Normally, the plan is visualized on a monitor close to the situs. The level of assistance during the surgery depends on the application and can be passive, semi-active or active.

Although such systems have been available for decades and promise increased accuracy and improved patient outcome, the majority of interventions is still performed in a conventional manual way without computer assistance [2]. There are several possible reasons why clinics and surgeons are critical in regard to such systems:

- The acquisition and maintenance of these systems entail considerable economic costs.
- Surgeons and nurses are required to carry out additional tasks not directly related to the medical intervention (robot setup, parameterization, technical details, etc.).
- The time consumption for trainings increases since surgeon and nurse perform a variety of different interventions whereas most applications are dedicated to one.
- Increased radioactive exposure due to additional CT that is required for a detailed plan.

- A predefined workflow restricts the surgeon in his reaction to unforeseen anatomical conditions.
- Missing possibility to adapt the plan after its confirmation could force the surgeon to abort the intervention.
- Surgeon is forced to continuously change his perspective between situs and monitor due to missing in-situ visualization of the plan.
- Long-term improvement in operative outcome compared to conventional approaches is not proven.

1.2 Goal

The improvement of these shortcomings is a key challenge for CAOS. The goal of this work is to create a CAOS environment representing a paradigm shift in the operative procedure. Instead of optimizing the environment to one specific intervention by dictating a predefined workflow, the presented environment allows the surgeon to plan arbitrary interventions using concepts known from computer-aided design (CAD) systems. Preoperative imaging becomes obsolete since the surgeon digitizes required objects directly in situ using a tracked pointing device. A touch screen allows the surgeon to assemble more complex objects from the digitized ones. The plan is visualized on the touch screen as well as superimposed on the situs using optical see-through glasses (OSTG).

Subsequently, the plan is carried out using a milling device or a novel handheld robotic device (HHRD) with three degrees of freedom (DoF). The former is already available in many operating rooms (OR) and the latter can be easily integrated since it is similar to a milling device. An HHRD combines the advantages of a robot with the flexibility of a handheld device and guarantees an accurate and safe intervention. Additionally, it is not constrained in motion and orientation as a stationary robot since it makes use of the dexterity of the surgeon. Surgeons should be easier to convince to use such a tool since they are already trained in using milling devices. These tools are also more cost effective and require less space in the OR than a stationary robot.

A robot control system (RCS) ensures a safe execution of the plan. In case of the HHRD, the system controls the end effector's position in such a way that it evades planned constraints as long as the kinematics allow it. When its maximal deflection is reached the device's power is turned off. Since a milling device has no joints, only its power is controlled.

The described surgical environment and procedure is more similar to conventional interventions than the classical robotic surgery. Therefore, this approach should help surgeons with the transition from conventional interventions to a computer-assisted one. Although this environment is presented in the field of orthopedics, it can be adapted to neurological, oral and maxillofacial surgery.

1.3 Challenges

The major challenges to achieve the previously described goals of an intraoperative and generic planning software for arbitrary orthopedic intervention using HHRDs are:

- Identification of the required functionality for a generic planning software by analyzing orthopedic interventions. Putzer et al. [3] analyzed orthopedic interventions and found out that all interventions can be assembled by a series of individual and distinct steps. These surgical steps include the creation and the execution of the plan. It has to be investigated if and in which way these surgical steps can be further broken down into technical steps.
- Development of new and intuitive interaction paradigms adapted to the surgical procedure, since those used in CAD applications (e.g. (3D) mouse) might not be applicable in the OR. This includes the digitization of objects using a navigated pointing device as well as the object interaction on a touch screen. The fact that the plan is not based on images further stresses the importance of an efficient interaction.

- Implementing an interface for additional input devices such as an ultrasound (US) probe or a 3D scanner since the digitization of larger parts of the patient's bone can be a time-consuming task. Such devices often run on an individual workstation, which requires a solution based on a network communication protocol.
- Offering just the right amount of information and functionality to the surgeon to prevent distraction by the multitude of objects and algorithms available in a generic planning environment. Thus, the information and functionality must be filtered according to the current state of the planning procedure.
- Development of an in-situ visualization allowing the surgeon to directly plan on the patient's bone. For an accurate overlay of plan and reality the OSTG need to be calibrated.
- Identification of an appropriate interface between planning and execution software. Orthopedic surgery environments including a robotic execution normally generate closed milling volumes based on a preoperative plan. Since the presented environment generates all data intraoperatively, the planning of closed milling volumes is impractical.
- Development of a robust RCS optimized for handheld surgical instruments such as a milling device or an HHRD. Compared to classical robotic control systems, the difference is that the user plays a major role since he holds and moves the device.
- Design of an autoclavable HHRD with dimensions comparable to standard milling devices. Additionally, a robust instrument tracking plays a major role in improving the accuracy of the final result.
- Development of a flexible intraoperative calibration technique for surgical instruments. Different tool tips can be intraoperatively inserted into a milling device as well as an HHRD. Additionally, the position of these tips can also be adjusted. Therefore, a calibration by the manufacturer is not feasible. The fact that the number of

possible tips and instrument combinations is too large to provide dedicated calibration jigs further emphasizes the importance of such a flexible intraoperative calibration technique.

1.4 Contribution and Outline

A background and review of literature of CAOS applications and components illustrates the contrast between the presented and previous works (see Chapter 2). From the described goals and challenges the following contributions are derived.

An intraoperative and generic planning application not based on pre- or intraoperative imaging and applicable to any orthopedic intervention is described in Chapter 3. CAD-concepts known from preoperative planning and commercial CAD-systems are brought into the operating room. As mentioned in the previous section, orthopedic interventions are assembled by a series of surgical steps. These surgical steps are transformed into technical functions. New and flexible interaction paradigms including touch and pointer interaction and other additional devices are required, since traditional input devices such as a computer mouse cannot be used inside the OR. Besides the touch screen visualization, an augmented in-situ view based on OSTG helps the surgeon to see the planned intervention directly on the patient.

In order to guarantee an accurate overlay of the augmentation, the OSTG have to be calibrated (see Chapter 4). The presented calibration is split into two parts: the system calibration and the user adaptation. Whereas the first part has to be performed once, the second part is a continuous task. This work concentrates on the first part. The system calibration is performed without using a parametric model, which means that every single display pixel is calibrated individually. For this purpose the calibration process is based on cameras and is completely automated.

Since the presented environment shall be as flexible as possible, a generic approach is developed allowing to use additional input devices (see Chapter 5). For example, an ultrasound probe or a 3D scanner running on a separate workstation and streaming the bone's surface to the planning software. This was realized by implementing an approach based on a network protocol.

An intraoperative calibration method for surgical instruments (e.g. milling device, saw) and HHRDs is described (see Chapter 6). A camera-based method reconstructs the surface of the device's tip relative to the device's coordinate system. Subsequently, appropriate geometries can be matched into the surface (e.g. a sphere) that will be used for planning and execution. In contrast to other intraoperative calibration methods, the proposed technique is able to calibrate arbitrary objects as long as they do not contain cavities.

An RCS for HHRDs with multiple degrees of freedom is presented (see Chapter 7). This system protects previously defined regions by evading them. The milling task is more intuitive than milling with a normal milling device, since the end effector position is corrected automatically by the control system. This system can process arbitrarily shaped constraints in the form of a surface rather than a closed volume or a path, which distinguishes this approach from previous works. Different control strategies, algorithms and modes tested on different robots and devices (HHRD, table-top robot, milling device) are presented. Although different robots are used, this work concentrates on the RCS and its algorithms rather than the robot itself.

An overall evaluation shows the final results when all components work together (see Chapter 8). Different interventions are planned and executed with different robots. The augmented in-situ view is shown and illustrates its effectiveness. An expert review states the importance and the potentials of this new system.

CHAPTER 2

Background and State of the Art

Contents

The word *Orthopedics* was originally introduced by Nicholas Andry as the correction and prevention of deformities in children [4]. Nowadays, it is used with a much broader meaning as treatment of illnesses and injuries affecting the musculoskeletal system. This treatment includes surgical and nonsurgical approaches. Surgical interventions can be split into three phases:

1. A preoperative phase in which the image acquisition, the diagnosis and the planning of the intervention is performed.
2. An intraoperative phase in which the intervention is executed.
3. A postoperative phase in which the aftercare and evaluation is carried out.

In the preoperative phase the surgeon performs a diagnosis, determines an appropriate strategy and plans the intervention. In most cases, this is based on 2D X-ray images and executed manually or with the assistance of computers (see Figure 2.1a and 2.1b). The plan consists of lengths and angles given with respect to characteristic landmarks visible in the X-ray image and on the patient's anatomy. The scale of the X-ray is transferred to the patient by an additional scaling object. Normally, the third dimension is only implicitly considered, at best by a second X-ray image being perpendicular to the first one. Intraoperatively, the surgeon transfers the most important landmarks, lengths and angles onto the patient and performs the intervention according to these measurements.

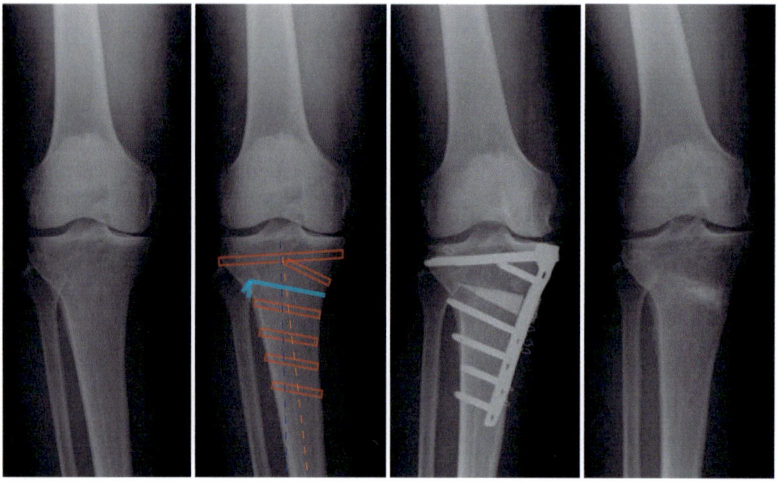

(a) Diagnosis **(b)** Planning **(c)** Evaluation **(d)** Evaluation

Figure 2.1.: X-ray images illustrating the procedure of a surgical intervention (medial compartment osteoarthritis). Two evaluation steps are shown, the first after two weeks and the second after 2.5 years. [5][1]

An osteotomy performed in such a way can last between two hours and one day. It is clear that the surgeon cannot perfectly execute the preoperative plan. Due to this, the quality of the result strongly depends

[1] Published in [5] by Takeuchi et al. and licensed under Creative Commons Attribution License (CC BY) (http://creativecommons.org/licenses/by/2.0/). Added planning data in (b).

on the experience of the surgeon. At certain intervals, the surgery is evaluated (see Figure 2.1c for an X-ray image taken directly after the surgery and Figure 2.1d for one after 2.5 years).

After this brief introduction of orthopedic surgery, the following section addresses computer-assisted orthopedic surgery and describes how existing works in this field can be classified. Subsequently, the planning and the execution system of existing works are explained in more detail (see Chapter 2.2 and 2.3). The visualization of the plan plays a major role in CAOS. Chapter 2.4 describes an augmented in-situ view complementing the standard monitor-based visualization. In Chapter 2.5, different methods to intraoperatively calibrate surgical instruments are presented. Due to numerous interconnected systems inside the OR, different communication protocols and their advantages are described in Chapter 2.6. Finally, a conclusion summarizes the advantages and disadvantages of CAOS.

2.1 Computer-Assisted Orthopedic Surgery

In computer-assisted orthopedic surgery, the three previously described phases still remain. However, many steps are executed with the assistance of a computer, some are even completed automatically by a robotic system. Nowadays, there is a wide variety of CAOS systems and each of them has different requirements. Since the shape of the bone is rigid, images can be acquired pre- and intraoperatively. Different anatomies (hip, knee, spine, etc.) need different planning procedures and different sets of surgical instruments. All these considerations influence the final design of a CAOS system. [6]

In order to give an overview of works about CAOS, the classification of Picard et al. [6] is introduced. They define a clinical classification based on two characteristics:

1. The activeness and autonomy of the executing component (active robots, semi-active robots, passive systems)

2. The imaging requirement (preoperative image-based, intraoperative image-based, image-free)

This classification is extended by a third characteristic: the generality and flexibility of the surgical workflow. A CAOS application is considered general and flexible if it is applicable to several different interventions and if one of the following criteria is fulfilled:

1. A fully flexible surgical workflow: intraoperatively, planning steps and their execution can be interchanged, e.g. planning of an osteotomy, performing the cut, planning drill holes, drilling.
2. Preoperative plan can be adapted intraoperatively.

Otherwise, it is considered to be an application with predefined workflow. In conventional interventions it is standard practice to change between planning and execution. In CAOS systems it heavily depends on the implementation.

Predefined workflows simplify the intervention and decrease the operation time. However, they mostly limit the ability to modify the plan once it is created. This is especially important in the following cases:

- intraoperative detection of anatomical structures not visible on preoperative scans
- deformation of the bone during the intervention (e.g. by splintering of the bone)

If these complications occur and the plan is unusable, the procedure has to be aborted or performed in a conventional approach. Hence, it is important to have the ability to modify the plan intraoperatively.

Table 2.1 shows works in the field of CAOS categorized according to the three described characteristics. The activeness and the imaging requirement are shown on the two axes of the tables whereas the generality is used to categorize them in two different tables. Different presented works and applications might fit into several of these combinations. The majority of works use preoperative image-based planning. Moreover, there are several categories that are not filled. Note that this table does not cover possible extensions of these approaches but simply which ones are available and published.

	Preoperative Image-based	Intraoperative Image-based	Image-free
Active	[7]–[12]	-	-
Semi-Active	[8], [13]–[17]	-	[18]
Passive	[19], [20]	[21]	[22], [23]

(a) Works with predefined workflow

	Preoperative Image-based	Intraoperative Image-based	Image-free
Active	-	[24]	-
Semi-Active	-	[24]	-
Passive	[25]	[24]	[25]

(b) Works with generic workflow

Table 2.1.: Classification of CAOS systems according to Picard et al. [6] with categorized works from the review of literature.

2.2 Planning Systems

Over the years, computer-aided planning in CAOS has been used by an increasing number of surgeons. The planning procedure comprises the image acquisition, the diagnostics and the actual planning. Besides the planning it also allows the simulation of several factors. Handels et al., for example, introduced a virtual planning tool for hip operations in orthopedic surgeries, where the influence of different operation scenarios could be simulated [26].

Computer-aided planning procedures can be categorized by two criteria: the image requirements, and the generality of the plan and the planning process. The majority of works perform the planning based on CT or MR images, which increases the accuracy and level of detail. On the downside, it has several drawbacks such as higher costs and increased radiation exposure for the patient. Moreover, certain anatomical structures (e.g. cartilage) do not appear well on CT images [25]. Since intraoperative changes are not visible on preoperative CT scans, [21] uses intraoperative fluoroscopy imaging. However, the drawback of increased radiation exposure still remains. Furthermore, the level of detail of the plan decreases due to smaller scanners in the OR.

In order to overcome these disadvantages, there are a few works performing an image-free planning. Image-free planning is always performed intraoperatively, since the surgeon needs direct access to the bone. Normally, it also involves a navigation system in order to record landmarks and keep track of the bone position. The surgeon uses a pointing device for digitizing the bone surfaces and landmarks. Anatomical structures, such as the center of the femur's head, can be measured by kinematic movements. The disadvantage is that the surgeon cannot verify the intraoperative plan with a more detailed image set [27]. Picard et al. [6] states that image-free planning reduces the costs and increases the speed of the procedures but also directly depends on the quality of the collected data.

Most works use a planning system adapted to one or few specific interventions. These dedicated planning applications guide the user through the procedure according to a rather rigid workflow, which makes individual modifications difficult to accomplish. A generic planning application allows the surgeon to plan any orthopedic surgery without a predefined workflow. The following sections further describe different planning approaches classified by the generality and the image requirements.

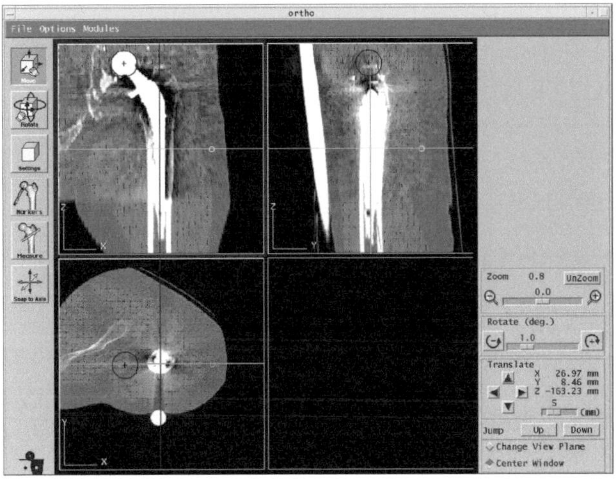

Figure 2.2.: ORTHODOC planning application [28].[2]

2.2.1 Dedicated Planning

Dedicated planning, adapted to one or few specific interventions, allows an optimized planning workflow. Hereby, the surgeon is guided through the individual steps, which decreases the time consumption. However, individual modifications of the plan not considered in the workflow are difficult to establish. Moreover, the clinical staff has to be trained in several applications.

Image-based

Most works in this category base their planning on a CT scan of the patient. The surgeon segments the CT image and plans the implant position and the resection of parts of the bone. For example, the ORTHODOC (Think Surgical, USA) preoperative planning application that

[2] Published in [28] by Yamamura et al. and licensed under Creative Commons Attribution License (CC BY) (http://creativecommons.org/licenses/by/3.0/)

is used in conjunction with ROBODOC allows the surgeon to choose, translate and rotate an implant directly inside the CT image (see Figure 2.2). Additionally, markers for the intraoperative registration have to be placed.

Subsequently, this plan is exported for the usage during the intervention. The format of this plan depends on the instruments and the robotic system being used. Song et al. [11] present a bone-attached surgical robot for joint arthrosplasty, which performs the milling process automatically. In their case, the planning application calculates the milling trajectory, which is then sent to the robot. As opposed to this, Kneissler et al. [15] use a power-controlled handheld milling tool. Since the surgeon holds and moves the tool, a precalculated trajectory is not applicable. Instead, the plan contains the regions that have to be removed and the ones not to be harmed. Therefore, the robotic system imports the plan in form of volumetric regions. Both works have in common that a preoperative CT-based planning is performed.

In contrast, Gottschling et al. [29] present an intraoperative, fluoroscopy-based planning system for complex osteotomies of the proximal femur. During the intervention, two fluoroscopic images are recorded to reconstruct a simple femur model. This allows the surgeon to simulate and determine the osteotomy parameters. Besides these images, no other imaging is needed. Compared to conventional approaches, there is an increased overhead but the surgery is performed with higher accuracy and lower radiation exposure.

Image-free

An image-free planning application requires a navigation system. In most cases, an optical navigation system is used. A tracking device is rigidly attached to the patient's bone(s) and a navigated pointing device can be used to digitize landmarks. Moreover, anatomical structures can be recorded by moving the patient, e.g. rotating the leg in order to find the center of the acetabulum. Such a system is used by Lonner [18]. He presents a system for unicompartmental knee arthroplasty. After setting up the navigation system, the hip center is calculated by rotating the patient's leg. Then, the axes of femur and tibia are digitized using a pointing device (see Figure 2.3a). Subsequently, the surgeon flexes the patient's knee through a full range of motion to determine the rotational axis of the knee (see Figure 2.3b). Finally, the surfaces of the femoral condyle and tibial hemiplateau are digitized using the pointing device (see Figure 2.3c and 2.3d). With this information, the system calculates a virtual model of the knee as well as the implant position.

2.2.2 Generic Planning

A generic planning application allows the surgeon to plan any orthopedic surgery without a predefined workflow. Such a planning application has to contain the functionality to perform any kind of orthopedic intervention. Putzer et al. [3] analyzed 30 randomly selected orthopedic interventions and found out that the planning workflow of these interventions is assembled by 14 distinct work steps. They further verified this finding on 243 orthopedic interventions described in Campbell's Operative Orthopedics atlas [30]. Therefore, a system similar to a CAD application containing this functionality should be able to perform any kind of orthopedic intervention.

Image-based

Brandt et al. [24] present an intraoperative planning application with robotic execution. The planning is based on at least two X-ray images taken from two different directions. The surgeon defines simple geometries such as drill holes and wedges. Implants can be imported and placed interactively. Although this planning application is generic, its usage is limited due to a restricted set of functionality.

A more advanced application is KasOp as presented bei Münchenberg [31]. KasOp is a preoperative planning system based on CT images allowing the surgeon to create plans consisting of different primitives such as points, lines, polygons and trajectories. With this set of primitives it should be possible to perform arbitrary orthopedic interventions despite the fact that Münchenberg originally presented this work for cranio-maxillofacial applications. In order to use a robot for the execution, the robot's trajectory has to be computed. Intraoperatively, this trajectory cannot

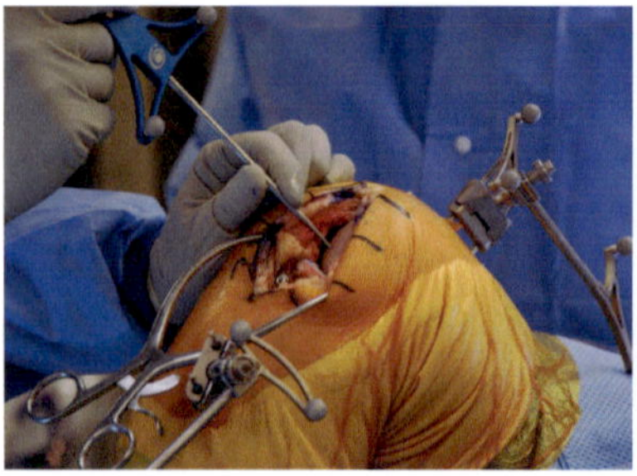

(a) Recording of landmarks using a pointing device

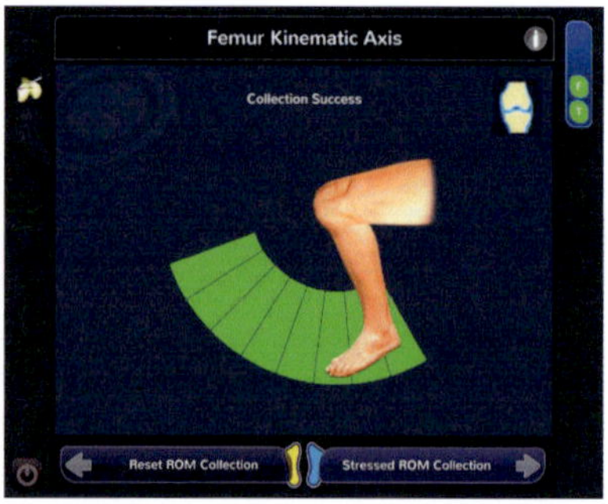

(b) Recording of the femur's kinematic axis

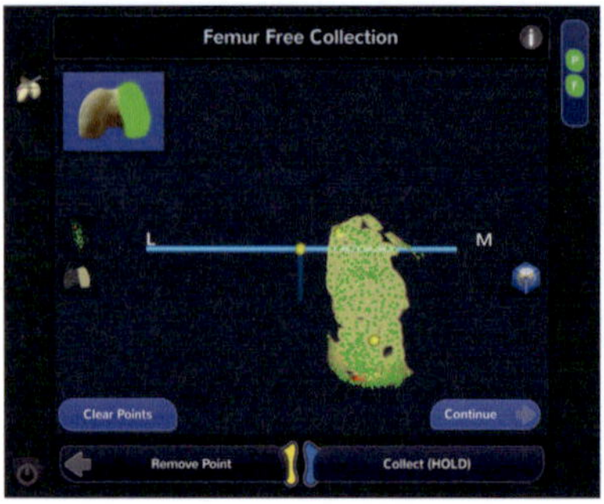

(c) Femur surface digitization

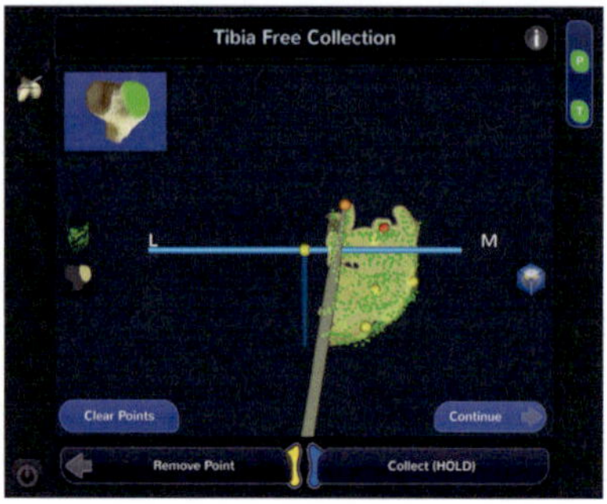

(d) Tibia surface digitization

Figure 2.3.: Image-free planning process using navigated pointing device as well as kinematic movements to record anatomical structures [18].[3]

[3] Published in [18] by Lonner and licensed under Creative Commons Attribution-NonCommercial-No Derivatives License (CC BY NC ND) (http://creativecommons.org/licenses/by-nc-nd/4.0/)

be adapted anymore. Wong et al. [19] present a planning system similar to KasOp. The difference is that this system is not cooperating with a robot but rather guides the surgeon.

Image-free

Sati et al. [25] present an in-situ guidance system originally designed for anterior cruciate ligament graft placement but also applicable to a variety of other surgical procedures. The system utilizes an optical navigation system with trackers mounted on the patient's bone. Landmarks and anatomical structures can be digitized using a pointing device (palpation hook), similar to the one in Figure 2.3a. The bone surface is calculated using the digitized points. The bone tunnels are defined by two points on the tunnel's axis. Since this work does not use a robotic device but rather represents a passive navigation system, the radius of the tunnel is not required. The surgeon simply aligns the direction of the drill with the one of the tunnel. The absence of a robotic system also allows the surgeon to switch freely between planning and execution.

2.3 Execution Systems and Robots

At the beginning of CAOS, research was mainly focused on active and passive execution systems. Whereas active systems promised high accuracies, passive systems were characterized by their simplicity. Active robots automatically perform certain surgical procedures, such as milling or drilling [6]. Such robots require image-based planning and intraoperative registration to bring the plan into relation with the anatomy. In a passive system, the surgeon is guided and keeps full control over the system (e.g. surgical navigation system or a cutting guide).

Over the time, active systems became less popular due to the missing control over the robot. Instead, the focus of attention turned towards semi-active systems. In a semi-active system, the robot shares the control with the surgeon. Instead of the robot, the surgeon moves the end effector. The robot only reacts in cases when the patient could be harmed or the surgeon is not following the plan. The following sections further explain these three types of execution systems, their characteristics and their differences.

2.3.1 Passive Systems

According to Picard et al. [6], passive systems are better accepted than active robotic systems, since they are safer and easier to adopt. There are three types of passive systems: surgical navigation, patient-specific instruments and robotic guides. Surgical navigation guides the surgeon by visualizing the pose of the instrument and the planned geometry, e.g. the drill pose and the direction of the drill hole. Patient-specific instruments as well as robotic guides implement the concept of cutting and drilling blocks that are adapted to the patient. Whereas patient-specific instruments are adapted to the anatomy of one patient, a robotic guide is a generic guide attached to the patient's bone that can hold different positions.

Patient-Specific Instruments

Patient-specific instruments are custom-made cutting or drilling guides adapted to the patient's bone and the according intervention (see Figure 2.4a). In order to calculate the fitting shape, preoperative CT or MRI scans are used. [32]

Scholes et al. [33] state that patient specific instruments for total knee arthroplasty do not match the preoperative plan assessed by intraoperative computer-assisted navigation.

Robotic Guides

Plaskos et al. [22] present a bone-mounted robot called Praxiteles (see Figure 2.4b). This robot positions a cutting or milling guide in accordance with the planned planes on the femur. The surgeon performs the resection under guidance. The robot has two motorized degrees of freedom with the motor axes arranged in parallel. The surgeon defines the cutting planes intraoperatively by using the navigation system. Koulalis et al. [23] compare conventional cutting guides with the automated cutting guide called iBlock, which is based on Praxiteles. They state that using automated cutting guides resulted in more efficient and accurate cuts. The first clinically available drilling guide for pedicle screw insertion was the Renaissance Guidance System (Mazor Robotics, Israel) [35]. This guidance system is based on a hexapod platform and places the screws with an accuracy in the range of 1 mm.

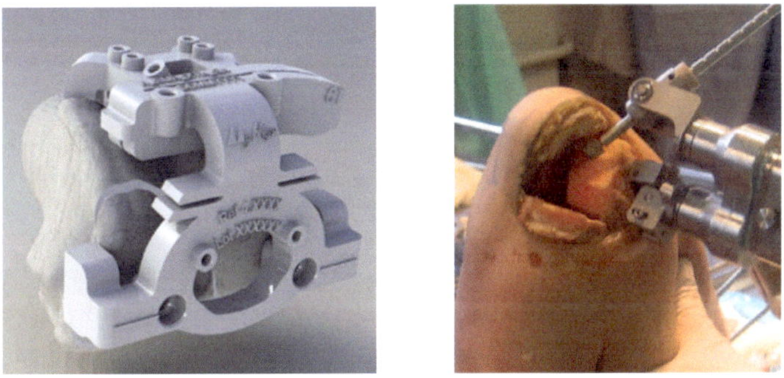

(a) Printed patient-specific instrument [34][4]

(b) Praxiteles, bone-mounted robotic cutting guide [22][5]

Figure 2.4.: Two examples of patient-specific templating approaches.

Surgical Navigation

The most common surgical navigation systems are based on optical tracking systems. For this purpose, three line or two area scan cameras are used to track infrared or retroreflective LEDs as well as black and white

[4] Published in [34] by Helmy et al. and licensed under Creative Commons Attribution License (CC BY) (http://creativecommons.org/licenses/by-nc-nd/4.0/)

[5] Published in [22] by Plaskos et al. and licensed by John Wiley & Sons, Inc.

markers. Figure 2.5a shows an FP6000 navigation camera (Stryker, USA) utilizing three line scan cameras. The position of a single LED can be determined with a standard deviation of 0.07 mm [36]. Figure 2.5b shows a pointing and a tracker device with active LEDs. Electro-magnetic navigation systems represent an alternative to optical system. However, they are not often used since surgical instruments, the robot and the implants contain or consist of metal and therefore interfere with the tracking.

Sati et al. [25] use a navigated drill or drill guide to accomplish the planned tunnels needed for the anterior cruciate ligament graft placement. The surgeon sees the current position and orientation of the planned tunnel and the drill visualized on a display. As soon as they coincide, the surgeon starts the drilling process. Thus, the drill is not directly controlled but only guided. Haider et al. [20] introduce a similar system in which a navigated saw is used for freehand bone cutting for minimally invasive total knee arthroplasty surgery. Their results show a 400% better alignment than conventional jigs. Figure 2.5c shows a similar system using a navigated saw.

Wang et al. [21] introduce a CT-free intraoperative planning and navigation system for high tibial opening wedge osteotomy aiming to support all common osteotomy techniques around the knee joint. After the intraoperative measurement and planning, the osteotomy is executed with a navigated saw and chisel. Wong et al. [19] describe a generic way of integrating CAD planning data into computer-assisted orthopedic surgery. Similar to the previous approaches, a navigated saw is used to perform the planned cuts.

Normally, navigation systems are dedicated and therefore optimized for one specific surgical intervention. For example, the eNact knee navigation system (Stryker, USA). The setup procedure contains the assembly of the navigation camera, the initialization of the trackers and the workspace optimization of the navigation camera. The surgical procedure starts by digitizing the predefined anatomical landmarks. Then, the system calculates an automatic plan. After the surgeon confirms thc calculated plan, he can execute the cuts fitting to the implant. In case that landmarks are digitized inaccurately, thus causing wrong cuts, the surgeon might not detect this until the cuts are already executed. Normally, in such a case, the only solution is to perform a conventional manual intervention.

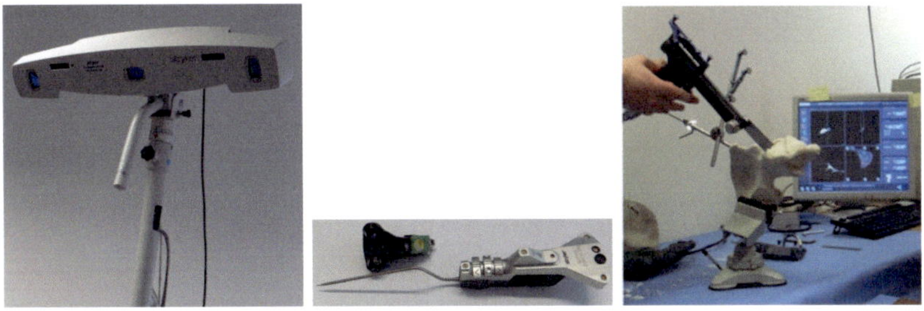

(a) Stryker FP6000 navigation camera **(b)** Stryker pointing and tracker devices used in conjunction with the FP6000 **(c)** Guided Saw based on another navigation system [37][6]

Figure 2.5.: Navigation system consisting of camera, pointing device, tracker and execution device (saw).

2.3.2 Active Robots

Active robots can execute surgical procedures automatically and autonomously. A registration is required bringing the anatomy into relation with the plan. Since the final result depends on the quality of the plan and, therefore, on its level of detail, the planning is based on pre- or intraoperative images. Table 2.1 shows that almost all systems using active robots are based on preoperative images. There is only one system that is primarily based on intraoperative images (see [24]).

[6] Published in [37] by Docquier et al. and licensed under Creative Commons Attribution License (CC BY) (http://creativecommons.org/licenses/by-nc-nd/4.0/)

During the surgical procedure it is essential to know the relation between the coordinate systems of the bone and the robot. For this purpose, an optical navigation system can be used. In the absence of such a system, the bone and the robot are normally rigidly fixed to the operating table. A third approach is to mount the robot directly onto the patient's bone.

Stationary

A stationary robot is a robot with a base that is fixed in position relative to the floor during the intervention. One of the first clinically applied automatic robotic systems was ROBODOC (Think Surgical, USA). The preoperative planning is performed on a computer workstation called ORTHODOC (see Figure 2.2). Intraoperatively, the plan is executed using a robotic arm with 5-DoF and a high speed milling device attached to its end effector [7]. Another early and similar approach that was approved as clinical product was CASPAR (Maquet, Germany) [12].

Brandt et al. [38] present a compact robot for orthopedic surgery based on a hexapod platform and intraoperative X-ray imaging. The surgeon plans the trajectory intraoperatively on the X-ray image and the robot subsequently executes the plan.

According to Jacofsky and Allen [27] the ROBODOC system has several weaknesses. Intraoperatively, modifications of the preoperative plan are only difficult to establish and there is no option to define additional bone resections. Once the milling process is started, the surgeon can not intervene the milling process. In case the system detects an error, the robot stops and only continues after a series of steps that brings it into a safe state. Clinical reports show that in many cases (approx. 10 %) complications occurred that forced the surgeons to abort the interventions. They state the following reasons:

- loosening of fixed registration pins
- inability to re-register the patient
- more than 30 minutes to recover from an error
- soft tissue in danger

Picard et al. [6] state that these first generation systems use relatively large industrial-like robots that are inadequately adapted to the operating room and the surgical procedures. Another drawback is that the bone has to be fixed on the operating table during the procedure due to the lack of a navigation system. Knappe et al. [9] present a position controlled surgical robot based on a navigation system. The patient as well as the robot-held instrument are navigated, which allows to move the patient during the surgery and even during the milling procedure.

Bone-Attached

Wolf and Jaramaz [10] present the Mini Bone Attached Robotic System (MBARS) that is used for bone cavity shaping in joint arthroplasty. The presented system is image-based and was initially implemented for patellofemoral arthroplasty surgery. They state that the system can be changed to an image-free approach collecting all data intraoperatively. The robot is placed on the bone and subsequently registered with the image data and the preoperative plan. The milling is executed automatically. Song et al. [11] present a bone-attached robot based on MBARS that uses hybrid kinematics consisting of two parallel and one serial joint.

2.3.3 Semi-Active Robots

Whereas active robots perform surgical procedures completely automatic, semi-active robots depend on the guidance of the surgeon. Instead of controlling the position of the end effector, the robot follows the movement of the surgeon as long as he follows the plan. In case the surgeon's movement differs from the plan, the robot tries to correct this or stops. Basically, there are two kinds of architectures: stationary robots placed on the ground and handheld robots held by the surgeon.

Stationary and Haptic

Harris et al. [13] present the Acrobot system. The basic difference compared to active robots is that the surgeon holds a force sensitive joystick mounted next to the end effector. Using this joystick, the surgeon controls three of four axes of the device. The fourth axis is controlled automatically to select the optimum position for side-milling actions. The robot responds to the surgeon's forces on the joystick by moving the cutter to remove allowed regions or with an opposing force in order to prevent him from removing too much bone or damaging soft tissue. The decision is made according to a preoperative image-based plan. Due to the absence of a navigation system, the patient's bone has to be rigidly fixed during the procedure. In the literature, such a robotic device is also referred to as haptic robot.

RIO, the Robotic arm Interactive Orthopedic system (Stryker, USA) is a Food and Drug Administration approved haptic robot with 6-DoF (see Figure 2.6a). Hagag et al. [17, p.222f] state that RIO is not designed to replace the surgeon but to enhance his skills. RIO defines a strict workflow requiring a big change compared to the conventional surgery. The procedure starts with the configuration and calibration of the robot. Then the robot is sterilely covered, the preoperative plan is uploaded and the navigation system and the robot are synchronized. Subsequently, the preoperative plan is matched onto the patient by digitizing predefined landmarks on the patient. The implant position is checked again (this is the last moment the plan can be adjusted without major changes) and then the resection process starts. Moreover, RIO is only approved for a few specific interventions.

Handheld

Handheld robotic devices are tools with an end effector such as burr or saw blade that can be dynamically relocated using one or several joints between the end effector and the handle (see Figure 2.6b).

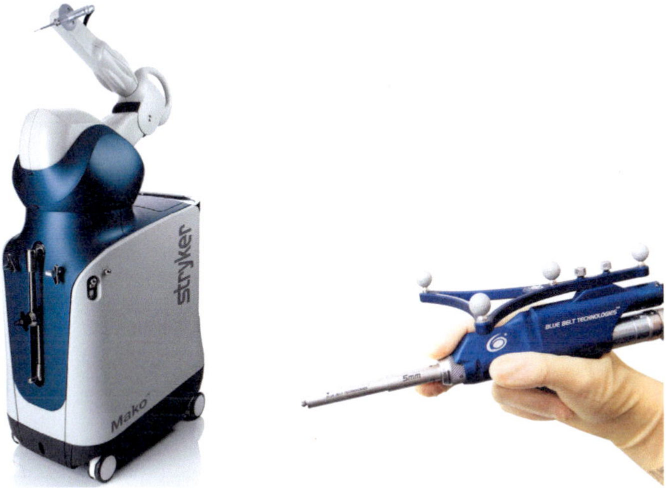

(a) Haptic semi-active robot with 6-DoF, RIO [39][7]

(b) Handheld semi-active robot with 1-DoF, Navio precision freehand sculptor [18][8]

Figure 2.6.: Two examples of semi-active robots.

This type of robotic device differs in several points from haptic ones:

1. Whereas stationary robots have higher degrees of freedom, HHRDs have only a limited range of motion but instead make use of the dexterity of the surgeon and his degrees of freedom.

2. A haptic feedback cannot be given since the surgeon holds the tool and the device has no rigid link to the ground.

3. Another difference also resulting from the missing link to the ground is that a navigation system is required to find the relation between the end effector and the patient.

[7] Copyright by Stryker. Published in [39]

[8] Copyright by Smith & Nephew. Published in [18]

First approaches in this field concentrated on navigated and controlled milling devices. Although these devices are rigid, big parts of the control algorithm are comparable to those of robots. Kneissler et al. [15] present such a system used for spine surgery in which the milling speed of the device is controlled depending on its position. The workspace of the device is defined by the preoperative plan, which is based on a CT or MRI scan. The surgeon holds and guides the milling device as usual. As soon as the surgeon leaves the boundaries of the plan, the milling speed is set to 0. They state that this approach results in accuracies comparable to robot controlled executions. Additionally, they report high-frequency speed changes in the border area of the target geometry. Every sudden change caused a jerk at the hand of the operator, which complicates the handling and produces ragged edges.

By using an HHRD with at least one joint, the milling speed and the end effector's position can be controlled. In case the end effector is located outside the boundaries of the workspace, its position is corrected. In case the maximal deflection of the HHRD is reached, the milling speed is set to 0. This decreases the frequency of the speed changes and improves the accuracy. Brisson et al. [14] introduce the precision freehand sculptor that uses a retractable rotary blade to control which part of the bone is removed. The surgeon simply glides the sculptor over the bone surface and the tool removes the defined parts. It can handle pre- and intraoperatively defined plans and utilizes an optical navigation system for the navigation. However, their system does not support a partial blade retraction. The Navio precision freehand sculptor (Smith & Nephew, UK) represents a similar device: A milling device with retractable milling tip that either controls the speed or the exposure of the end effector depending on the proximity to the constraints. Lonner [18] states that this HHRD is able to place implants in unicompartmental knee arthroplasty as accurate as stationary robots and more accurate than conventional techniques. A different approach is presented by Kane et al. [16]. They introduce a handheld mobile robot for craniotomy that can actuate on the bone surface by using two wheels.

The surgeon places a device in 6-DoF and the milling surfaces are not just planar but also contain cavities and edges. Therefore, controlling the exposure of the end effector might be insufficient since it only moves the end effector along one axis (1-DoF). Hence, there should be at least 3-DoF in order to be able to evade perpendicular to the tool axis. Riviere et al. [40] present Micron: a 3-DoF micromanipulator with a 6-DoF inertial sensor able to compensate the surgeon's tremor. Becker et al. [41] implemented different control modes for Micron. Besides others, a "standoff-regulation" mode prevents from accidental unwanted contact by repulsing the end effector within a defined range to the center of a sphere. This does not prevent the end effector to enter the area but only repulses it away from the center.

Control Systems for Semi-Active Robots

Although stationary and handheld robots seem similar, their control system differs. Stationary cooperative robots are often force-controlled: the surgeon applies a force to the handle of the end effector and the robot reacts with a motion. On HHRDs, force-control is not implementable since the surgeon holds the device and no force can be applied between the HHRD and the surgeon's hand. Therefore, control systems for HHRDs are normally based on the hand motion of the surgeon and the position of the device. Another elementary difference is the relation between the end effector position and the hand: Whereas the end effector position of stationary robots stays rigid relative to the surgeon's hand, it varies in HHRDs.

A high level collaborative control strategy, called virtual fixtures (VF), provides assistance to the user by controlling the robot in such a way that predefined regions or targets are either protected or approached. The name virtual fixtures was originally published by Rosenberg [42] and is inspired by mechanical fixtures that anisotropically limit the motion of tools, e.g. a ruler. However, virtual fixtures are more flexible according to positioning and modification. Virtual fixtures can be split into two categories:

- Regional VF restrict the pose of the device to predefined regions in order to prevent the device from harming this region.
- Guidance VF assist the user in moving the device along a specific path or towards a specific target.

Conventionally, these virtual fixtures (constraints) are evaluated by calculating the proximity (or collision) between the VF and the robot's end effector. Subsequently, the robot motion is determined. Rosenberg states that virtual fixtures reduce mental workload, execution time and errors. An extensive survey of virtual fixtures and active constraints is given in [43]. Virtual fixtures were already applied on many types of robots in different fields. Rosenberg originally developed VF for teleoperation tasks, therefore it is reasonable that VF were implemented on teleoperated surgical robots such as ZEUS (Intuitive Surgical, USA) [44]. Xia et al. [45] and Haidegger et al. [46] describe the skull base neurosurgery project from John Hopkins University, which implements VF on a stationary cooperative milling robot. Another robotic system from John Hopkins University implementing VF is the microsurgical steady-hand eye robot [47]. Becker et al. [41] describe a handheld microsurgical robot based on guidance VF.

2.4 Augmented Reality

Most CAOS systems use a visualization that is shown on a monitor next to the situs. This monitor visualization forces the surgeon to switch his gaze between the situs and the monitor while controlling the instrument at the same time. This requires a good hand-eye coordination [48]. Thus, an augmented reality (AR) visualization is beneficial and could run complementary to the monitor. The surgeon looks onto the situs and sees the plan superimposed on the anatomy. Therefore, this kind of visualization can be used for a fast and efficient verification of accuracy and object placing.

Chen et al. present a surgical navigation system based on optical see-through glasses and preoperative CT scans. After the registration of the preoperative plan with the real scene, the surgeon is able to see the planning directly on the anatomy of the patient [49]. In a cadaver experiment they show that their system is accurate enough to place a sacroiliac joint screw into the pelvis. Wang et al. perform a pilot study about a precision insertion of percutaneous sacroiliac screws based on the system of Chen et al. [50].

Badiali et al. present a system based on video see-through glasses and preoperative CT scans that allows the surgeons to simulate certain bone alignments intraoperatively [51]. Elmi-Terander et al. prove in their cadaver-study about thoracic pedicle screw placement that a surgical navigation system based on AR (on the screen, without see-through) and intraoperative imaging (C-arm) is superior to free-hand techniques referring to the overall accuracy [52]. However, since the visualization is shown on the monitor, the surgeon has to switch continuously his gaze between the situs and the monitor.

2.4.1 Technologies

Nowadays, there are different devices that allow the use of augmented reality in the OR. Besides see-through glasses, a projector or a monitor with attached camera can be used. This work concentrates on see-through glasses since they promise a better contrast than projectors and a higher flexibility compared to the monitor. For the purpose of an augmented in-situ view, the monitor would be placed between the situs and the surgeon, thus, blocking the direct view onto the situs.

There are two types of see-through glasses used for AR:

- Optical see-through glasses (OSTG) that allow the surgeon a direct view through the glasses with a superimposed augmentation.
- Video see-through glasses in which displays are placed in front of the surgeon's eyes showing the augmented image originating from an attached camera.

Figure 2.7 shows the two kind of glasses. Both glasses have advantages and disadvantages and a completely different augmentation process. In video see-through glasses the real-world view is captured with one or two miniature video cameras mounted on the glasses (see Figure 2.7b). The images of the cameras are displayed in the background whereas the virtual objects are rendered in the front. The advantage of these glasses is their ability to compensate the effects caused by the processing delay, which can be done by delaying the camera images. Thus, camera images and virtual objects are shown at the same time. But then the movement of the user is inconsistent with the shown movement. A delay of more than 100 ms makes it impossible to use such a system [53]. Furthermore, since cameras record the real world, there are digitization errors caused by low resolutions. The fact that the cameras can not be mounted at the eyes' positions, introduces an error in the viewpoint for the real-world images. This causes a shift in the perceived scene for each eye that may lead to perceptual anomalies [53].

Optical see-through glasses allow the view onto the surrounding world through a semitransparent mirror (combiner) placed in front of the user's eye. This mirror also reflects the virtual objects directly into the view of the user and therefore it combines real- and virtual-world view (see Figure 2.7a). Since the combiner is semi-transparent, the background always shines through the reflected image. Therefore, a complete superimposition of the reality is impossible. Another disadvantage is the delay of the virtual objects caused by the processing time needed for tracking and rendering. Some milliseconds can already disturb the user [53]. However, real objects are always shown in the correct place and this may be crucial for CAOS systems. In CAOS systems a direct view of the situs must be guaranteed. For this reason, most CAOS systems using AR are based on OSTG.

2.4.2 Limitations

Despite its advantages, AR has to be used reasonably in orthopedic surgery. Dixon et al. show in a user study that surgeons can be blinded by enhanced navigation (AR) in such a way that certain anatomical structures were overseen [55]. Therefore, it is important that the shown objects in the see-through glasses are limited to only the most important ones. Navab et al. [56] further state that an AR visualization is only

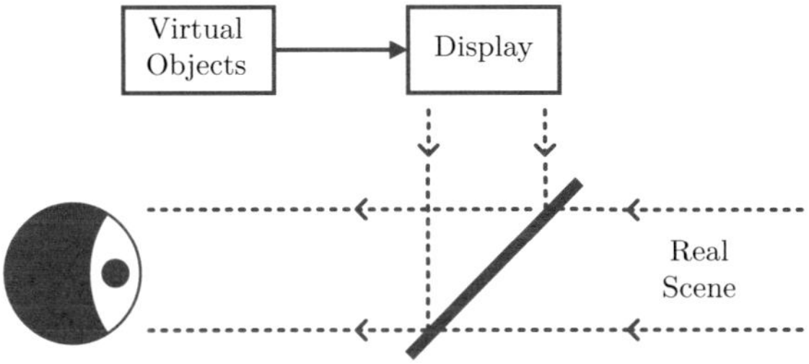

(a) Optical see-through glasses

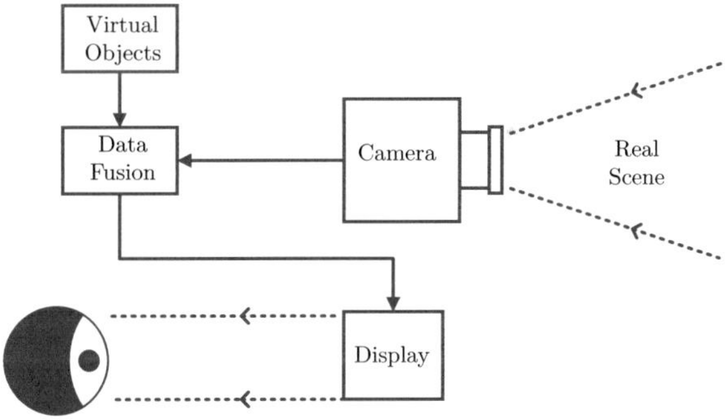

(b) Video see-through glasses

Figure 2.7.: Different types of see-through glasses [54].

needed in certain moments of an intervention. In others, it might stress the surgeon and distract from important things. Therefore, an AR visualization needs to be workflow dependent. During certain steps of the workflow the visualization is on; for others, when it is not needed, it is turned off. Besides these considerations, there are certain issues that still limit the usage of AR in CAOS:

- current glasses are too big and heavy to wear
- the mobility is restricted since the glasses are either connected to a PC or require an additional battery pack due to battery limitations
- fixed depth of focus optimized for the consumer field ($\approx$3 m) does not fit to the working distance in CAOS ($\approx$0.8 m)
- restricted field of view
- not autoclavable

There are many research groups and companies currently working on improving these issues. The conflict between depth of focus and working distance is also known as vergeance-accomodation conflict and became a major research focus in this field [57].

2.4.3 Calibration

Optical see-through glasses are usually shipped uncalibrated and have to be calibrated before they can be used for applications requiring accurate overlays. Since the display itself is not able to provide feedback for the processing unit, the user is normally an inseparable part of the eye-display system. For this reason, the majority of calibration techniques are based on user interaction. Janin et al. [58] described the first technique to calibrate OSTG by relying completely on user interaction. There are several works that improved this way of calibration [59]–[65]. Currently, the most commonly used one was presented by Tuceryan et al. [62] and is called SPAAM. All these works have in common that the user has to align points, displayed on the OSTG, with defined points in the working space. Since the system has several unknown parameters, the user has to collect numerous point correspondences, which is a frustrating and time-consuming task. Aside from that, it is necessary to have trained staff knowing the procedure. Nevertheless, the main problem is that wrong or inaccurate point correspondences have a direct influence on the calibration result. McGarrity et al. [66] state that wrong user interaction often results in errors in the range of centimeters.

Owen et al. [67] split the calibration process into two phases in order to “limit human involvement in the calibration process”:

1. An automated calibration procedure to acquire all intrinsic parameters of the display system
2. An adaptation to the user’s eye by gathering point correspondences

In the first phase, the OSTG are mounted on a jig with a 5 megapixel camera behind them. At the beginning, a Tsai camera calibration [68] is performed. Then, the OSTG are moved in front of the cameras, the setup is covered and a pattern with known fiducials is shown on the displays. These steps are repeated five times from different positions in order to triangulate the virtual position of the display pixels. In the second phase, the display system is adapted to the eye position of the user by gathering point correspondences. Whereas several point correspondences were necessary in previous works, Owen et al. reduced them to exactly one. For this purpose, the user has to align a virtual crosshair displayed on the OSTG with a known world point.

Itoh and Klinker [69] also split the calibration procedure into an “offline” and an “online” phase. The offline phase determines the parameters of the rigid setup of the OSTG/camera system, whereas the online phase is based on dynamic eye tracking. The calculated eye position is then used to adapt the offline calibration. Moser et al. [70] state in their subjective evaluation of semi-automatic OSTG calibration techniques that Itoh and Klinker’s calibration procedure is more accurate and stable than the commonly used SPAAM [62] calibration.

All approaches mentioned use a parametric model similar to Tsai’s pinhole camera model [68]: six extrinsic and five intrinsic parameters together with coefficients for modeling distortion effects are used to describe the OSTG displays. This model is based on the assumption that the optical axis of the system is perpendicular to the image plane and that the principal point equals the distortion center. As investigated by Lee and Hua [71], the principal point normally differs from the distortion center and, thus, makes this model inadequate. They developed a new model that is able to handle this fact and were the first ones considering the radial and tangential distortion up to the third order. However, not even their model is able to map arbitrary distortions.

Itoh and Klinker [72] divide the OSTG calibration even further. The optics of the OSTG distort the "direct view" of the real world and the "augmented view" from the display in different ways. Therefore, they suggest calibrating them simultaneously but separately. Their method is camera-based and consists of an offline learning and an online adaptation phase. Correspondences collected from different camera positions and given calibration patterns are used to determine two mappings, one between undistorted and distorted viewing rays and another one between undistorted pixels and distorted viewing rays.

Parametric models have the advantage that they can be computed with only a few point correspondences generated by a human in the loop. At best, accurate calibration techniques should consider as many display pixels as possible. Although Owen et al. [67] use an automatic calibration, they use a parametric model that defines a parabolic surface. Their measured data points are too noisy, which is why they fit a radially symmetrical parabolic into these points. Gilson et al. [73] also describe a system where point correspondences are generated automatically. They are used to perform an advanced Tsai calibration, which results in the definition of the OpenGL frustum that is used to render the scenes in the display.

2.5 Intraoperative Calibration of Surgical Instruments

Computer-assisted surgery (CAS) systems often utilize tracking systems with tracked surgical instruments. These instruments can be simple pointing tools as well as tracked burrs or saws (active instruments) that are used for bone resections in orthopedic surgery. In this kind of intervention the pointing tool can be used to define resection areas, which are removed by the tracked instrument. To ensure that the active instrument only removes the defined regions, a calibration is required that not only includes the pose of the tool tip but also its surface.

Brisson et al. [14] calibrate their navigated saw with an optical-tracking-based procedure in which the blade is registered to its tracker by touching previously measured registration pins. They state that "the largest sources of modelling error in this experiment were calibration errors".

Cao et al. [74] describe a calibration technique of surgical instruments using a stereo camera. This camera is used as tracking system and for the calibration. Their approach is basically a pivoting of a tracked instrument on a tracked calibration plate. Pivoting means rotating the tracked instrument while its tip is placed in a mold on the calibration plate (see Figure 2.8a). Hence, the path of the tracked instrument lies on the surface of a sphere. The transformations from the tracked instrument to the world coordinate system are used to calculate the center of this sphere. This procedure requires no additional calibration hardware besides the calibration plate but it is not able to determine instrument shapes. De Leon Cuevas et al. [75] present a similar calibration that is also based on pivoting.

Pivoting has the drawback that it can only determine the rotation center of instruments. Due to this limitation some manufacturers have dedicated calibration jigs that allow a more accurate calibration. Many commercially available image-guided surgery systems also provide universal trackers, which can be attached to an arbitrary surgical instrument [76], [77]. This means that in principle any instrument in the OR can be used as a navigated tool by simply attaching a universal tracker. Moreover, most of the active instruments have interchangeable attachments that allow the use of different instrument tips such as drill bits, burrs and blades (see Figure 2.8b).

Tracked instruments can either be shipped precalibrated by the manufacturer or they are calibrated pre- or intraoperatively in the OR. The first case does not work reliably for instruments including interchangeable instrument tips. The position of the tip is altered every time it is changed.

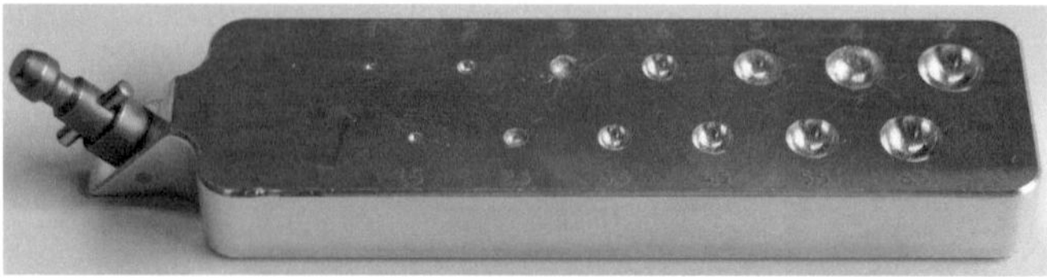

(a) Pivoting calibration plate with different molds

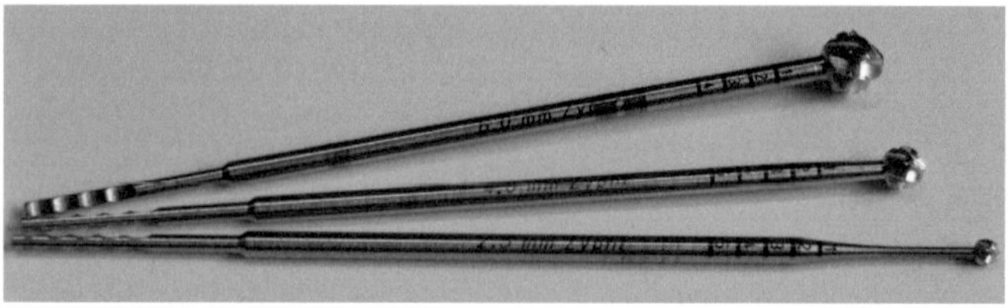

(b) Interchangeable instrument tips

Figure 2.8.: Calibration plate as used for pivoting instrument tips and a small selection of interchangeable instrument tips for a milling device.

This can even be the case when exchanging a tip with a tip of identical construction due to production tolerances or wear and tear. Therefore, the second approach is preferable if it can be ensured that a calibration takes clearly less than a minute.

2.6 Communication between Devices and Toolkits in the OR

Nowadays, a CAS OR is a network of many devices and software components. From planning software over navigation control to robot execution there are many components interacting with each other. These components do not always run on the same system. For example, planning and execution are often separated from each other since they have different requirements. Whereas the planning software must run a visual front-end adapted to the needs of the surgeon, the executing back-end has to run on a real-time system. There are different protocols used in the OR but most of them are proprietary ones (e.g. VectorVision Link, BrainLab, Germany, [78, p. 207ff]). Since these are designed for specific hardware and software, the clinics are bound to the proprietary products of these companies. In order to overcome this limitation and to create a more modular OR for CAS, different standardized and open communication protocols were developed (e.g. CORBA [79] or an interface based on the OpenTracker library [80]). Tokuda et al. [81] state that they failed to become standard protocols due to "overgeneralization, overabstraction and limited portability" causing impractically long training periods. In order to minimize this time consumption, a "simple and easy-to-implement network protocol" was developed by Tokuda et al. [81]. The open image-guided therapy link protocol is an open source network protocol originally developed for IGT environments and is the de facto standard in the medical research field. OpenIGTLink can be used for the communication between software components and devices since it is based on TCP/IP. It has proven its functionality in many different applications, such as MRI-guided robotic prostate interventions for communication between scanner, workstation and robot or neurosurgery for communication between a commercial navigation system and 3D Slicer [81]. A wide range of toolkits such as 3D Slicer [82], IGSTK [83], MUSiiC [84], MeVisLab [85], PLUS [86] and NifTK [87] already support this protocol.

Thus, this system allows connecting arbitrary components, which represents a flexible way to increase the functionality of a software. Zettinig et al. [88] present a system for real-time visual servoing for interventional navigation based on ultrasound. Their system relies heavily on the OpenIGTLink protocol. On one workstation, 3D US images are acquired using PLUS [86] and are then sent to a client workstation running the ImFusion Suite (ImFusion, Germany). This suite is an "extendible GPU-based image processing framework for medical images". This system generates a volumetric representation from the incoming 2D ultrasound images. This volumetric representation is then processed to calculate the target position of the robot that is then sent to the robot via OpenIGTLink.

Another example is presented by Tauscher et al. [89] in which they use OpenIGTLink to communicate between 3D Slicer and a KUKA robot control workstation. Yet another good example is the combination of PLUS and 3D Slicer [86], [90]. While PLUS is acquiring and processing the data, 3D Slicer is used to visualize it.

2.7 Conclusion

This chapter presented a background and state of the art of computer-assisted orthopedic surgery and its methods. System components and technologies from the planning phase to the execution phase were shown and explained in detail. This includes the planning, the visualization, the intraoperative instrument calibration and the execution as well as the communication between systems in the OR.

Although many CAOS systems have been available for the last ten to twenty years, the majority of interventions is performed in a conventional way. This implies that plans are based on 2D X-ray images and executed manually without computer-assistance. The plan consists of lengths and angles given with respect to characteristic landmarks visible in the X-ray image and on the patient's anatomy. In CAOS applications, this basic procedure still remains, however, many steps are executed with the assistance of a computer. Apart from the advantages such as the increase of accuracy, these systems also include certain disadvantages such as high acquisition costs and time-consuming training.

The majority of works in this field plan preoperatively and image-based (CT or MRI), which results in a detailed plan. This in turn causes an increased exposure to radiation and produces higher costs. Moreover, certain anatomical structures (e.g. cartilage) and intraoperative changes are not visible on the images. Intraoperative image-free planning represents an alternative approach. Here, all information is digitized from measurements on the bone surface or from measurement of movements of the bone. Intraoperative image-free planning reduces costs and increases the speed of procedures. However, the quality of the accuracy directly depends on the quality of the data acquisition.

Active robots perform certain surgical procedures automatically. Such a robot requires an image-based plan and intraoperative registration. A semi-active robot shares the control with the surgeon and passive systems simply guide the surgeon while the surgeon has the full control. Whereas stationary robots result in higher accuracies, handheld robots are integrated more easily into existing surgical procedures and environments. The less degrees of freedom of handheld robots are compensated by the dexterity of the surgeon.

Predefined workflows simplify the intervention and decrease the operation time but they also limit the ability to modify the plan once it is created. This might be important if anatomical structures are not visible on the preoperative plan or if the bone is deformed during the intervention. Such cases often invalidate the plan and, in the worst case, the intervention is performed conventionally. However, most works concentrate on CAOS systems with predefined workflow (image-based and image-free). There are just a few works presenting a planning system with flexible workflow. As shown in Table 2.1b, there is no system available with a generic and image-free planning application utilizing a semi-active robotic system.

Optical see-through glasses enable an augmented in-situ view of the situs that visualizes the plan directly on the patient's bone. Examples and technologies, showing the advantages of these systems, are described: Instead of switching his view from the monitor to the situs, the surgeon can concentrate on the situs during the execution of the plan. Different calibration techniques are shown and the necessity of a pixel-wise calibration is stressed.

A surgical instrument calibration is required since the tool tips of certain instruments can be replaced. Dedicated calibration jigs are impracticable due to the large number of possible tool tip/instrument combinations. For this purpose, a flexible intraoperative calibration technique is necessary.

Different communication protocols utilized in the OR are listed and described. It is shown that OpenIGTLink is the most used open-source protocol in the OR. Therefore, an OpenIGTLink implementation allows using a variety of intelligent surgical instruments (e.g. an ultrasound probe). Moreover, planning as well as navigation data can be streamed to other applications.

The following chapters describe an intraoperative system for computer-assisted surgery that can be used for arbitrary orthopedic surgeries. An orthopedic CAD planning system forms the basis of the system. Optical see-through glasses can be used for an augmented in-situ view of the patient and the plan. Their calibration process is explained in detail. A handheld robotic device allows the integration of a robotic tool without time-consuming training. An intraoperative calibration process for navigated instruments is presented. Additional instruments can be added via OpenIGTLink. The overall system allows the surgeon to perform the intervention with an accuracy that are comparable to stationary robots.

CHAPTER

3

OrthoCAD: Generic and Intraoperative Planning of Orthopedic Surgeries

Contents

Nowadays, most CAOS applications are optimized and therefore limited to only a few specific interventions. Their flexibility depends on several factors, such as the image requirements and the way of execution (e.g. guided or automatic). On the one hand, the optimization of the surgical planning and execution procedure simplifies the individual intervention and decreases the operation time. On the other hand, every intervention needs a different application, which requires additional training and leads to increased costs.

OrthoCAD, a CAD system for orthopedic interventions, follows another approach. Many orthopedic interventions are still carried out conventionally based on 2D X-ray images and without computer assistance. The goal of OrthoCAD is to give the surgeon the opportunity to change from this conventional procedure to a computer-assisted method with only minimal changes in his workflow.

The overall workflow starts with the image acquisition that is required for the diagnosis. After the diagnosis, the surgeon creates a preliminary plan on the 2D X-ray image as in conventional interventions. Intraoperatively, the surgeon repeats these planning steps in further detail directly on the patient's bone. Subsequently, the plan is executed. If necessary, the surgeon can switch between planning and execution. This workflow equals the conventional approach with the difference that the planning is computer-assisted and the execution is guided. Additionally, together with the robot control system (see Chapter 7), OrthoCAD offers the execution with two different tools:

1. Power-controlled handheld navigated tools that are already available in many ORs
2. Novel handheld robotic devices with movable end effector

The following two sections, Chapter 3.1 and 3.2, list OrthoCAD's requirements and give an overview of the system. Chapter 3.3 describes the software architecture. The derivation of technical functions from given surgical steps is explained in Chapter 3.4. Interaction and visualization approaches suitable for the OR are presented in Chapter 3.5. Subsequently, the features of OrthoCAD are described and illustrated in Chapter 3.6 till 3.11. In order to evaluate the presented system, a femur neck osteotomy is planned (see Chapter 3.13). Finally, the results of this chapter are summarized in Chapter 3.14.

3.1 Requirements

The following requirements were identified for OrthoCAD as an intraoperative CAD system for orthopedic surgeries:

1. Identification and implementation of surgical planning steps and therefrom derived technical functions
2. The ability to switch on-the-fly between planning and execution
3. A data structure to synchronize planned constraints with the robot control system
4. Flexible interaction and visualization paradigms adapted to orthopedic interventions and the surgeon's needs
5. Control of diverse hardware systems
    a) Navigation system including trackers and pointing device as input
    b) Touch screen for visualization and interaction
    c) Optical see-through glasses for in-situ visualization
6. Extensibility for new input methods such as ultrasound or 3D-scanners

3.2 System Overview

OrthoCAD's OR system is arranged in such a way that all inputs and instruments are placed close to the surgeon and the situs. Figure 3.1 shows the overview of the operating room when using OrthoCAD. A touch screen is placed next to the situs and can be positioned flexibly. Different input instruments are available: an obligatory pointing device and optional ones such as an ultrasound probe. If OrthoCAD is not only used as planning and navigation system but also to execute the plan, a milling or cutting device must be available. These devices can be simple power-controlled or power- and position-controlled robotic devices. A handheld as well as a stationary robot can be used to execute the plan, however, this work concentrates on handheld robots (see Chapter 7). In order to calibrate intraoperatively the tool tips of these devices, an optical calibration device is available (see Chapter 6). Optionally, the surgeon can wear optical see-through glasses for an augmented in-situ view (see Chapter 4). The patient's bones, the instruments and the OSTG are tracked using an optical navigation system. The milling devices are enabled by pressing a foot pedal.

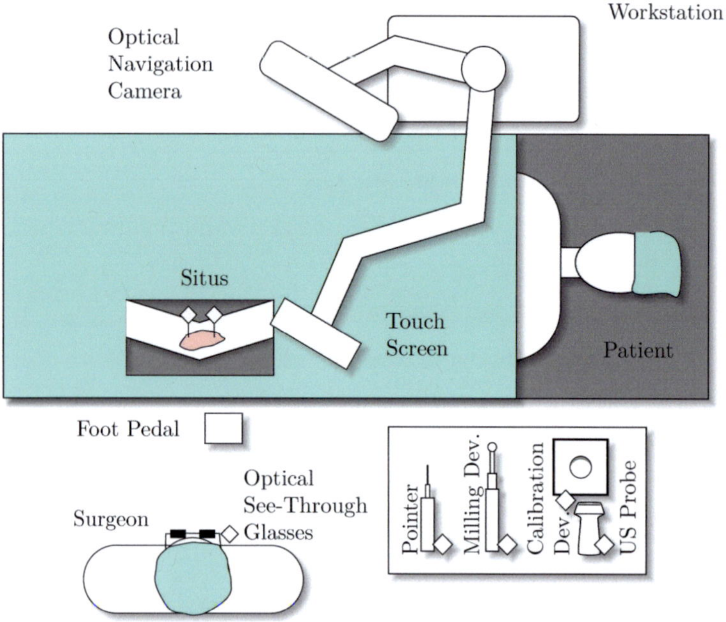

Figure 3.1.: OrthoCAD components overview.

3.3 Software Architecture

The software implementation is based on open-source toolkits, particularly the Medical Imaging Interaction Toolkit [91] and its dependencies. MITK is a framework for interactive medical image processing and combines and extends the features of the Insight Toolkit (ITK) [92] and the Visualization Toolkit (VTK) [93]. Qt is used as a platform-independent application framework. OpenIGTLink was integrated into the MITK framework (see Chapter 5) and is used to extend the functionality of MITK by connecting to other applications and hardware. The Armadillo C++ Library [94] is used as linear algebra library. The robot control system uses the Bullet Collision Detection and Physics Library as a basic framework for the collision detection (see Chapter 7.3). The only proprietary libraries used in OrthoCAD are the drivers necessary to connect to the Stryker navigation system and milling device, and CUDA, which is used to efficiently undistort the visualization of the OSTG (see Chapter 4.7).

3.4 From Surgical to Technical Planning Steps

Putzer et al. [3] analyzed 30 randomly selected orthopedic interventions and found out that the planning procedures of these interventions consist of 14 distinct functions (e.g. defining a landmark or aligning a plane perpendicular to a certain axis). These functions are assembled in a different order and amount depending on the procedure. They further verified this finding on 243 orthopedic interventions from Campbell's Operative Orthopedics atlas [30]. The identified surgical planning steps are:

1. Define a landmark.
2. Define a plane passing through a cloud of digitized points.
3. Define a plane parallel to another one.
4. Define a plane perpendicular to a certain axis.
5. Define a line on a plane.

6. Swing plane around an earlier defined line on plane.
7. Define a generic milling volume.
8. Define an osteotomy plane.
9. Define a drill hole.
10. Define areas, which should not be exceeded during the milling process.
11. Define a surface deepening.
12. Convert osteotomy plane to dome-shaped cut.
13. Define milling volume from a 3D object for bone transplantation.
14. Perform free hand milling.

These steps enable the surgeon to perform any kind of orthopedic intervention and are further divided into technical planning steps:

1. Define a primitive (landmark, point cloud, line segment, cylinder, plane, wedge).
2. Apply algorithms, e.g. calculation of regression plane through point cloud.
3. Assemble primitives to compound objects (complex cuts, osteotomy planes, triangle meshes).
4. Place a primitive relative to another one (parallel, perpendicular, projected, through).
5. Adjust the position and orientation of objects.
6. Show measurements (angle and distance) between objects.
7. Define objects as milling constraints.

Dome-shaping can be achieved by using the complex cut functionality. The definition of a milling volume from a 3D object for bone transplantation is not yet implemented. However, the milling volume could be planned step by step using the previously described primitives.

3.5 Interaction and Visualization

Any CAD system needs functionality to digitize primitives and assemble them to more complex objects. In standard CAD systems, a keyboard and a (3D) mouse are used as input devices. In contrast, they cannot be used in OrthoCAD since they are not autoclavable and not easy to drape. Therefore, a navigated pointing device and a touch screen digitize primitives and construct compound objects, respectively. The surgeon digitizes the primitives directly on the patient's bone using the pointing device. Then he selects them on the touch screen and assembles them to new objects.

Additional to the pointing device and the touch screen, primitives can be sent to OrthoCAD via OpenIGTLink (see Chapter 5). An OpenIGTLink server running inside OrthoCAD allows receiving primitives sent by external tools. This functionality was tested by receiving the bone surface generated by an ultrasound scanner. Moreover, preoperatively generated objects can be imported and registered.

Figure 3.2 shows the visualization on the touch screen. On the left, the digitization menu contains the available primitives that can be digitized. The selected primitive is added to the tip of the pointing device (see Figure 3.3). The half circle shown inside the digitization menu is used to switch between the planning and the execution mode. The status bar shows information about the tracking devices and instruments such as visibility or milling speed. Furthermore, the entries in the status bar are clickable and can be used to call the context menu of the devices. The main menu on the upper right corner contains the view menu and several other entries. The most important ones are the following:

- import of preoperatively generated data objects
- export and import of the objects of the current plan
- visualization of all previously hidden objects in the current plan

Selecting an object on the touch screen opens the context menu as shown exemplarily for a point in Figure 3.4a. The context menu contains options concerning the current selection. Objects are added to the selection by pressing the selection option followed by opening the context menu for

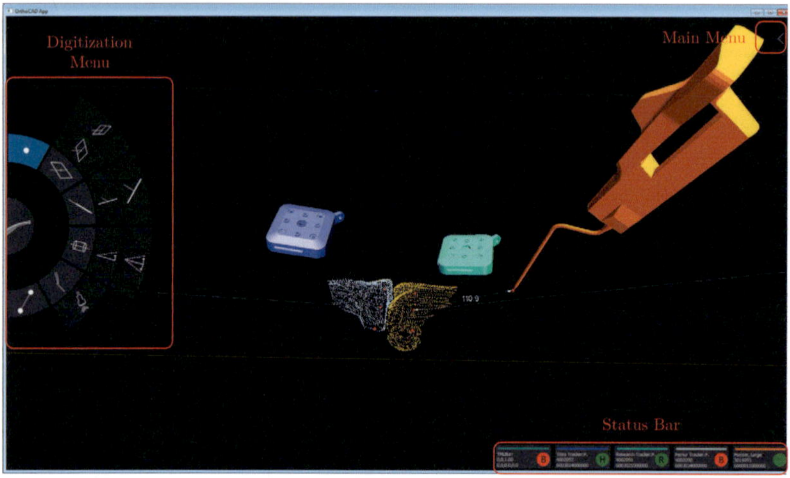

Figure 3.2.: OrthoCAD visualization and GUI. The digitization menu allows selecting the objects on the pointer tip (a landmark in the shown scene). The status bar shows the tracker status of the tools. The main menu is hidden since it is not used very often. The scene shows two point clouds digitized on the femur and tibia around the knee joint and the trackers attached to the two bones.

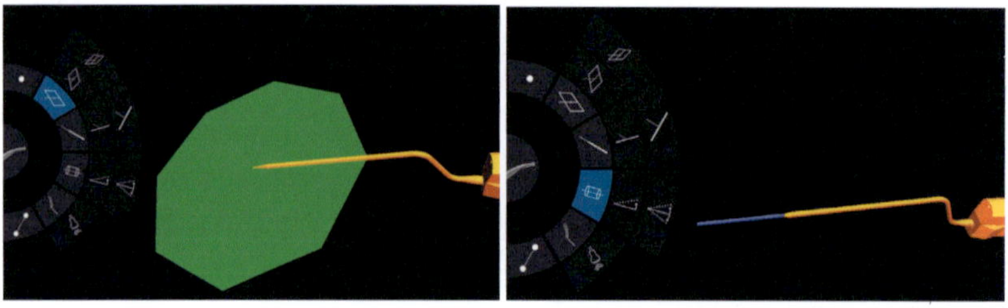

(a) Plane on pointer tip **(b)** Cylinder on pointer tip

Figure 3.3.: Different selection of objects in digitization menu.

the next object. Subsequently, the selection contains both objects and the context menu shows the options for the combination of both objects (see Figure 3.4b). The context menu contains several levels from which the current level and its children are shown (see Figure 3.4c).

The surgeon can interact with the virtual camera of the visualization using two distinct methods:

1. Using touch gestures:
   a) Rotation by one-finger pan, which only changes the camera position (camera moves around the focal point)
   b) Panning by two-finger pan, which changes the focal point and the camera position (translational change of view)
   c) Zooming by two-finger pinch/zoom gesture, which moves the camera position closer to or further away from the focal point
2. Using the pointing device

In the latter case, the virtual camera is placed on the tip of the pointing device. After finding the optimal position the surgeon confirms it using the pointer button. On startup, the surgeon defines two virtual camera settings of the situs using the pointing device:

1. Oriented according to the anatomy of the patient (see Figure 3.5a)
2. Oriented according to the view of the surgeon (see Figure 3.5b)

Additionally, there is a camera setting defining the view of the navigation camera (see Figure 3.5c). By using the view menu the surgeon can easily switch between the settings (see Figure 3.5d), which allows him to quickly see the plan from different perspectives. The anatomical and surgeon's view can be adjusted whereas the navigation camera view stays rigid.

Besides the touch screen, the surgeon can use optical see-through glasses for an augmented reality view of the situs (see Figure 3.6). The touch screen visualizes low and high-level information whereas the OSTG only visualizes essential information (objects and measurements). Menus are not shown on the OSTG. Showing all information on the situs could distract the surgeon. If the surgeon looks at the monitor the AR view is blank and he only sees the content of the touch screen visualization.

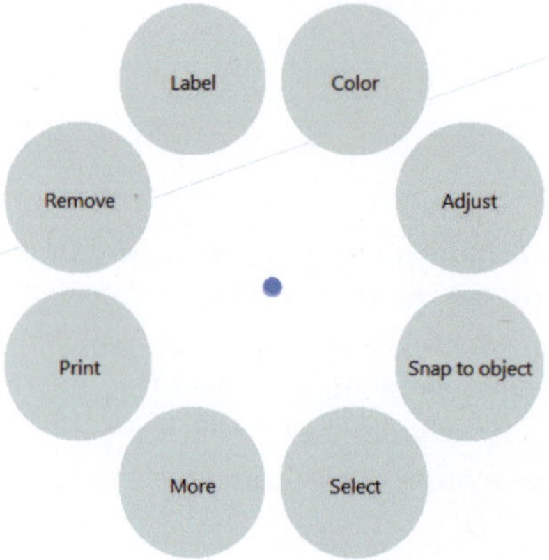

(a) Context menu after selecting a point

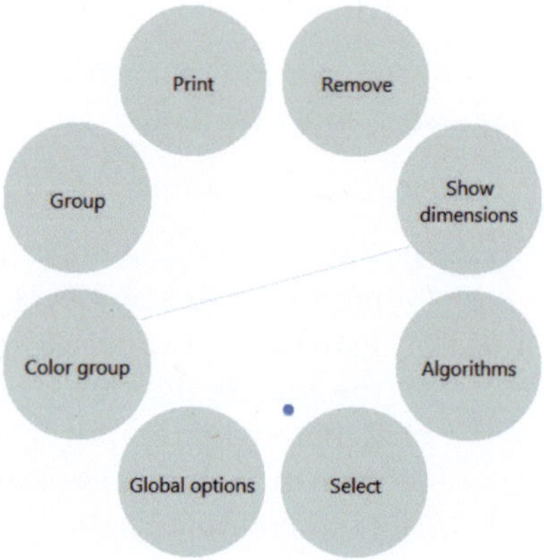

(b) Context menu after selecting a point and a line

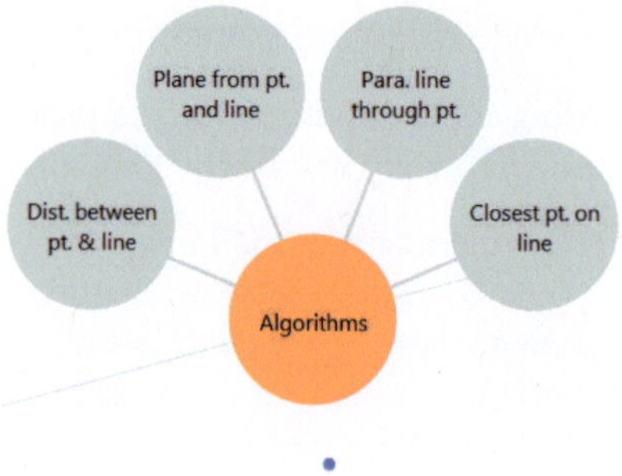

(c) Algorithms of the selection in (b)

Figure 3.4.: Context menu in OrthoCAD. In (a) the user selected a point and chose the "Select" option. After selecting a line, the context menu in (b) shows the options for a combination of point and line. The user selects "Algorithms" and sees the algorithms applicable for a point and a line.

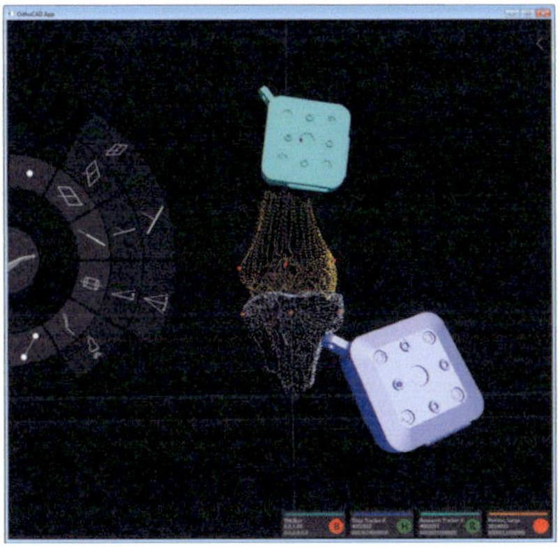

(a) Anatomical view

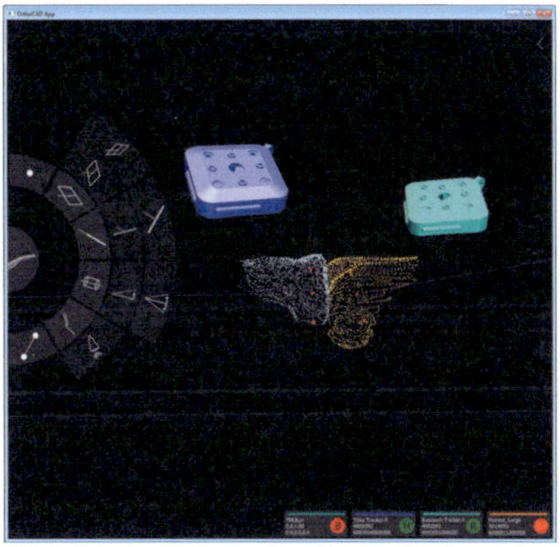

(b) Surgeon's view

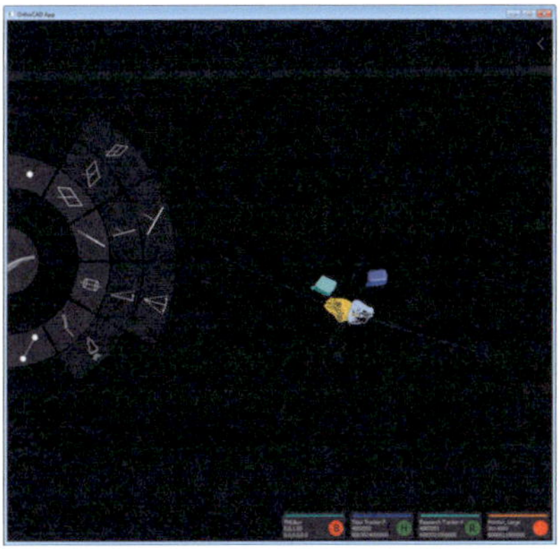

(c) Navigation camera view

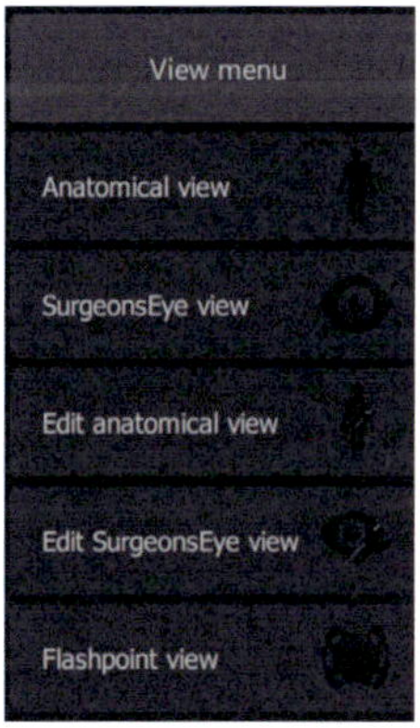

(d) View menu

Figure 3.5.: The available views (a to c) and the view menu (d) in OrthoCAD.

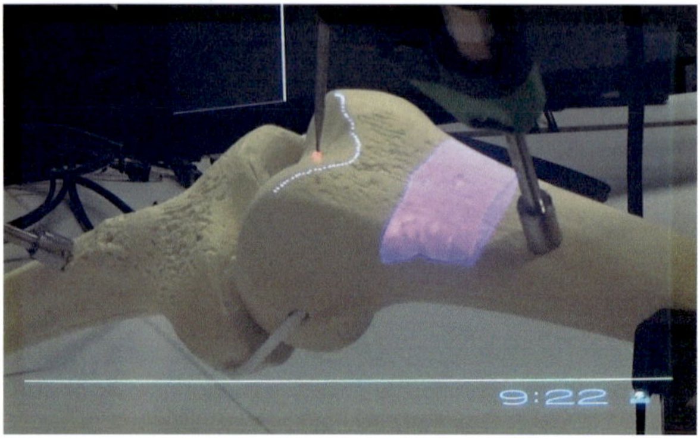

Figure 3.6.: Precise overlay in AR visualization using optical see-through glasses.

The augmented in-situ view complements the visualization on the touch screen. Without this additional view, the surgeon operates on the situs while looking onto the touch screen. The in-situ view improves this issue since the visualization and point of view coincide with the situs. Therefore, the AR visualization can be used for a fast and efficient object placement. Even though the OSTG is calibrated, some issues remain:

1. For a good calibration the user's eye position has to be known but most OSTG lack the ability of eye tracking. A simple GUI is used, which allows the user to manually move the virtual eye position until a virtual pattern coincides with the real world.

2. Most OSTG have a fixed focus length of around 2 m, meaning that the virtual display appears at this distance. Surgeons, however, work at a distance of around 80 cm, which forces the surgeon to switch his focus continuously from 80 to 200 cm.

3. Currently, these devices are still bulky and sometimes become quite hot. However, future devices will be smaller and more efficient.

Since the AR view is complementary and not essential for the outcome of the intervention, the surgeon can decide if he wants to wear the OSTG or not. It is also possible to use it only temporarily during certain procedures.

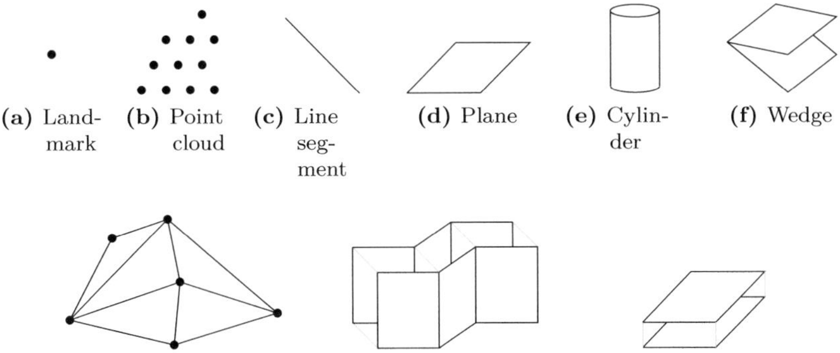

(a) Landmark (b) Point cloud (c) Line segment (d) Plane (e) Cylinder (f) Wedge

(g) Triangle mesh (h) Complex cut (i) Osteotomy plane

Figure 3.7.: Overview of primitives and compound objects.

3.6 Primitives and Compound Objects

Primitives such as points, lines or planes form the basis of every CAD software. In OrthoCAD, the following primitives can be digitized: landmarks (points), point clouds, line segments, cylinders, planes and wedges (see Figure 3.7a-3.7f). Planes are understood as regular polygons. A wedge is understood as two squares sharing one edge and it can either open symmetrically in both directions or asymmetrically.

Primitives are used to assemble compound objects, e.g. a triangle assembled from three points. In OrthoCAD, the following compound objects are available: triangle meshes, complex cuts and osteotomy planes (see Figure 3.7g-3.7i). A triangle mesh is the most generic of these types. The basis of a complex cut is an assembly of several rectangles sharing one edge with the neighboring rectangle and these edges are parallel to each other. The final complex cut results from inflating the rectangles perpendicular to their surface normals. An osteotomy plane is defined by two parallel planes at a certain distance. Additional to these "pure" compound objects, primitives can also assemble other primitives, e.g. a line segment defined by two points or a wedge by two planes. Objects can be created using the following list of implemented algorithms:

- center of mass from points
- intersection point from
  - multiple line
  - multiple plane
  - line and plane
- closest point on
  - line
  - plane
- intersection line of two planes
- project line onto plane
- point at percentage of
  - distance
  - line segment
- parallel line through point
- line segment from two points
- plane from
  - three points
  - point and line
  - parallel lines
- parallel plane through point
- align plane's normal pointing towards point
- regression plane from points
- osteotomy plane from plane
- wedge from
  - line and plane
  - plane
- cylinder fit of points
- cylinder from line
- merge
  - surfaces
  - points
- surface from points
- clip surface with planes
- cut out volume from surface
- cut out wedge from
  - surfaces
  - point cloud
- create complex cut from
  - planes
  - line segments

After an object is created from one or more primitives, these primitives are hidden since they are normally not needed anymore. OrthoCAD saves the relationships between objects. Therefore, each object knows its parents objects. In case that they are needed additionally to the created objects, they can be shown again. Sometimes, it might be necessary to remove objects. In case that the removed object has parent objects, they are shown automatically.

3.7 Object Representation

The data representation of an object is shown in Figure 3.8a. An object is basically structured in three parts:

- data and mathematical parameters
- geometry
- additional properties

The data and parameters describe the object mathematically. An osteotomy plane, for example, is described by a hesse normal vector, a hesse constant, a span, a thickness and the number of corners. A surface is described by a collection of vertices and edges. In order to further explain this structure, it is necessary to introduce the coordinate systems concerning an object (see Figure 3.8b). Data and mathematical parameters are given in index coordinates I. The index coordinate system stands in direct relation with the object itself. In case of an osteotomy plane, the origin of I coincides with the center of the plane, the z-axis coincides with the plane's normal and the x- and y-axis lie inside the plane. Every object is assigned to one tracking tool (tracker or pointer). The transformation $F_{T \leftarrow I}$ from index coordinates I to tracker coordinates T is one of two transformations saved in the geometry of the object. The other transformation is F_{WT} from tracker coordinates T to world coordinates W. The world coordinates are defined by the navigation camera. This separation of transformations facilitates the handling of the data object. In a background process, the tracker to world transformations F_{WT} of all objects are updated. Rotating and translating an object is further explained in Chapter 3.9 and is based on the index to tracker transformation F_{TI}. The data and mathematical parameters are not changed by these transformations. The third part of the data representation is a database of properties that is basically used for management and rendering. This includes, for example, the parent object(s), the color, the visibility or the surface model representation (wireframe or surface).

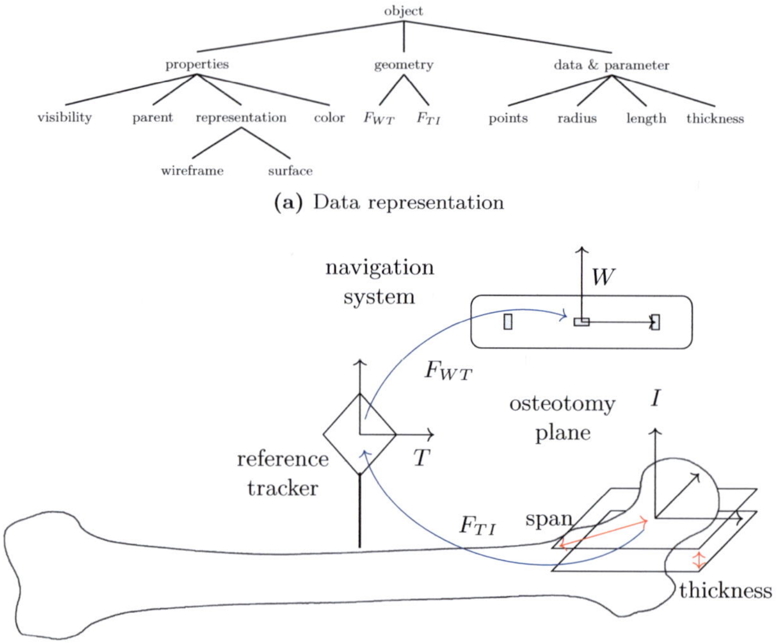

(a) Data representation

(b) Geometry concept

Figure 3.8.: Object representation.

3.8 Object-Relative Placement

Placing primitives relative to other ones is a major requirement in an orthopedic CAD system. This feature allows the surgeon, for example, to place a plane perpendicular to a previously digitized bone axis. This component helps the surgeon to precisely place objects by limiting the number of degrees of freedom of the placement. A plane, for example, can be placed with 6-DoF (3 parameters for the position and 3 for the orientation). If the surgeon wants to place a plane such that it passes through a given landmark, the 3 positional DoF are fixed and he can concentrate on finding the best orientation.

In order to use the object-relative placement, the surgeon selects the previously digitized primitive and chooses the placement option. Subsequently, the primitive on the pointer tip is adapted accordingly. The available options in the context menu (see Table 3.1) are object-specific, since not all algorithms are suitable for all primitives.

Table 3.1.: Object-relative placement options with examples. Not all options are suitable for all primitives.

Option	Description	Example
Perpendicular	The new primitive is perpendicular to the reference object, e.g. a plane perpendicular to a line	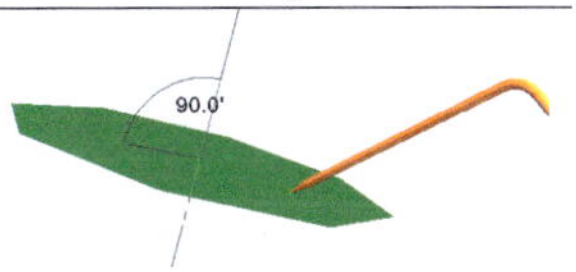
Parallel	The new primitive is parallel to the reference object, e.g. a plane parallel to another one	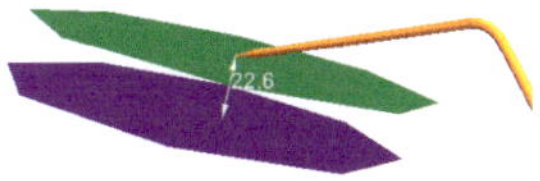
Projected	The new primitive is projected onto the reference object, e.g. a point projected onto a plane	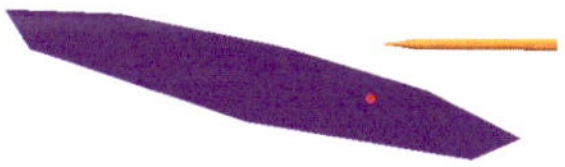
Through	The new primitive passes through the reference object, e.g. a plane passing through a line	
Through and Cut	The new primitive passes through the reference object and is cut by the reference object, e.g. a plane constrained by a line	

3.9 Object Adjustment

After objects are created, they can be adjusted. This includes their pose and geometry-dependent parameters. In case of an osteotomy plane, configurable values are the number of corners, the span and the thickness. In case of a cylinder, the diameter and the length can be changed. The pose can be adjusted using handles as shown in Figure 3.9. The three rings are used to rotate the primitive and the three arrows translate it. The surgeon can either use these handles or the adjustment dialog next to it. The current change (angle or distance) is shown directly on the object and in the adjustment dialog. Several transformations can be applied and undone.

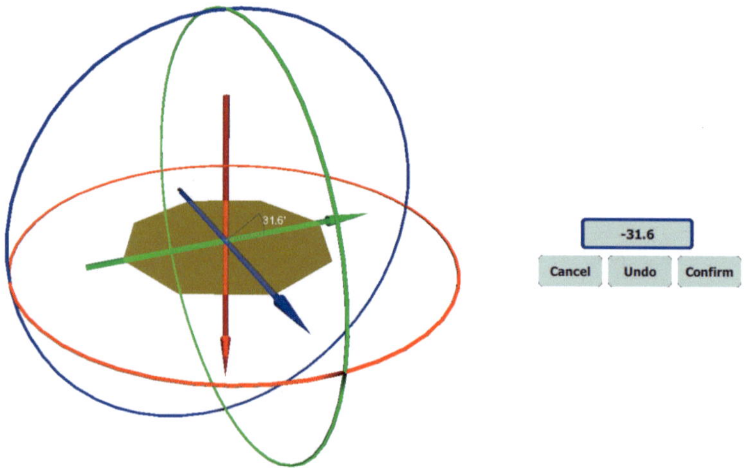

Figure 3.9.: Direct object adjustment: The rings rotate and the arrows translate the object. In the adjustment dialog exact numbers can be entered, changes can be reversed and the final pose can be confirmed or canceled.

3.10 Complex Cut Creation

Complex cuts are assembled by a series of rectangles in which two of them share one edge that is parallel to all other shared edges. They also have a thickness, similar to osteotomy planes. Different orthopedic interventions utilize different cuts. Here, a hallux valgus correction shall be used as an example. A hallux valgus is a deformity of the joint connecting the big toe (hallux) and the foot (more specific the metatarsal). The deformity causes the joint to further stand out in medial direction (pointing to the other foot). Typical cuts in a hallux valgus surgery are chevron and scarf cuts (see Figure 3.10a and 3.10b). The goal of a chevron or scarf osteotomy for hallux valgus is to translate the deformed joint in lateral direction (to the side) to establish a more natural position of the joint. First, the surgeon defines the cut. Then, after the cut is prepared, the bone can be translated along the axis of the cut. Once it is in the proper position, the bone is fixed with one or two screws (see [95] for a more detailed explanation).

For certain osteotomies, a dome-shaped cut is required that helps the surgeon to correct the axis of femur or tibia. Here, the concept is similar to a scarf cut, however, instead of moving the cut along the cut direction it is moved around the curvature of the cut.

In OrthoCAD, an abstracted version of these cuts is implemented. Such a cut consists of multiple planes whose surface normals lie in one plane. Therefore, it can be defined in two distinct ways: By several parallel line segments or by several planes with appropriate orientation. Since OrthoCAD does not require a robotic execution system, the complex cut cannot directly be converted into a path. Instead, the thickness of the cut has to be specified manually. Therefore, after designing the cut, the surgeon has to define its thickness. A dome-shaped cut is approximated with several densely placed lines or planes.

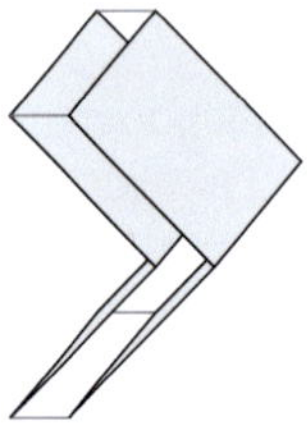

(a) Chevron cut

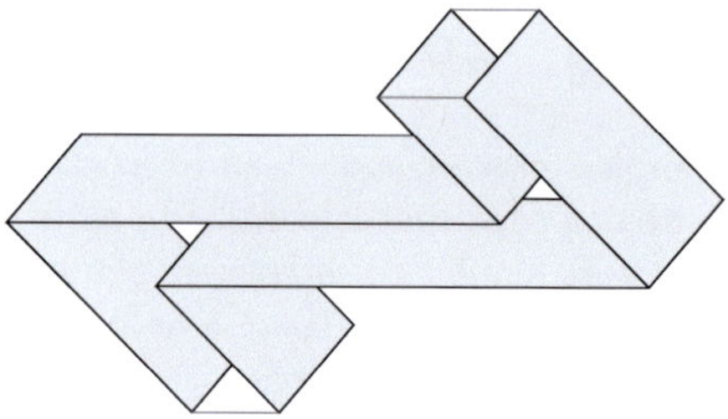

(b) Scarf cut

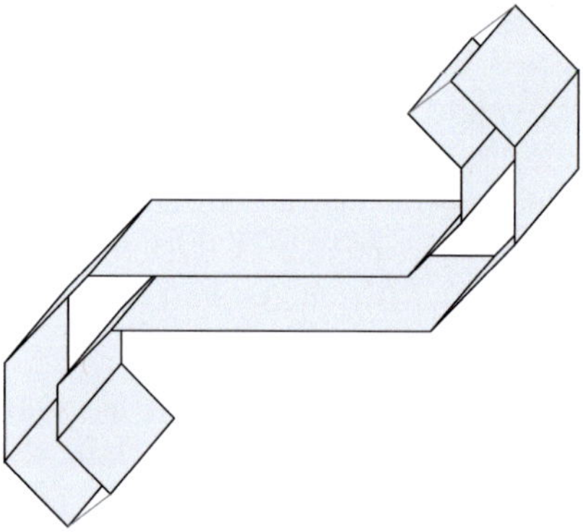

(c) Abstracted complex cut

Figure 3.10.: Chevron, scarf and abstracted complex cut.

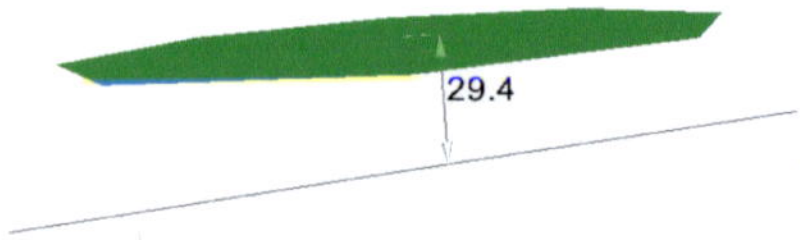

(a) Distance measurement

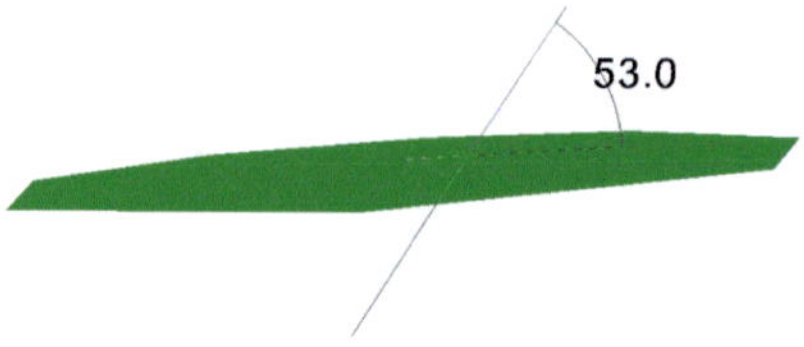

(b) Angle measurement

Figure 3.11.: The virtual ruler and triangle.

3.11 Virtual Ruler and Triangle

OrthoCAD allows the surgeon to measure distances or angles between objects by using a virtual ruler or triangle, respectively. This is also a key feature in commercial CAD tools. Currently, the two objects have to be selected manually. However, future versions will be able to visualize the measurements automatically depending on the focus of the surgeon.

3.12 Data Structure for Synchronization with Robot

Once the planning is finished, the planned constraints must be sent to the robot. For this purpose, the constraints are converted into a data structure that the robot control system can process. The type of this structure differs from those in existing applications. Existing applications construct dedicated milling volumes. Since all data in OrthoCAD is digitized intraoperatively and image-free and some structures cannot be reached, it is not always possible to create such volumes. Therefore, OrthoCAD follows another approach. The surgeon explicitly constructs constraints that the executing tool cannot pass through. Thus, instead of a volume, a surface is constructed. The synchronized data structure consists of a collection of triangle meshes that are virtually connected to a tracking device. Therefore, all objects that are used to constrain the end effector movement are converted into a triangle mesh and then stored in a database. The robot control system, as described in Chapter 7, accesses this database. Intraoperatively, the surgeon can add, modify and remove these constraints individually.

3.13 Exemplary Surgical Intervention

A femoral neck osteotomy is used as an exemplary surgical intervention to evaluate the functionality of OrthoCAD. In a hip arthroplasty (hip replacement) the femur's head is completely removed and replaced by an implant (see Figure 3.12a for the theoretical plan). The acetabulum that, together with the femur head, forms the hip joint is extended and an implant is inserted. Before the implant can be inserted into the femur, the head and neck have to be removed. This preparation of the femur is called femoral neck osteotomy. The surgeon performs an osteotomy of 1 cm, which is rotated 45° to the femoral axis and has a distance to the trochanter minor of 8 mm. These values are determined by the surgeon according to the preoperative X-ray scan and the surgeon's experience. The cut of 1 cm is necessary since the surgeon needs space to remove the femur head from the acetabulum. The intraoperative planning steps are:

1. Digitize points on femur neck for easier orientation.
2. Digitize landmark on saddle point and trochanter minor.
3. Digitize landmark on medial and lateral epicondyle.
4. Create transepicondylar axis center using medial and lateral epicondyle landmarks.
5. Create femur axis using transepicondylar axis center and saddle point.
6. Define a plane passing through saddle point.
7. Enable measurements between this plane, the femur axis and the trochanter minor.
8. Place plane in such a way that the angle between axis and plane is 45° and the distance to the trochanter minor is 8 mm.
9. Create osteotomy plane from this plane.
10. Set thickness of the osteotomy plane.
11. Set as constraint.

See Figure 3.12b for the created plan in OrthoCAD. Subsequently, the surgeon uses a saw or a milling device to resect the bone. The femur head is removed from the acetabulum and the surgeon starts planning the implant position. See Chapter 8.2.2 and 8.2.1 for the execution of this intervention.

3.14 Conclusion

Most CAOS applications are dedicated to specific interventions. This, however, requires individual training that produces increased costs. In contrast, OrthoCAD follows a more generic approach. The surgeon is able to plan arbitrary interventions intraoperatively and image-free. Moreover, the surgeon can flexibly change between planning and execution. Different levels of computer assistance are available:

- none (OrthoCAD is only used for planning)
- navigation
- power-controlled handheld navigated tool
- power- and position-controlled handheld navigated tool

The plan is visualized on a touch screen that the surgeon also uses to construct the plan. Primitives are digitized using a pointing device. The touch screen is used to interact with the primitives and the objects. Optical see-through glasses are used for an augmented in-situ view allowing the surgeon to see the plan directly on the patient's bone. The software implementation is heavily based on open-source toolkits. Features known from commercial CAD systems, such as object-relative placement or a virtual ruler and triangle, are implemented and adapted to the OR. Instead of using dedicated milling volumes for the execution of the plan, OrthoCAD only requires constraints that can be seen as walls that the executing tool cannot pass through.

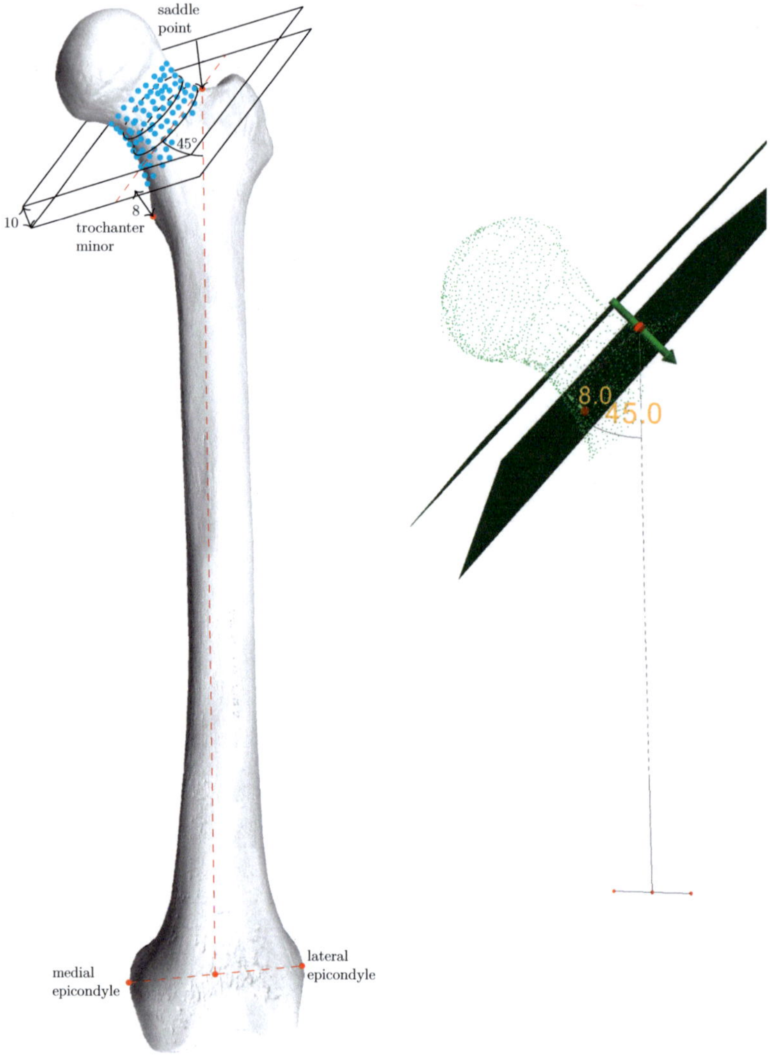

(a) Theoretical plan **(b)** OrthoCAD plan

Figure 3.12.: A theoretical plan and its representation in OrthoCAD.

CHAPTER 4

High Accuracy Pixel-Wise Calibration of Optical See-Through Glasses

Contents

Due to diverse influences mainly caused by the optics of the OSTG, the virtual display is not a simple plane. The virtual display of the Vuzix STAR 1200XLD, for example, is a curved surface (see Figure 4.1). A parametric model can map such surfaces well at their centers but normally it deviates close to the edges. Moreover, the current and upcoming generations of OSTG mainly utilize a waveguide-based display technology. This technology uses special components like gratings or reflectors to guide the light into the user's field of view [96], [97]. These optical components introduce non-linear distortions that a parametric model cannot map appropriately. Therefore, it might be better to consider the display pixels individually.

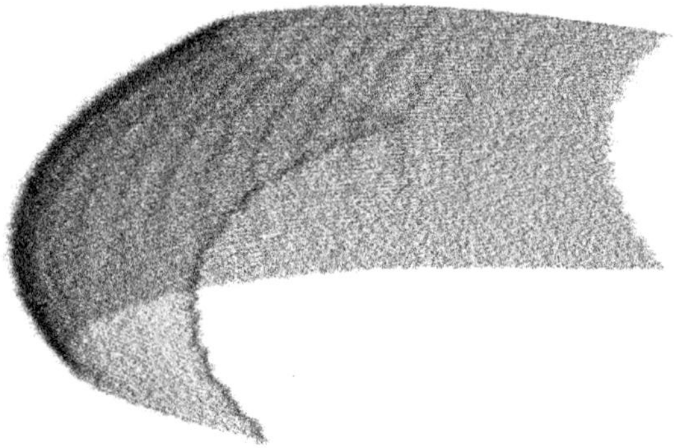

Figure 4.1.: An example of a virtual OSTG display. Depicted are the virtual display positions of the pixels. While looking through the OSTG the display seems to be a flat surface but in reality it is curved.

In a first approach, the virtual location of every single display pixel was triangulated in order to obtain a non-parametric calibration. Figure 4.2 shows the principal setup used for the triangulation. The triangulation is based on the viewing rays passing through a particular pixel and the camera's projection centers for different camera positions (viewpoints). In a waveguide-based OSTG, different eye positions might result in viewing rays passing through different waveguide plates or gratings. This jumping between gratings could falsify the triangulation. In the following sections it is shown that the triangulation approach, as described in [98] and [99], does not work for OSTG with more complex optics.

In this chapter, a non-parametric camera-based calibration of OSTG is described. The calibration procedure and results were previously published in [100] and extend the results from [99]. The calibration process is split into two parts: a one-time system calibration and a continuous user's eye adaptation. The system calibration determines all parameters of the OSTG system except for the user's eye position, which has to be found continuously while the user wears the OSTG. This work concentrates on the system calibration. See [69] for an implementation of a continuous eye adaptation.

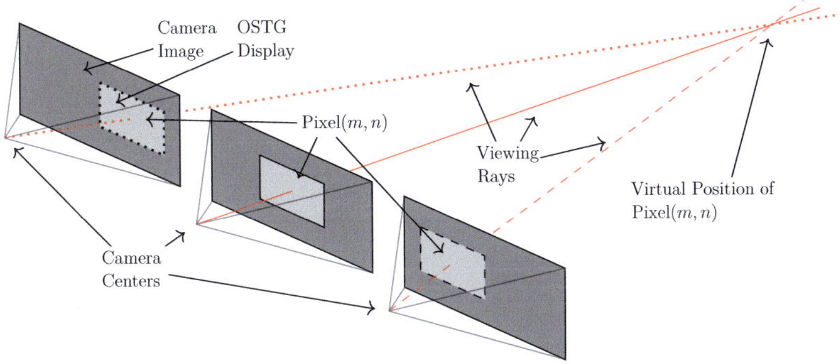

Figure 4.2.: Triangulation of the pixels' virtual positions. In reality the camera centers are much closer together and camera as well as OSTG display images overlap.

The whole calibration process is automated and works without error-prone user interaction. Furthermore, not only the displays are calibrated using a non-parametric approach, but also the attached or integrated reference camera and the display calibration cameras. For this purpose, the approach of Hoppe et al. [101] is used. Calibrating every single pixel of the cameras and the OSTG individually, guarantees so far unmatched accuracy and precision. Whereas Itoh and Klinker [72] explicitly calibrate the distortion of the optics, the proposed method integrates this implicitly by calibrating the display cameras while looking through the optics. Additionally, both displays of the OSTG are calibrated simultaneously. An evaluation of the calibration result is provided and compared to previous approaches. Parts of this chapter were previously published in [100].

The following two sections (see Chapter 4.1 and 4.2) give an overview of the calibration procedure. The contributions of this chapter are: 1. A calibration method that (a.) maps every single display pixel to individual viewing rays (Chapter 4.4 and 4.5), (b.) calculates a precise distortion map and an optimized OpenGL frustum (Chapter 4.6 and 4.7) and (c.) can be rendered in real time (Chapter 4.8). 2. A calibration procedure that is completely automated (Chapter 4.3). 3. A demonstration of the previous triangulation approach by [99] with two different OSTG and its drawbacks (Chapter 4.9.1 and 4.10.1). 4. An accuracy analysis of the proposed method (Chapter 4.9.2 and 4.10.2).

4.1 Procedure

The final result of the presented calibration is an optimized OpenGL frustum together with a collection of projection centers and distortion maps that can be interpolated in order to account for the user's current eye position. The procedure can be split into three steps, which are repeated for nine different display camera positions:

1. (Re-)calibration of all cameras (including relative transformations and optimized projection centers)
2. Determination of the display cameras' viewing rays for all display pixels (together with the optimized OpenGL frustum for the center position)
3. Calculation of the distortion map for the rendered OpenGL image

It can already be noted that the OpenGL frustum is only optimized for the center position. In all other camera positions it is reused with adapted projection centers. This does not lead to any inaccuracies since the distortion maps account for any deviation originating from the linear projection model.

4.2 Coordinate Systems

Figure 4.3 shows a schematic overview of the calibration coordinate systems. This figure and the following sections refer to these coordinate systems:

W … calibration coordinate system of the reference camera used for observing the scene in front of the OSTG
S … calibration coordinate system of an optional camera forming a stereo camera system with the reference camera
L … calibration coordinate system of the left display camera
R … calibration coordinate system of the right display camera
H … ancillary coordinate system not rotated with respect to W but translated in such a way that its origin equals the approximate projection center of the left or right camera
E … OpenGL's eye coordinate system with z_E pointing inside the user's eye
C … OpenGL's clip coordinate system
N … OpenGL's normalized device coordinate system
G … OpenGL's pixel coordinate system
P … pixel coordinate system of the left or right OSTG display
K … pixel coordinate system of the left or right display camera

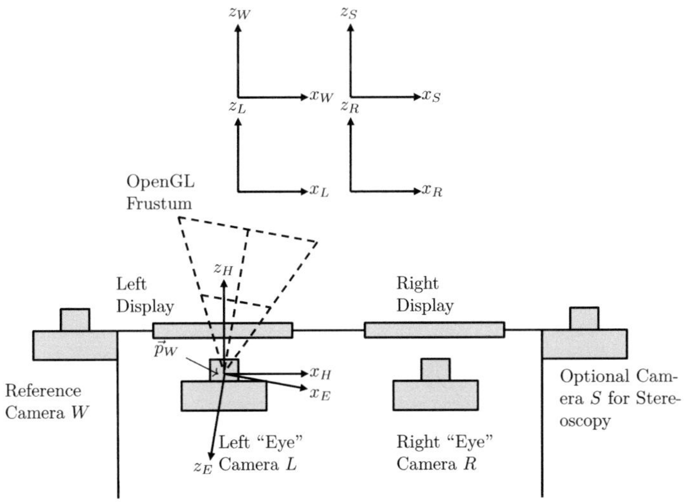

Figure 4.3.: Schematic overview showing the coordinate systems used in this calibration. $\vec{p}_W$ is the approximate projection center of the camera.

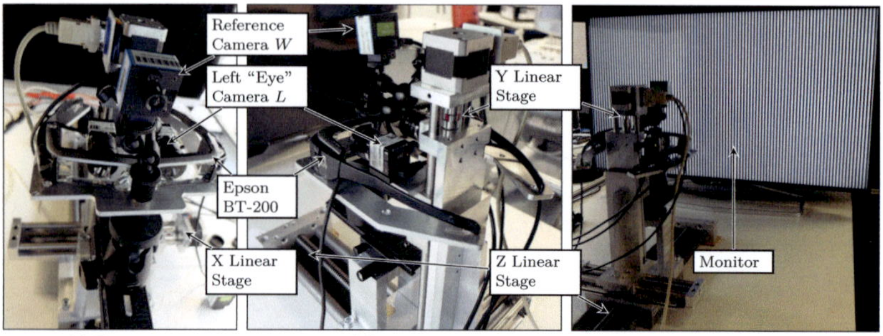

(a) Front view (b) Rear view (c) Rear view with monitor showing sinusoidal pattern

Figure 4.4.: The hardware setup used for the calibration.

4.3 Setup

The calibration was tested on two OSTG: the STAR 1200XLD (Vuzix, USA) and the Moverio BT-200 (Epson, Japan). The attached reference camera is a DMK22AUC03-F (The Imaging Source, Germany) and the displays are calibrated by two 1.3 MP cameras (MQ013MG-E2, XIMEA, Germany). The non-parametric monitor-based camera calibration (see Chapter 4.4) was performed using a BDM4065UC monitor (Philips, Netherlands). See Figure 4.4 for the hardware setup.

The automation of the calibration process is implemented using three translation stages. Two of them are used to place the display cameras at different x- and y-positions behind the displays. The third one places the whole setup at different distances with respect to the monitor used for the camera calibration.

The BT-200 consists of the glasses that are connected to an Android-based control unit. When using the control unit, the images needed for the calibration are transferred via USB or WLAN using a streaming app (e.g. IDisplay). Since this produces high latencies, the control unit was replaced with the conversion board DM484CS (Colorado Video, USA), which allows connecting the BT-200 directly to the PC.

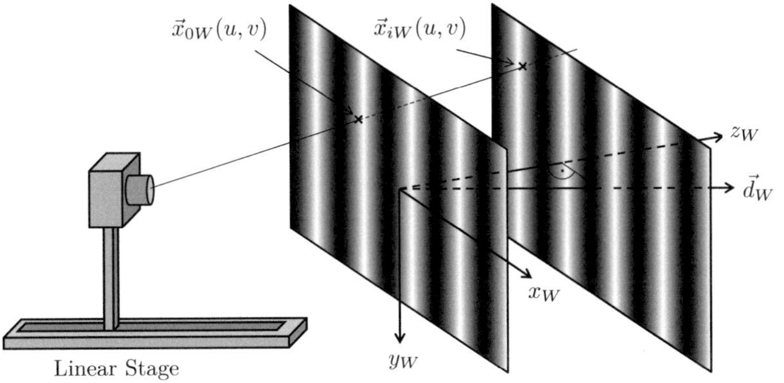

Figure 4.5.: Schematic setup of the non-parametric monitor-based camera calibration. The direction $\vec{d}_W$ is parallel to the linear stage.

4.4 Camera Calibration

The display cameras are used to measure feature points lying behind the optical components of the OSTG. Therefore, these optics become an integral part of the camera, which means that the display cameras have to be calibrated while looking through the OSTG. Since the cameras are moved with respect to these optical elements, they have to be recalibrated for each of the nine positions. See Section 4.11 for more details.

In order to be able to calibrate the OSTG as accurate as possible, an accurate camera calibration is crucial. Therefore, the camera calibration is performed using the non-parametric monitor-based calibration method described in [101]. The basic idea behind this calibration approach is that the viewing rays of the camera pixels are calibrated individually and independently from each other instead of using a pinhole model together with radial and tangential distortion parameters. The automation process of this model-free calibration is implemented using a linear stage and an off-the-shelf monitor (see Figure 4.5).

The camera is attached to the linear stage and observes the monitor showing a horizontal alternatively vertical sinusoidal gray value pattern that is shifted horizontally alternatively vertically by one period in N equidistant steps. Each pixel (u, v) observes two gray value oscillations $g_n(u, v)$ with $0 \leq n \leq N - 1$ that are approximated by $g_n(u, v) \approx b + a \cos\left(\varphi - \frac{2\pi n}{N}\right)$. Solving the underlying minimization problem results in $\varphi = \text{atan2}(a_s, a_c)$ with

$$a_c = \frac{2}{N} \sum_{n=0}^{N-1} g_n(u, v) \cos\left(\frac{2\pi n}{N}\right) \tag{4.1}$$

$$a_s = \frac{2}{N} \sum_{n=0}^{N-1} g_n(u, v) \sin\left(\frac{2\pi n}{N}\right) \tag{4.2}$$

This relative phase shift (within one period) is accurate even if the measured oscillation is not perfectly sinusoidal (e.g. compressed or clipped). Subsequently, it can be converted to a monitor pixel using $p = \frac{P}{2\pi} \cdot \varphi$ where P is the period width alternatively height in monitor pixel. It is straightforward to convert this relative to an absolute phase shift by adding or subtracting multiples of P whenever phase shift jumps occur. By multiplying the results with the pixel width alternatively height the metric coordinates are calculated.

All this results in accurate 3D world points $\vec{x}_{0W}(u, v)$ for each camera pixel where the z-coordinate of the first monitor position is set to zero. This step is repeated several times for different camera positions. Given that the normalized direction $\vec{d}_W$ of the linear stage is parallel to the normal direction of the monitor, only the z-coordinate of the subsequently measured monitor points $\vec{x}_{iW}(u, v)$ has to be adjusted according to the relative movement along the stage. If this is not the case, this direction can either be measured or reconstructed from rotated test positions of the monitor. The correct 3D position can then be found by de-shearing the measured points. Finally, the viewing rays are calculated as regression lines through the measured world points $\vec{x}_{iW}(u, v)$. These viewing rays are shown in Figure 4.6.

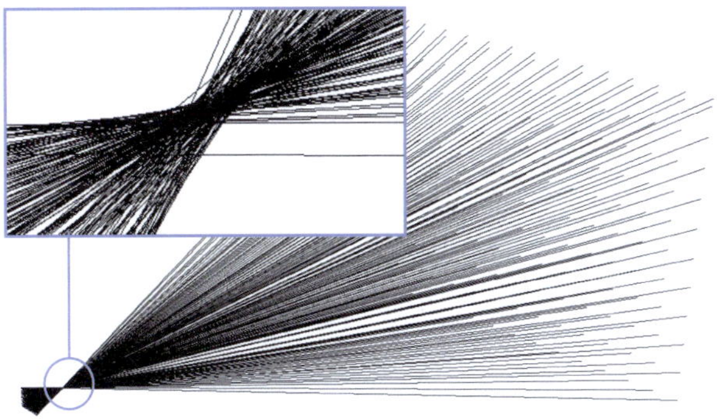

Figure 4.6.: An example of a non-parametric camera calibration. Depicted is every 10th pixel. In the upper left corner a zoom to the approximate projection center is shown.

Since the monitor defines the calibration coordinate system, all simultaneously calibrated cameras are calibrated in the same coordinate system. In other words, the coordinate systems L, R, S and W are all the same. Nevertheless, the following algorithm is written in terms of different calibration coordinate systems in order to be able to allow for other calibration methods.

This pinhole-model-free calibration technique results in the absence of a definite projection center (see Figure 4.6). Nevertheless, it is still possible to calculate the approx. projection center $\vec{p}_L$ or $\vec{p}_R$ by intersecting all rays in a least-squares sense and to use these points as origin for OpenGL's eye coordinate system E.

4.5 Cosine Pattern Calibration

After calibrating the cameras, they can be used to find the viewing rays of all OSTG display pixels in L and R coordinates, alternatively. This is realized using the same calibration technique. A series of horizontally and vertically shifted cosine patterns is displayed on the OSTG display. Each camera pixel observes two phase-shifted gray value oscillations.

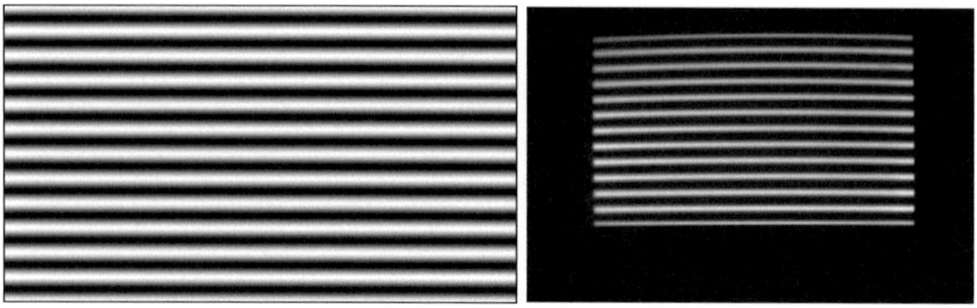

(a) Rendered cosine pattern **(b)** Recorded cosine pattern

Figure 4.7.: Example of a cosine pattern shown on the display and recorded by a camera.

The resulting phase shifts are used to calculate the observed OSTG display pixel position (x_P, y_P) with subpixel accuracy. For an overview of alternative patterns see [102]. Figure 4.7 shows the rendered cosine pattern and how it is seen by one of the display cameras.

In summary, this calibration results in a mapping between non-integer display pixel positions (x_P, y_P) and integer camera pixels (x_K, y_K). Subsequently, a reverse bilinear interpolation is used to inverse this map: for each integer display pixel $x_P = m$ and $y_P = n$ with $m, n \in \mathbb{N}_0$ and $m \leq w - 1$ and $n \leq h - 1$ the corresponding non-integer camera pixel (x_K, y_K) is calculated with subpixel accuracy. Here, the width w and height h of the OSTG displays were introduced. Figure 4.8a depicts this mapping.

The camera calibration is now used to calculate the viewing rays corresponding to the found camera pixel positions (x_K, y_K). All in all, this results in a mapping between integer OSTG display pixels $x_P = m$, $y_P = n$ and the corresponding viewing rays $\vec{x}_L(m, n) = \vec{a}_L + s \cdot \vec{d}_L$ and $\vec{x}_R(m, n) = \vec{a}_R + s \cdot \vec{d}_R$ of the left and right display camera, respectively.

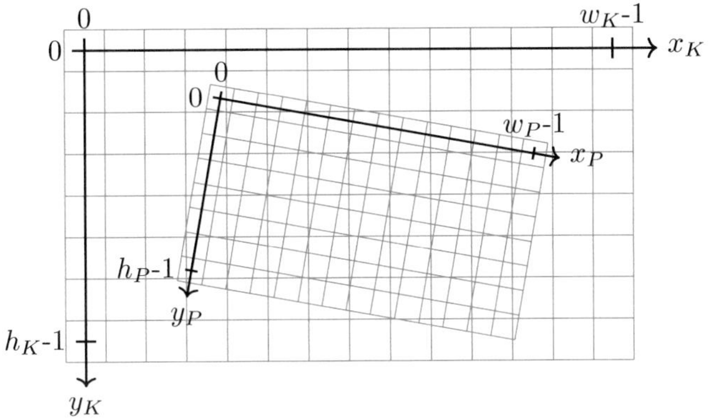

(a) Camera coordinate system K with respect to OSTG display coordinate system P.

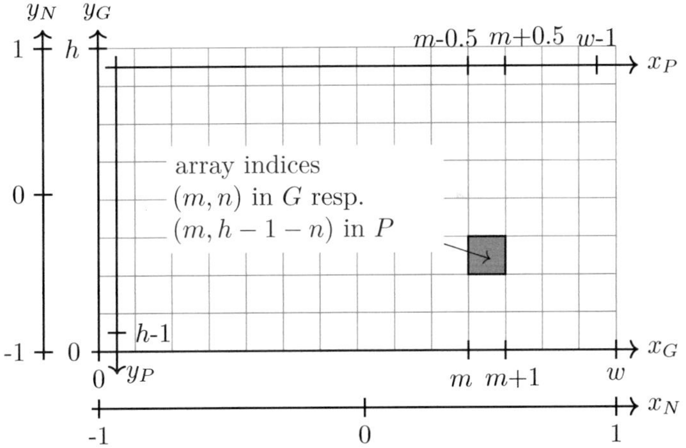

(b) OpenGL's normalized device coordinate system N and pixel coordinate system G with respect to OSTG display coordinate system P.

Figure 4.8.: The pixel coordinate systems used in this calibration.

4.6 Frustum Optimization

Initially, the correspondences between OSTG display pixels $\vec{x}_P$ and the corresponding viewing rays $\vec{x}_L$ and $\vec{x}_R$ are used to calculate an optimized OpenGL frustum for a specific viewpoint of the left and right OSTG display, respectively. Then, the frustum and the correspondences are used to define distortion maps for the rendered images such that each image pixel is located at exactly the right position. This approach ensures that the rendering process is both fast and precise.

In the following paragraphs, the description will concentrate on the OSTG' left display. The right display is processed analogously. The transformation chain between camera L and the clip coordinates of the OpenGL frustum is defined as:

$$\begin{pmatrix} x_C \\ y_C \\ z_C \\ w_C \end{pmatrix} = F_{CE} \cdot F_{EH} \cdot F_{HW} \cdot F_{WL} \cdot \begin{pmatrix} x_L \\ y_L \\ z_L \\ 1 \end{pmatrix} \tag{4.3}$$

F_{WL} is the rigid transformation from the left eye camera coordinates L to the reference camera coordinates W, which results from calibrating the two cameras. In case of a simultaneous non-model-based calibration, this transformation equals identity, since all cameras are automatically calibrated in the same coordinate system. The ancillary coordinate system H is not rotated with respect to W but only translated into the approximate projection center of the left alternatively right camera. Therefore, the transformation from W to H is

$$F_{HW} = \begin{pmatrix} E_3 & -\vec{p}_W \\ \vec{0}^T & 1 \end{pmatrix} \tag{4.4}$$

where $\vec{p}_W = F_{WL} \cdot \vec{p}_L$ is the approximate projection center of the left camera in W coordinates and E_3 the 3×3 identity matrix. E and H share the same origin. Therefore, the transformation from H to E equals

$$F_{EH} = \begin{pmatrix} R_{EH} & \vec{0} \\ \vec{0}^T & 1 \end{pmatrix} \tag{4.5}$$

R_{EH} is the corresponding rotation matrix and will be optimized by this algorithm. F_{CE} is the well known OpenGL projection matrix

$$F_{CE} = \begin{pmatrix} \frac{2n}{r-l} & 0 & \frac{r+l}{r-l} & 0 \\ 0 & \frac{2n}{t-b} & \frac{t+b}{t-b} & 0 \\ 0 & 0 & -\frac{f+n}{f-n} & \frac{2fn}{f-n} \\ 0 & 0 & -1 & 0 \end{pmatrix} \tag{4.6}$$

with the parameters l (left), r (right), b (bottom), t (top), n (near) and f (far) defining the OpenGL frustum.

The origin of the pixel coordinate system P describing the OSTG display is located in the center of pixel $(0, 0)$, which can be found in the upper left corner. x_P points right along the columns and y_P points down along the rows of the OSTG image. In contrast to that, the origin of OpenGL's pixel coordinate system G is located in the lower left corner of pixel $(0, 0)$, which is located in the lower left corner of the image. x_G points right along the columns and y_G points up along the rows of the image (see Figure 4.8b).

It can be easily derived that $x_G = x_P + 0.5$ and $y_G = h - 0.5 - y_P$. Furthermore, OpenGL's pixel coordinates can be transferred to normalized device coordinates using $x_N = \frac{2}{w} \cdot x_G - 1$ and $y_N = \frac{2}{h} \cdot y_G - 1$ (see Figure 4.8b). The still missing link between N and C is

$$x_N = \frac{x_C}{w_C} \text{ and } y_N = \frac{y_C}{w_C} \tag{4.7}$$

Given an OSTG pixel (x_P, y_P) and the corresponding viewing ray of the left camera $\vec{a}_L + s \cdot \vec{d}_L$, the pixel coordinates can be transformed to normalized device coordinates (x_N, y_N). Then a specific point on the viewing ray $\vec{x}_L$ is chosen and transformed to H using $\vec{x}_H = F_{HW} \cdot F_{WL} \cdot \vec{x}_L$. The transformation from H to C can be written in the form

$$\begin{pmatrix} x_C \\ y_C \\ w_C \end{pmatrix} = \underbrace{P_{CE} \cdot R_{EH}}_{=:Q} \cdot \begin{pmatrix} x_H \\ y_H \\ z_H \end{pmatrix} \text{ with } P_{CE} = \begin{pmatrix} f_x & 0 & x_0 \\ 0 & f_y & y_0 \\ 0 & 0 & -1 \end{pmatrix} \tag{4.8}$$

with the abbreviations $f_x = \frac{2n}{r-l}$, $f_y = \frac{2n}{t-b}$, $x_0 = \frac{r+l}{r-l}$, $y_0 = \frac{t+b}{t-b}$ and the (3×3)-matrix Q. This leads to the following equations for the nine unknown elements of Q:

$$x_N = \frac{x_C}{w_C} = \frac{q_{11}x_H + q_{12}y_H + q_{13}z_H}{q_{31}x_H + q_{32}y_H + q_{33}z_H} \tag{4.9}$$

$$y_N = \frac{y_C}{w_C} = \frac{q_{21}x_H + q_{22}y_H + q_{23}z_H}{q_{31}x_H + q_{32}y_H + q_{33}z_H} \tag{4.10}$$

which can be rewritten as

$$x_H q_{11} + y_H q_{12} + z_H q_{13} - x_N x_H q_{31} - x_N y_H q_{32} - x_N z_H q_{33} = 0 \tag{4.11}$$

$$x_H q_{21} + y_H q_{22} + z_H q_{23} - y_N x_H q_{31} - y_N y_N q_{32} - y_N z_H q_{33} = 0 \tag{4.12}$$

All in all, each correspondence between an OSTG display pixel $x_P = m$, $y_P = n$ and a corresponding point $\vec{x}_L(m,n)$ on the viewing ray of this pixel results in two equations for the nine unknown elements of Q. This overdetermined homogeneous linear equation system can be solved, for example, by means of an eigenvector analysis. Since the equation system is homogeneous, Q can only be found up to a so far unknown scaling factor.

By defining the row vectors of matrix R_{EH} to be $\vec{r}_1^T$, $\vec{r}_2^T$ and $\vec{r}_3^T$ matrix Q equals

$$\begin{pmatrix} \vec{q}_1^T \\ \vec{q}_2^T \\ \vec{q}_3^T \end{pmatrix} = \begin{pmatrix} f_x & 0 & x_0 \\ 0 & f_y & y_0 \\ 0 & 0 & -1 \end{pmatrix} \cdot \begin{pmatrix} \vec{r}_1^T \\ \vec{r}_2^T \\ \vec{r}_3^T \end{pmatrix} = \begin{pmatrix} f_x \cdot \vec{r}_1^T + x_0 \cdot \vec{r}_3^T \\ f_y \cdot \vec{r}_2^T + y_0 \cdot \vec{r}_3^T \\ -\vec{r}_3^T \end{pmatrix} \tag{4.13}$$

It can be seen that the normalized third row $\vec{r}_3^T$ of R_{EH} equals $-\vec{q}_3^T$. Therefore it is necessary to scale Q such that its third row is normalized: $Q \rightarrow \frac{1}{|\vec{q}_3|} \cdot Q$. Furthermore, it is known that

$$\det(Q) = \det(P_{CE}) \cdot \underbrace{\det(R_{EH})}_{=1} = -f_x \cdot f_y \tag{4.14}$$

Since f_x and f_y are positive scaling factors, it can be concluded that $\det(Q)$ has to be negative. Therefore, if $\det(Q) > 0$, Q has to be replaced by $-Q$.

Utilizing the fact that the row vectors of a rotation matrix are normalized and perpendicular to each other, the scalar products of $\vec{r}_3 = -\vec{q}_3$ with the first and second row of Q result in:

$$\vec{q}_1^T \cdot \vec{r}_3 = \left(f_x \cdot \vec{r}_1^T + x_0 \cdot \vec{r}_3^T\right) \cdot \vec{r}_3 = x_0 \tag{4.15}$$

$$\vec{q}_2^T \cdot \vec{r}_3 = \left(f_y \cdot \vec{r}_2^T + y_0 \cdot \vec{r}_3^T\right) \cdot \vec{r}_3 = y_0 \tag{4.16}$$

With $f_x \cdot \vec{r}_1 = \vec{q}_1 - x_0 \cdot \vec{r}_3 =: \vec{h}_1$ and $f_y \cdot \vec{r}_2 = \vec{q}_2 - y_0 \cdot \vec{r}_3 =: \vec{h}_2$ it follows that

$$f_x = \left|\vec{h}_1\right|, \quad f_y = \left|\vec{h}_2\right|, \quad \vec{r}_1 = \frac{\vec{h}_1}{f_x}, \quad \vec{r}_2 = \frac{\vec{h}_2}{f_y} \tag{4.17}$$

In a final step, the positive z-coordinates of the near and far clipping plane n and f can be chosen such that the particular scene elements lie inside this region. Now the whole transformation chain from L to P including the projection matrix F_{CE} of the optimized OpenGL frustum are known and can be used to render the scene and to calculate a distortion map such that the pixels of the rendered scene appear at their exact location (see below). If desired, the frustum parameters l, r, t and b can be derived from n, f_x, f_y, x_0 and y_0 as follows:

$$l = \frac{n}{f_x}(x_0 - 1) \qquad r = \frac{n}{f_x}(x_0 + 1) \tag{4.18}$$

$$b = \frac{n}{f_y}(y_0 - 1) \qquad t = \frac{n}{f_y}(y_0 + 1) \tag{4.19}$$

4.7 Calculating the Distorsion Map

After calculating the optimal OpenGL frustum, it is possible to render a specific scene given in W coordinates. The resulting image J is rendered off-screen and not displayed to the user but taken as texture or, more specifically, pixel source for the actual and precise image D, which accounts for distortion effects of any kind.

A specific integer pixel of image D with array indices (m, n) with $m, n \in \mathbb{N}_0$ ranges from m to $m + 1$ alternatively n to $n + 1$ in G coordinates. In P coordinates, this pixel is located at the integer position $x_P = m$

and $y_P = h - 1 - n$ (see Figure 4.8b). Since the corresponding viewing ray $\vec{x}_L(m, h-1-n) = \vec{a}_L + s \cdot \vec{d}_L$ of this pixel is known, the position in image J, where the information for this pixel has been projected on, can be calculated as

$$x_G(m,n) = \frac{w}{2} \cdot \left(\frac{x_C}{w_C} + 1 \right) \qquad y_G(m,n) = \frac{h}{2} \cdot \left(\frac{y_C}{w_C} + 1 \right) \tag{4.20}$$

with $\vec{x}_C = (x_C, y_C, w_C)^T = F_{CL} \cdot \vec{x}_L(m, h-1-n)$. The collection of all $x_G(m,n)$ and $y_G(m,n)$ is called distortion map and used to find the correct pixel color for all pixels of image D using bilinear interpolation in image J. This correction can be performed independently for each pixel and is therefore parallelizable. High frame rates are achieved by executing this algorithm on the graphics card using CUDA.

Remark: The distortion map is calculated using specific points $\vec{x}_L$ on the viewing rays $\vec{a}_L + s \cdot \vec{d}_L$. As long as the viewing rays share the same projection center, neither the OpenGL frustum optimization nor the distortion map depend on the choice of the parameter s. Given that the OSTG's optical elements result in the absence of a joint projection center (which can be calibrated using non-model based camera calibration techniques), the distortion map gets depth dependent.

4.8 Accounting for the Eye Position

So far, the calibration is correct for the viewpoint of the left resp. right camera. Now it has to be taken into account that the user's eye positions do not coincide with these viewpoints. While viewpoint displacements perpendicular to the displays result in negligible projection errors, even small displacements parallel to the displays result in significantly mismatched overlays.

Therefore, the calibration process described above is performed nine times with nine different camera positions lying on a rectangular (3×3)-grid (see Figure 4.9). In a subsequent step, the user's eye position is (dynamically) set within this rectangle and the calibration parameters are interpolated between four of the nine calibrated positions. As mentioned

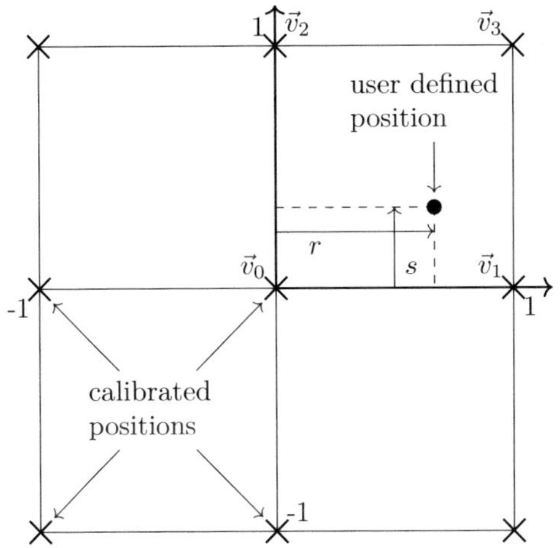

Figure 4.9.: The calibrated and the user defined positions on a (3×3)-grid. The distortion map parameters of the user defined eye position are interpolated between the neighboring calibration positions.

in the previous section, this interpolation process runs on a GPGPU in real time. Since it is difficult to interpolate the OpenGL frustums resp. projection matrices F_{CE}, only the frustum of the center position is optimized. The resulting projection parameters are used for all nine viewpoints. This does not lead to undesired inaccuracies, since the individual distortion maps of all nine positions account for all projection and distortion errors. But it is absolutely essential to use the correct projection centers $\vec{p}_W$ for all nine positions, which result from calibrating the left resp. right camera.

Given that the user's eyes are not tracked (which requires another calibration step for aligning this tracking coordinate system with W), the user has to perform an initial one-time adjustment of his eye-position. This can be realized by moving the eye position away from the initial center position (left, right, up, or down) until a displayed sample image matches a real calibration object. In fact, he defines a certain position between -1 and 1 in horizontal and vertical direction where $(0, 0)$ equals the calibrated center position, $(1, 1)$ equals the upper right position, etc. (see Figure 4.9). The projection center as well as all entries of the distortion maps are then interpolated bilinearly in the correct quadrant using

$$\vec{v}_{res} = (1-r)\cdot(1-s)\cdot\vec{v}_0 + r\cdot(1-s)\cdot\vec{v}_1 + (1-r)\cdot s\cdot\vec{v}_2 + r\cdot s\cdot\vec{v}_3 \quad (4.21)$$

where $\vec{v}_{res}$ can either be the interpolated projection center $\vec{p}_W$ or the pixel coordinates of the distortion map (x_G, y_G).

4.9 Experiments

Two different experiments were performed: 1. An evaluation of the triangulation approach described in [99] using OSTG with complex optical elements. 2. An accuracy analysis of the proposed method.

4.9.1 Evaluation of Triangulation Approach

To evaluate the triangulation calibration method, two different OSTG were calibrated:

- the STAR 1200XLD by Vuzix using a single planar light-guide
- the BT-200 by Epson using several free-form light-guides

If the triangulation method is generally valid, it must apply that the pixel locations are independent from the eye position. Therefore, the selection of viewpoints should not influence the calibration result. In the case of the triangulation approach, five viewpoints (Center, Center Right, Center Left, Top Center, Bottom Center) are used. For this evaluation nine viewpoints (the ones from the proposed calibration) are calibrated. From these nine positions two independent calibrations are calculated:

(+) Center, Center Right, Center Left, Top Center, Bottom Center

(×) Center, Top Right, Top Left, Bottom Right, Bottom Left

If there is a difference between these two, the calibration result is viewpoint dependent. Therefore the triangulation method is not applicable.

4.9.2 Accuracy Analysis of Proposed Method

In order to evaluate the presented calibration technique, an accuracy analysis is performed. The monitor that was used for calibrating the involved cameras (see [101] for further details) now displays filled circles at certain 3D positions. These positions are known since the cameras are calibrated in the world coordinate system W that is defined by the monitor. The corresponding 3D scene consisting of the collection of circles with given radii at known positions is rendered as described in Chapter 4.1. The left and right display camera can now be used to find the centers of the circles shown on the monitor (with OSTG overlay switched off) and the OSTG display (with monitor switched off), successively. This results in a set of center deviations given in camera pixels. This accuracy analysis was performed six times with different settings:

1. Camera viewpoint at calibrated center position with distortion map switched off
2. Camera viewpoint at calibrated center position with distortion map switched on
3. Camera viewpoint at intermediate point with interpolated distortion map switched off
4. Camera viewpoint at intermediate point with interpolated distortion map switched on
5. Camera viewpoint at calibrated top right position with distortion map switched off
6. Camera viewpoint at calibrated top right position with distortion map switched on

All results are converted from deviations in camera pixels to viewing angle deviations and absolute deviations in millimeter at a distance of 500 mm. For this test a Epson Moverio BT-200 was used.

4.10 Results

The following sections describe the evaluation results of the two previously explained experiments.

4.10.1 Triangulation Method

Figure 4.10 shows the results of the evaluation of the triangulation approach. The results for the Vuzix OSTG are as expected. The pixels are located on a curved surface (Figure 4.10a), which appears to be a rectangular grid from the user's perspective (Figure 4.10c). Figure 4.10e shows the difference between the two calibrations (+) and (×). It is shown that the pixels in the center of the display are influenced by the different configurations while the border pixels seem to be steady. The difference is up to 400 mm.

The calibration of the Epson BT-200 produced a corrugated surface (Figure 4.10b) that also appears to the user as rectangular grid (Figure 4.10d). Figure 4.10f shows that the calibration differences of the BT-200 are much higher than the ones of the Vuzix OSTG. Besides being up to three times larger, they are also more uneven and unsymmetrical. In this case the border area has larger differences than the center.

4.10.2 Proposed Method

Figure 4.11 and Figure 4.12 show the overlay of circles drawn on the OSTG display. Whereas Figure 4.11 shows an overview, Figure 4.12 shows the close-up of circles in the upper right corner of the right OSTG display for the upper right calibration position. Each image represents one test. Figure 4.12a shows the overlay in the upper right position without distortion map correction. It is apparent that the calculated frustum is not able to produce a good overlay. Figure 4.12b shows the same situation with the distortion map switched on, which demonstrates a perfect overlay.

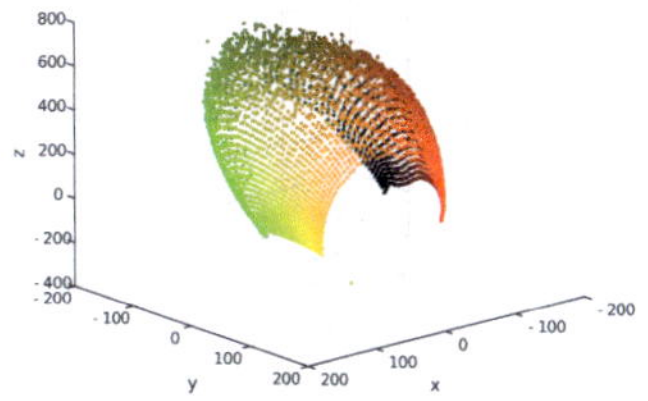

(a) STAR 1200XLD Virtual Display

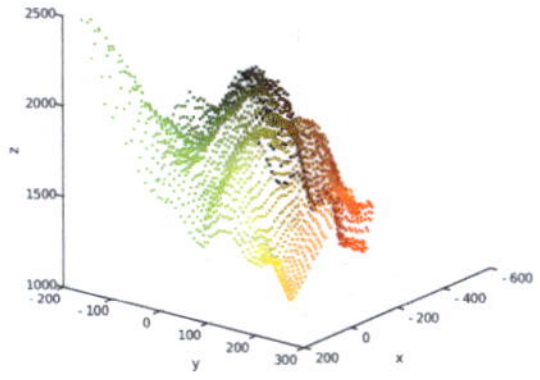

(b) BT-200 Virtual Display

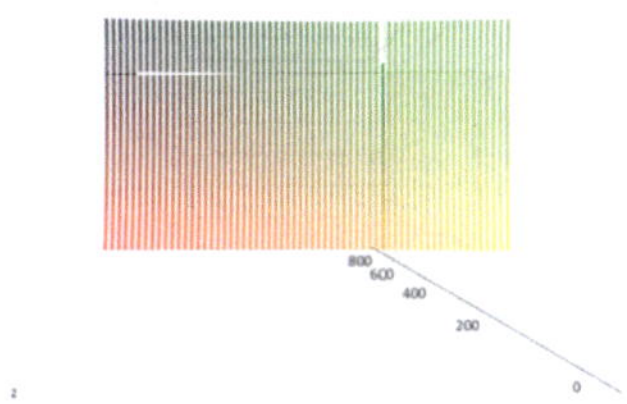

(c) STAR 1200XLD Eye View

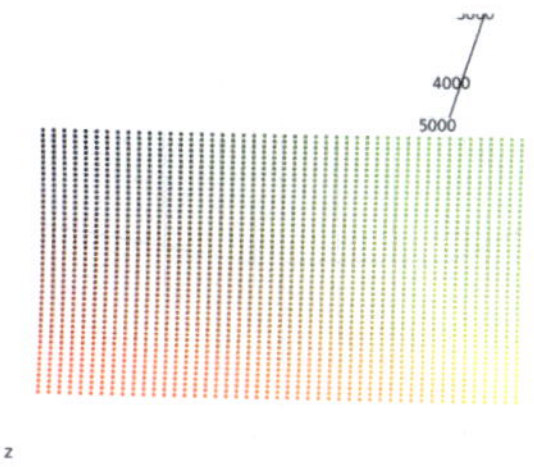

(d) BT-200 Eye View

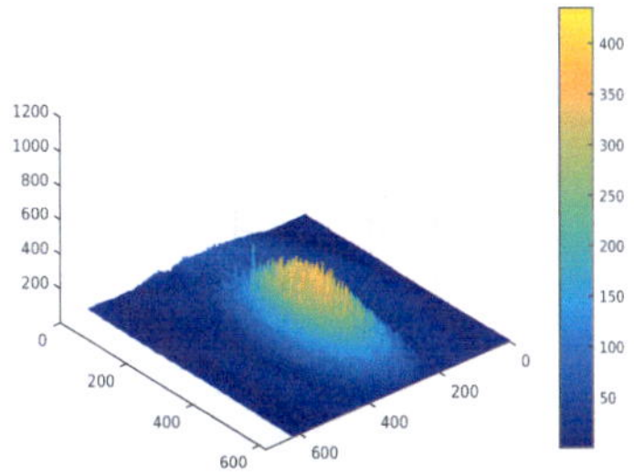

(e) STAR 1200XLD Calibration Difference

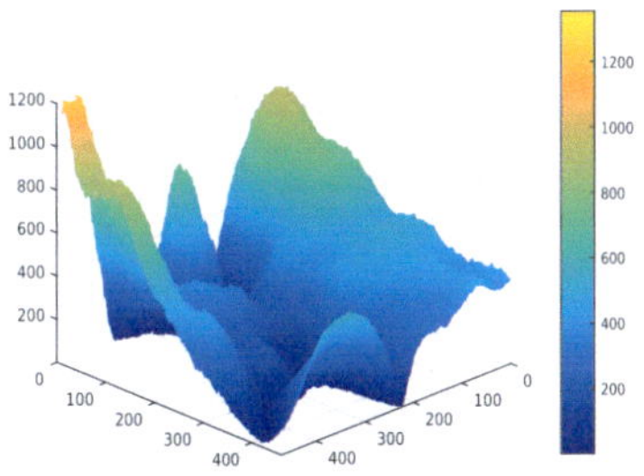

(f) BT-200 Calibration Difference

Figure 4.10.: Results of the calibration method presented in [99] for two different OSTG (Vuzix STAR 1200XLD and Epson BT-200): (a) and (b) show the positions of the virtual display pixels, (c) and (d) show the virtual display seen from the user's perspective and (e) and (f) show the difference of two calibrations with different calibration viewpoints. All values are given in millimeters.

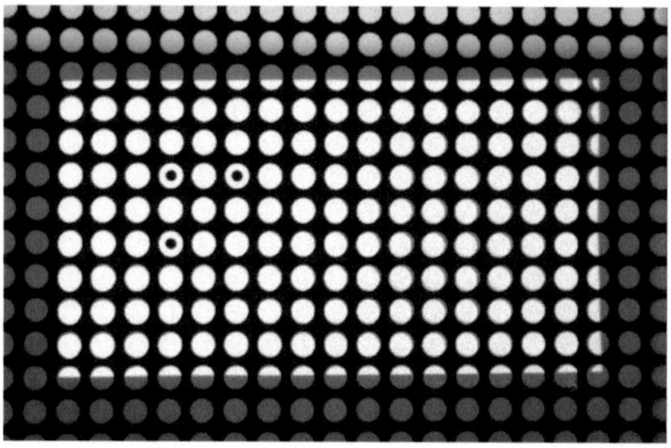

(a) Test (5)

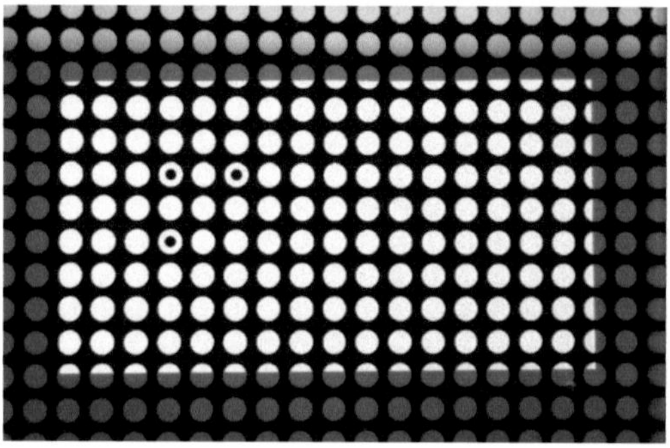

(b) Test (6)

Figure 4.11.: OSTG overlay with distortion map switched off (a) and on (b). Shown is only the region of interest (845×540 pixel) of the camera image.

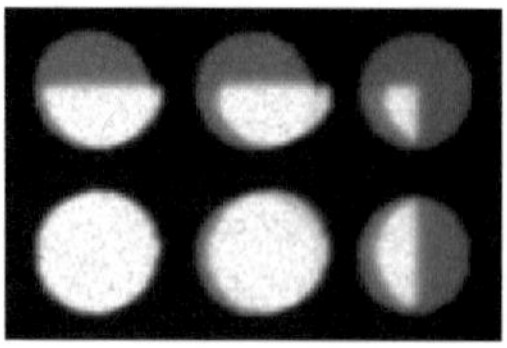

(a) Test (5)

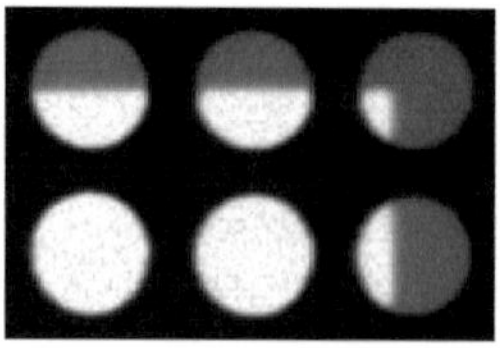

(b) Test (6)

Figure 4.12.: Close-up (125×125 pixel) on the OSTG edge area showing an overlay with distortion map switched off (a) and on (b).

Test	Number of circles	Reprojection error [pixel]		Angular error [arcmin]		Absolute error [mm]	
		mean	max.	mean	max.	mean	max.
1.	247	0.77	3.55	1.27	5.86	0.19	0.85
2.	248	0.24	0.80	0.40	1.31	0.06	0.19
3.	244	1.75	4.65	2.89	7.67	0.42	1.12
4.	248	0.53	1.37	0.88	2.26	0.13	0.33
5.	240	2.58	4.88	4.26	8.04	0.62	1.17
6.	244	0.46	0.79	0.76	1.30	0.11	0.19

Table 4.2.: Results of the accuracy analysis given in arcminutes ($1\,\text{arcmin} = \frac{1}{60}^{\circ}$), camera pixel and mm. The absolute error in mm depends on the distance and is calculated for 500 mm.

Table 4.2 and Figure 4.13 show the deviations between the center positions of the monitor circles and the overlaid ones. The maximal deviations in Test (1), (3) and (5) are in the range of 3.5 to 5 pixel. However, by using the distortion map to correct the pixels, the maximal deviation decreases to under 1.4 pixel or 2.26 arcmin. These values translate to a deviation of 0.33 mm at a distance of 500 mm. All results are generated with the Epson Moverio BT-200 and averaged over the left and right display.

4.11 Conclusion

Drawback of a triangulation-based approach The performed tests show that the triangulation-based calibration works for the STAR 1200-XLD but not for the BT-200. Whereas the STAR 1200XLD uses a simple curved mirror, the BT-200 uses three free-form light guides. The results show that different eye positions cause different results. In the case of the BT-200, it results in a completely different calibration. The STAR 1200XLD is also influenced by a different viewpoint setup, though only at its center. These results show that the triangulation approach only works for OSTG with simple optics and that it is not a universal approach.

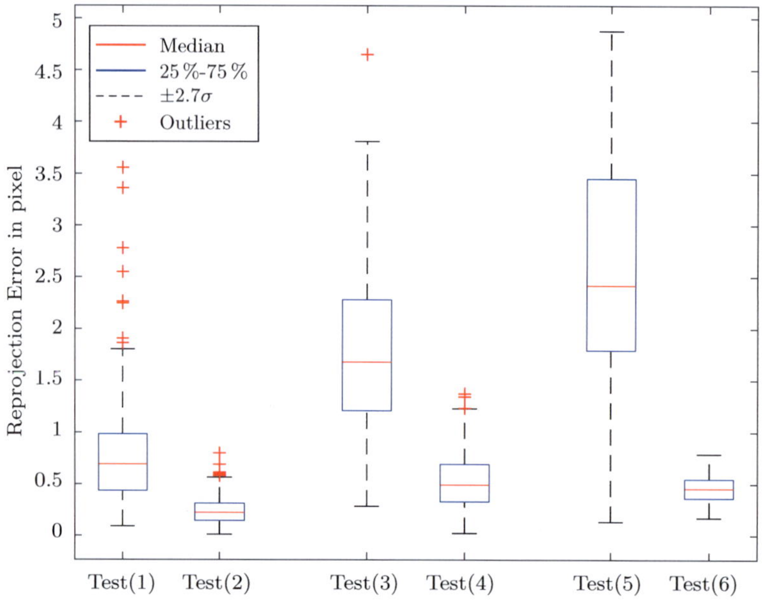

Figure 4.13.: The reprojection errors in pixel for each test.

Comparison with the direct/augmented view distortion method The calibration described by Itoh and Klinker [72] might seem similar to the proposed method but differs in several points:

1. The proposed method considers the distortion of the direct view implicitly, whereas [72] calculates it explicitly. This is discussed in more detail in the following paragraph.

2. The direct view correction [72] uses a 4×11 asymmetrical circle grid, whereas the proposed method utilizes the full resolution of the calibration monitor and camera. Thus, the proposed method collects many more point correspondences.

3. In the proposed method a given world point is projected onto the 2D image plane using the optimized OpenGL frustum. The resulting 2D point is subsequently corrected with the distortion

maps. This approach ensures that the rendering process is both precise and fast. In [72] the projection function is not a simple perspective projection. In order to find the resulting 2D point, a light-field regression function is utilized that maps undistorted 3D light rays to distorted 2D points. They state that their approach is not running in real time and that a sampling approach similar to ray tracing could improve this.

4. The cameras in the proposed method are calibrated with a non-parametric approach, whereas [72] utilizes cameras with a standard calibration model.

Camera calibration through the OSTG optics The integrated reference camera with coordinate system W is used to observe the scene in front of the user. Given that this camera observes something at point $\vec{x}_W$ that should be overlaid, the pixel that lies on the viewing ray from the eye's projection center $\vec{p}_W$ through this world point has to be found. For this purpose, the user's eye position and the display's pixel positions or pixel directions in W coordinates are needed.

It can be assumed that the display pixels in W coordinates are located straight in front of the (left) glass as shown in Figure 4.14. Given that a precalibrated camera was used to measure these locations or directions of the display pixels, it would make the user believe that these pixels are displaced as shown in the same figure. Intersecting the viewing ray from the real projection center $\vec{p}_{1W}$ through $\vec{x}_W$ with the displaced pixel positions would result in the incorrect overlay pixel $\vec{q}_{1W}$ since from the user's viewpoint, the overlay pixel is left whereas the to be overlaid world point is right.

Therefore, the display camera L, which is used for calibrating the OSTG display pixels, has to be calibrated through the optical elements of the OSTG such that it observes the scene in front of the display exactly the same way as the OSTG user observes it. This results in the fact that the display camera appears to be at the virtual camera position L'.

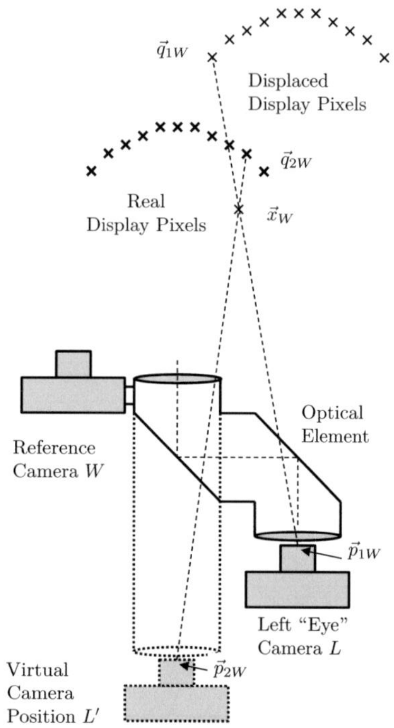

Figure 4.14.: Exemplary OSTG system stressing the necessity to calibrate cameras through the optics.

Intersecting the viewing ray from the virtual projection center $\vec{p}_{2W}$ through $\vec{x}_W$ with the real display pixel positions yields the right overlay pixel indicated with $\vec{q}_{2W}$ in Figure 4.14.

It can be argued that it is still possible to precalibrate the intrinsic (projection) parameters of camera L to place it behind the left display and to optimize the rigid transformation $F_{WL'}$ from the virtual camera position L' to W. This could be implemented by placing a calibration object in front of camera W and camera L' looking through the left display. But due to the fact that the distortion effects of the left display were not part of the camera calibration of L', camera L' now observes a distorted calibration object that does not fit to the one observed by camera W.

In short, if camera L is placed behind the display in order to measure something that lies in front of the display, the displacement and distortion effects of the display become an integral part of camera L. Therefore, camera L has to be calibrated through the display. Only in this case camera W and camera L observe the same measurable scene lying in front of the glasses.

Itoh and Klinker [72] use these effects the other way round. They calibrate their cameras in advance, which makes them independent from the optics. Then, they record the scene from different viewpoints and calculate a mapping between undistorted viewing rays and distorted ones. Therefore, both methods include the influence of the optics: Itoh and Klinker [72] explicitly calculate it, whereas the proposed method implicitly includes it in the camera calibrations and the final distortion maps.

Accuracy comparison with previous works Figure 4.15 shows the accuracy of a simultaneous direct and augmented view distortion calibration [72], a triangulation-based non-parametric calibration [99] and the proposed calibration. The results from previous works have to be compared carefully, since all of them used different OSTG. However, Figure 4.15 shows that the proposed calibration is at least a factor of two more accurate than the other approaches.

Compared to the resolution of the human eye A healthy human eye has a resolution of 0.6 to 0.8 arcmin. This means that two objects cannot be distinguished from each other if the angle between them is smaller than the resolution. For the best case (0.4 arcmin, see Test (2) in Table 4.2), this means that the user cannot spatially differentiate between the real object and its overlay as long as the eye position is detected correctly. However, the maximal errors of up to 2.26 arcmin (Test (4)) are still visible to the user.

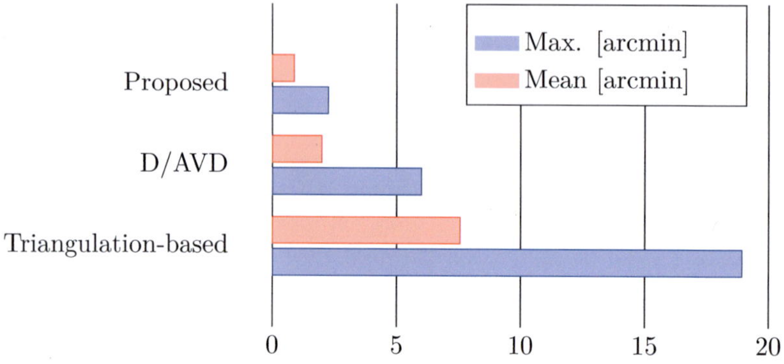

Figure 4.15.: Accuracy comparison between different calibration methods. The red and blue plots represent the mean and the maximal angular errors, respectively. Values for the simultaneous direct and augmented view distortion calibration (D/AVD) and for the triangulation-based approach are taken from [72] and [99], respectively. All values are given in arcmin.

Number of calibration viewpoints Although a fixed number of nine different calibrated viewpoints was suggested, it is straightforward to extend the presented method to an arbitrary number of viewpoints. The processing time is not influenced by a higher number of viewpoints, though the memory need increases.

Evaluation by the user The proposed method only covers the system calibration and disregards the continuous eye tracking adaptation. All presented results were observed by cameras in a static scenario. The final accuracy, however, will also depend on how well the user's eyes are tracked.

Summary A camera-based method for calibrating OSTG was presented in this chapter. The calibration is automated and therefore completely interaction-free. It results in an optimized rendering frustum together with an arbitrary number of distortion maps from different viewpoints. In order to render a scene the current eye position is needed. It is used to adapt the frustum and to interpolate the distortion map. Then the scene is rendered off-screen and subsequently corrected by using the distortion map. It is shown that the proposed method works well and produces so far unmatched accuracy. The maximal deviations are less than 2.26 arcmin, which are 0.33 mm at a distance of 500 mm.

It is shown that a triangulation of the display pixels is not possible in OSTG with free-form light-guides as used in the Epson BT-200. However, for OSTG using simple light-guides (e.g. STAR 1200XLD by Vuzix) a triangulation is applicable.

In this work the calibration and the rendering was performed on the PC and the rendered scene was streamed to the OSTG device. In future, the device shall use these calibration results (frustum and distortion maps) by itself. Moreover, an eye tracking will be implemented and the accuracy of the whole setup will be evaluated in a user study.

CHAPTER 5

OrthoCAD I/O Services

Contents

In CAOS, the amount of different input devices is as high as the diversity of interventions. Their usage depends on the preferences of the surgeon and the availability inside the clinic. OrthoCAD only requires a pointing device and a touch screen. However, in certain cases it is beneficial to use additional devices, for example a 3D scanner, which helps to digitize a larger part of the bone's surface. In order to allow OrthoCAD to perform any CAOS intervention, a method to allow arbitrary input devices was integrated. The same applies to the other data flow direction. The planning data and additional other information inside OrthoCAD can be provided to different execution devices as well as visualization or simulation environments (e.g. MATLAB).

For this purpose, OpenIGTLink is used as protocol allowing arbitrary input and consumer devices to be connected to OrthoCAD. They can connect at runtime and send or receive single data objects or streams of data. As explained in Chapter 3, OrthoCAD is based on MITK. OpenIGTLink was integrated into MITK, since an efficient implementation required adaptations of core components of MITK. The integration was contributed to the official open sourced MITK repository. Additionally, a performance analysis was carried out. This implementation, together with the results, were previously published in [103].

This chapter starts with the requirement analysis (Chapter 5.1), followed by the architectural overview (Chapter 5.2) and the methodology for validating the developed architecture (Chapter 5.3). The results of the validation are presented, discussed and finally concluded (Chapter 5.4 and 5.5).

5.1 Requirements

In order to connect to arbitrary input and output devices and send or receive data from them, the OpenIGTLink protocol was integrated into MITK, which so far did not support OpenIGTLink. Thereof, the following requirements were derived for MITK-OpenIGTLink as a communication layer for MITK:

Extensibility The new module must easily integrate into the pipeline structure of MITK and its modules to allow for interchangeability of e.g. data processing methods. Using new and customized OpenIGTLink message types must be possible.

Flexibility The data transmission and its processing inside the MITK pipelines have to be connected in a flexible way in order to easily exchange the processing steps.

Performance High frame rates and low latency are necessary for real-time applications. The US image data transfer shall run with 30 Hz, since typical real-time US devices run with such frame rates. Tracking data shall be transmitted with up to 1000 Hz in order to cover robotic applications [81]. The latency for tracking data caused by MITK shall be one order of magnitude smaller than the latency caused by the tracking device, which is the time from when the tracking device is sampled until tracking data is available on the PC.

Application-wide availability The module should provide an application-wide availability of all filters and devices that are necessary for an OpenIGTLink connection. This makes multiple configurations of the same component unnecessary.

Portability MITK-OpenIGTLink should be implemented in C++ and run on Windows, Linux and Mac.

Robustness Messages must not be discarded as long as the user wants to process all of them. It must be configurable to keep only the latest message or all.

Usability The module must be easy to integrate for developers and the resulting application or plugin should be easy to use for the end user.

5.2 Architecture

OpenIGTLink support is implemented as a module within the MITK toolkit providing standardized independent communication across toolkits and medical devices. The implementation complies with the MITK software process [91] using a continuous integration, a database for tracking changes and a dedicated release process with manual tests at the application level.

An architectural overview of MITK-OpenIGTLink is given in Figure 5.1. MITK-OpenIGTLink is structured in the following three layers:

Network Layer: handles the communication with the OpenIGTLink SDK

Processing Layer: processes incoming and outgoing messages

Application Layer: handles the management of connections

Figure 5.1 shows the classes used to connect MITK pipelines to other OpenIGTLink devices. A pipeline is a concatenation of processing filters, where each filter does a particular job and sends the result to the next stage of the pipeline. This approach is based on ITK [104]. In ITK, pipelines are implemented as pull-pipelines, meaning that the processing is triggered on demand by any filter inside the pipeline (in general the last one). This stands in contrast to a push pipeline in which the processing is started from the first pipeline component.

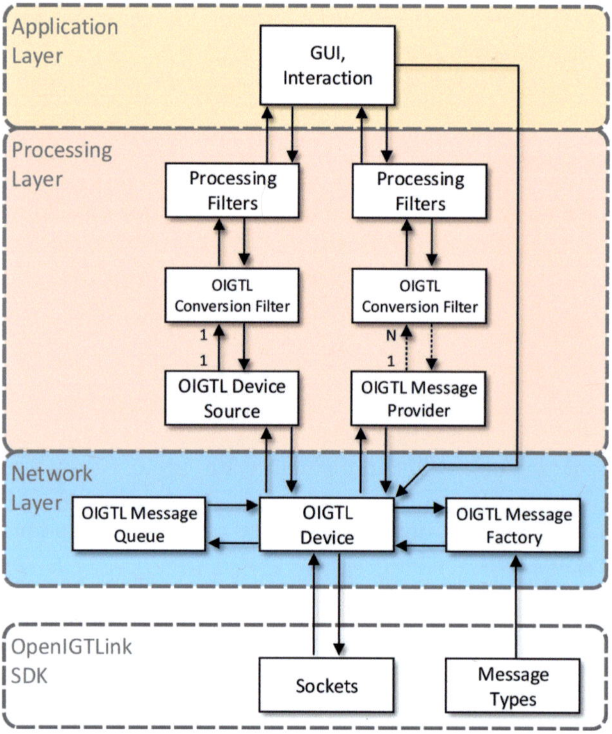

Figure 5.1.: The MITK-OpenIGTLink layered architecture. The network layer wraps the OpenIGTLink classes and manages the communication. The processing layer connects the OpenIGTLink device to the processing pipeline. The OIGTLDeviceSource is used for 1-to-1-connections, whereas the OIGTLMessageProvider can handle several conversion filters and supports streams. The OIGTLDeviceSource is statically coupled to the conversion filters, whereas the OIGTLMessageProvider is only loosely coupled to them. Both versions can run in parallel but normally only one of them is used.

5.2.1 OpenIGTLink SDK

The OpenIGTLink SDK consists of two parts: a low level C library and a higher level C++ library. OpenIGTLink is designed to run on top of the transmission control protocol (TCP) stack. As an alternative to TCP, the user datagram protocol (UDP) is supported. There is no session management, which is the reason why an OpenIGTLink message contains all necessary information for the receiver to interpret it (data type, etc.). This simplifies the protocol but also increases the overhead of each message. Besides the standard messages for exchanging tracking data, images, control and monitor information, custom message types can be defined. The protocol version 2 also specifies a querying mechanism used to request single messages or streams of a given message type.

5.2.2 Network Layer

The network layer interfaces with the OpenIGTLink protocol and encapsulates its implementation as provided in the SDK. It contains all classes for establishing and managing OpenIGTLink communications and messages.

Client-Server Architecture

The central class in the network layer is the OIGTLDevice. An OIGTLDevice is responsible for the communication with other toolkits or devices supporting OpenIGTLink. For sending and receiving messages it uses the OpenIGTLink sockets. The device runs three different threads to continuously check for new connections, receive messages and send messages. This allows the server to accept new client connections while it is already communicating with other clients. The OpenIGTLink client-server architecture is implemented by two specializations of the OIGTLDevice: OIGTLClient and OIGTLServer.

In OpenIGTLink a server can connect to an arbitrary number of clients but each client can only connect to one server. Server and clients are classified by their role during the connection establishment and not during the connection itself. The client is the device that requests the connection with the server. During the connection both devices (client and server) can request or send data.

Messages

Incoming and outgoing messages are stored in an OIGTLMessageQueue. These queues can be configured in two different modes. Depending on the application, it might be necessary to process all incoming messages or only the latest one. The outgoing message buffer is used when messages are created faster than they can be sent. An additional command queue stores the incoming commands. The standard defines four different querying commands:

- a message requesting a single object of the specified data
- a message informing that the requested data is not available
- a message requesting a stream of the specified data
- a message stopping the current stream

The query mechanism that results from these command messages can be used for a two-way communication, e.g. to send control commands to an US machine and receive image data. This query mechanism is not used by all existing OpenIGTLink implementations. In these cases the stream automatically starts as soon as client and server are connected to each other. To be compatible with such implementations it is possible to configure MITK-OpenIGTLink to also send messages upon connection. The commands are received and sent from the OIGTLDevice, however, the handling of these commands is done in the processing layer.

Custom message types can be created and have to be registered in the OIGTLMessageFactory before they can be used. This can be done at compile and at run time. Standard types are automatically added to the factory at compile time.

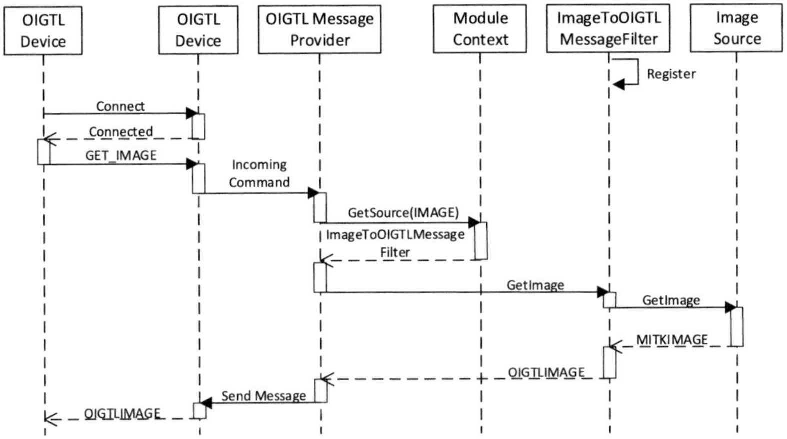

Figure 5.2.: Sequence diagram for the query of an image. An OIGTL device is requesting an image. The message provider looks for available image sources inside the module context, connects itself to the fitting conversion filter (ImageToOIGTLMessageFilter) and requests an image. Subsequently the image is provided, converted and sent to the requesting device.

The factory is registered as a C++ Micro Service allowing a system-wide access to the factory. C++ Micro Services are a low level mechanism for a service-oriented modular system [91] . The goal of this architecture is to hide complex tasks behind a simple service interface and to provide it to other components during run-time. After registering a service in one module it is available to other modules. The selection of services is based on properties and priorities and is managed by the so-called module context. In this way functionality can be easily extended by registering a new service with a higher priority.

5.2.3 Processing Layer

The processing layer holds the components establishing the connection between ITK style pipeline filters and the OpenIGTLink devices in the Network Layer. This conversion is important since existing MITK-IGT components are mainly implemented as such filters. The first step, a so-called conversion filter, converts either MITK data types into OpenIGTLink messages or vice versa. Custom conversion filters can be easily integrated, however, for the most common data types used in MITK, conversion filters are already available. In the second step, the message has to be sent or received. Alternatively, MITK-OpenIGTLink can also be used without the pipeline by directly sending OpenIGTLink messages to the OIGTLDevice as indicated in Figure 5.1 by the connection from the application layer to the OIGTLDevice. This might be useful if the pipelining concept is not used.

5.2.4 Application Layer

The application layer consists of ready-to-use MITK plugins and the MITK-OpenIGTLinkUI module. The latter contains several Qt GUI widgets that allow the developer to easily integrate the new module into his application. An OpenIGTLinkManager widget, for example, can be used to manage the OpenIGTLink devices. In addition to these new plugins, existing plugins for IGT and US applications were updated in such a way that, instead of hardware devices, these modules can also connect directly to OpenIGTLink network devices.

5.3 Performance Analysis

In order to assess the performance of latency and frame rate parameters in realistic and reproducible environments, two recently set up high-end computers[1] were used. To neglect any falsification caused by the network, the two PCs were directly connected to each other.

The experiments were performed on Linux. Time synchronization between both computers was achieved by using the precision time protocol [105] and its implementation, the precision time protocol daemon (PTPd). PTPd is open-source and only available on Linux.

Previous experiments with the OpenIGTLink protocol [81], [87] mainly focused on the network performance. Clarkson et al. and Tokuda et al. tested the latency from the generation of the OpenIGTLink message to the receiving in a second PC. In contrast, the proposed analysis covers the whole pipeline, from the data generation in MITK to the rendering of the data in the other MITK instance.

In order to evaluate the latency of all steps of the pipeline presented before, six measurement points (MP) are defined as illustrated in Figure 5.3. In each MP the current timestamp and the index of the current message were recorded. The rendering process was considered in the tests by performing the tests one time with rendering and one time without. However, in both cases the messages are received, converted and processed in the pipeline. There is no MP inside the rendering, since it normally runs slower than the processing. Certain processes need to run with high frame rates (e.g. 500 Hz), whereas the rendering is limited by the refresh rate of the monitor (typically 60 Hz). For this analysis the rendering was set to 30 Hz.

[1] CPU: Core i7-5960X 3.5 GHz 8 cores, RAM: 32 GB, Storage: SSD, GPU: Geforce GTX970 4 GB PCI-E x16, OS: Ubuntu 14.04

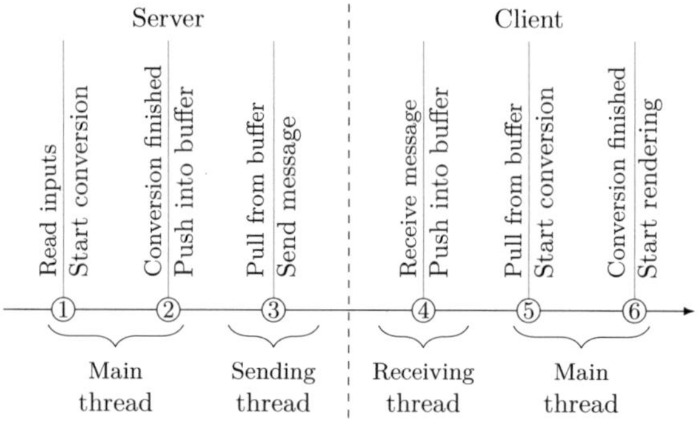

Figure 5.3.: Measurement points used for the performance analysis.

5.3.1 Experiment 1: Transmission of Tracking Data

In order to test the transmission, 10000 messages containing tracking data in 16 channels with four frame rates of 128, 256, 512 and 1000 Hz were transmitted. The tracking data was previously generated and read from file. During this experiment the rendering was turned off, since it is application-specific how this data is visualized. In the easiest case every channel could be rendered as a single point. However, on a modern computer this would not have an influence on the test results.

5.3.2 Experiment 2: Transmission of Image Data

An US stream was simulated by transmitting 1000 grayscale image messages with an US-typical resolution of 640×480 with varying frame rates of 16, 32, 64, 128, 256 and 512 Hz. The images were taken from a standard USB webcam. All measurements were performed two times, with rendering enabled and with rendering disabled.

5.3.3 Experiment 3: Transmission of HD Image Data

Similar to Experiment 2, 1000 grayscale image messages with a Full-HD resolution of 1920×1080 with frame rates of 16, 32, 64 and 128 Hz were transmitted. All measurements were performed two times, with rendering enabled and with rendering disabled.

5.4 Results

The first part of this section depicts two usage scenarios based on the MITK-OpenIGTLink module as they are used in OrthoCAD. The second part shows the results of the tests described above.

5.4.1 Usage Scenarios

The integration of the OpenIGTLink protocol into MITK allows several interoperability usage scenarios. They range from intra-toolkit communication on the same computer to intra-toolkit communication on different platforms and communication with medical devices and robotic systems. The next two sections present use cases used in OrthoCAD.

Interfacing with Visualization and Simulation Environments

Through MITK-OpenIGTLink, OrthoCAD can now be easily connected to other toolkits to exchange data and additional information. OrthoCAD, for example, interacts with a simulation environment running in MATLAB (see Figure 5.4). This environment is used to experiment on new control strategies and algorithms for an HHRD (see Chapter 7.6). Additionally, it can be used to compare the real control system with the simulation. The two applications can run on different platforms (e.g. Windows and Linux) and on different CPU instruction set architectures (x86 or x64).

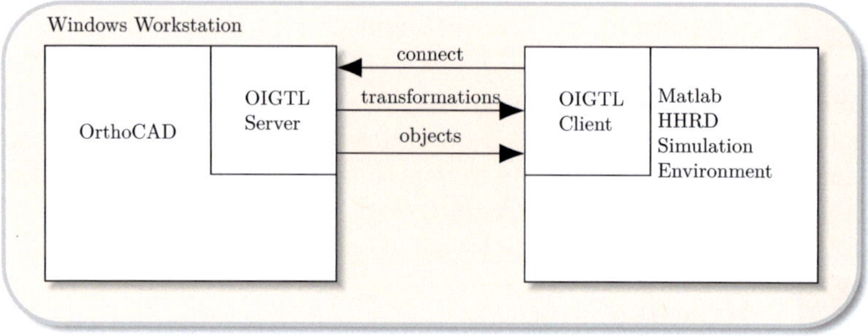

Figure 5.4.: OrthoCAD streaming data to an HHRD simulation environment in MATLAB. Both toolkits can run on different platforms. After connection OrthoCAD automatically starts streaming data.

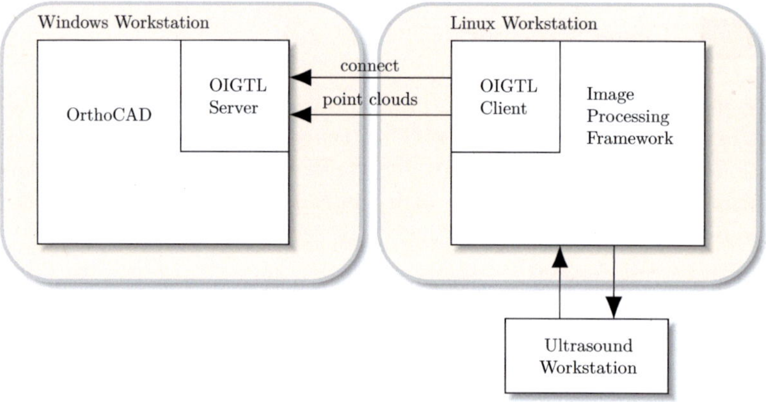

Figure 5.5.: OrthoCAD receiving input data from an US workstation. US workstation extracts the bone surface and sends it to OrthoCAD.

Interfacing with Arbitrary Input Devices

Through MITK-OpenIGTLink, arbitrary input devices can now be utilized in OrthoCAD. After the surgeon selected the OpenIGTLink input method inside the OrthoCAD GUI, the application listens to connected input devices. Once the data is received and understood it is added to the data storage. This is illustrated by interfacing OrthoCAD with an ultrasound workstation (see Figure 5.5). The US workstation runs an image processing framework that is able to extract the bone's surface shown in the US scans. This surface, in form of a point cloud consisting of the vertices, is sent to OrthoCAD and is subsequently visualized there. Whereas OrthoCAD runs on a Windows workstation, the US application runs on Linux.

5.4.2 Performance Analysis

In the following sections, the results of the performance tests are shown for the tracking data transfer (Section 5.4.2), the image transfer (Section 5.4.2) and the HD image transfer (Section 5.4.2). For each of those individual evaluations, the results are presented in two ways. First, a boxplot diagram is given showing the latency produced by the components of the pipeline. Since these values do not change significantly from one test run to another, only one diagram per experiment is shown. Each test run uses a different frame rate and calculates the mean values for transmitting 10000 tracking or 1000 image messages. Second, tables showing the average, median, minimal and maximal values of the test runs are given.

Tracking Data Transfer

Figure 5.6 shows a boxplot diagram of Experiment 1. The first boxplot shows the time required for data generation. The second and fourth boxplot show the time a message lies in a buffer. As explained above this is not processing time but idle time and has a major influence on the total result. The third boxplot is the time the message is sent from one socket to the next one. The fifth one is the time necessary to convert the incoming message into an MITK datatype and the sixth boxplot shows the total latency from generation till conversion. As shown in the figure, the two buffers produce the highest latencies in the pipeline. The higher the frame rate the lower the buffer idle time and, thus, the lower the total latency. This behaviour can also be seen in Table 5.1. The average latencies, depending on the frame rate lie between 2.81 and 7 ms.

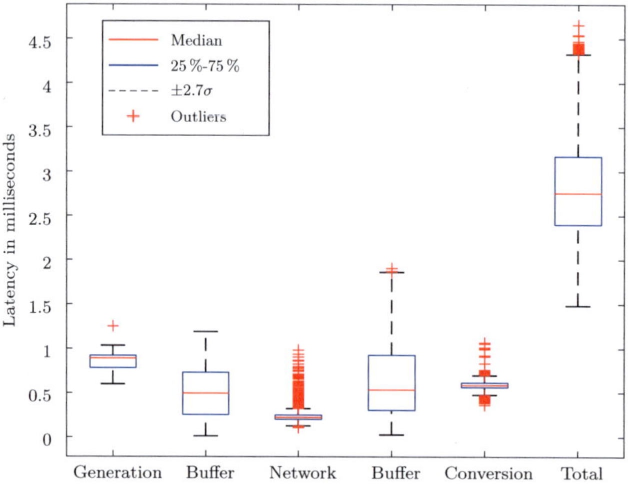

Figure 5.6.: Experiment 1: Latency in transmission of tracking data. 10000 messages with tracking data of 16 channels were sent at 1000 Hz. The average total latency was 2.81 ms.

Frame rate [Hz]	Average [ms]	Median [ms]	Min [ms]	Max [ms]
128	7.00	8.38	1.89	10.65
256	3.13	3.08	1.95	6.19
512	2.90	2.84	1.64	4.81
1000	2.81	2.76	1.48	4.65

Table 5.1.: Measurement result for tracking data with different frame rates and 10000 recorded messages.

Image Transfer

Figure 5.7 shows the result for Experiment 2 in which image data with a fixed resolution of 640×480 pixel was sent over the network. Compared to Experiment 1, the major part of the latency is not produced by the buffers but by the network itself. The average latency, depending on the frame rate and if rendering is enabled, lies between 10.5 and 21 ms (see Table 5.2 and 5.3). Until 128 Hz the rendering only causes minor latencies. However, for higher frame rates it causes a significant increase in latency of almost 100 %.

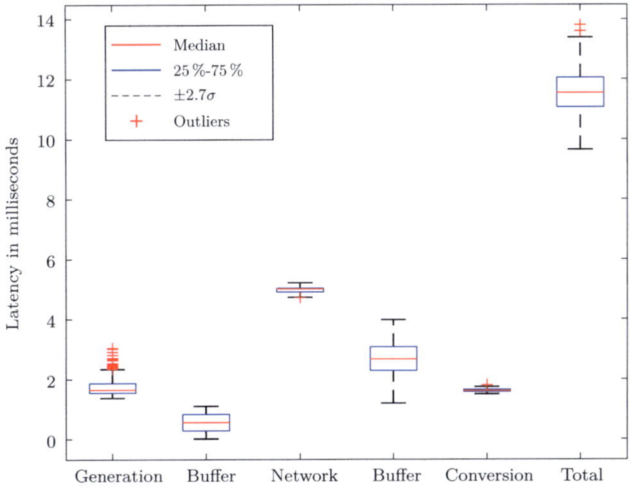

Figure 5.7.: Experiment 2: Latency in transmission of image data (640×480 pixel). 1000 messages were sent at 128 Hz with disabled rendering. The data transmission is the most time consuming step.

Frame rate [Hz]	Average [ms]	Median [ms]	Min [ms]	Max [ms]
16	13.77	13.75	12.44	15.20
32	13.01	13.00	11.57	14.96
64	12.57	12.58	10.65	14.42
128	11.55	11.54	9.66	13.79
256	10.55	10.31	8.54	23.01
512	11.20	10.52	8.36	25.43

Table 5.2.: Measurement result for image data with different frame rates and 1000 recorded messages (rendering disabled).

Frame rate [Hz]	Average [ms]	Median [ms]	Min [ms]	Max [ms]
16	14.17	14.11	11.12	18.68
32	13.66	13.57	10.69	19.09
64	12.60	12.61	8.99	17.80
128	12.64	12.48	9.56	20.57
256	18.36	18.84	8.87	30.86
512	21.71	14.28	8.47	53.44

Table 5.3.: Measurement result for image data with different frame rates and 1000 recorded messages (rendering enabled).

HD Image Transfer

Figure 5.8 shows the latencies for Experiment 3 in which HD grayscale image data with a fixed resolution of 1920×1080 pixel was sent over the network. Due to the increased message size, the major part of the latency is produced in the network itself. The average latency, depending on the frame rate, lies between 65 and 69.5 ms (see Table 5.4). Unlike the results in Experiment 2, these results are only slightly influenced by the rendering.

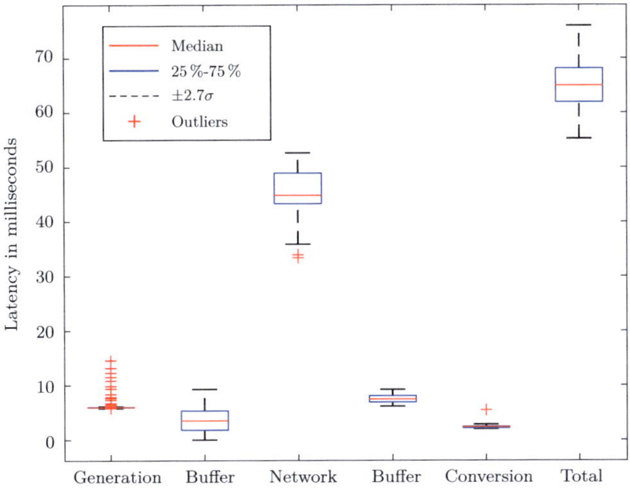

Figure 5.8.: Experiment 3: Latency in transmission of HD image data. 1000 messages were sent at 128 Hz with disabled rendering. The data transmission is by far the most time consuming step.

Frame rate [Hz]	Average [ms]	Median [ms]	Min [ms]	Max [ms]
16	69.45	69.57	60.75	74.72
32	60.86	60.86	51.07	71.13
64	68.90	68.96	50.29	84.47
128	65.09	64.99	55.21	75.95

Table 5.4.: Measurement result for HD image data with different frame rates and 1000 recorded messages.

5.5 Conclusion

The experiments were carried out under Linux utilizing the PTPd implementation. Due to a missing open-source alternative on Microsoft Windows and missing hardware for OS X, tests were not performed on these platforms.

Tokuda et al. [81] state that the frame rate of tracking devices is in the range of 40 - 375 Hz and the one for robotic applications in the order of kHz. The experiments show that tracking data can be sent with more than 1000 Hz. The highest measurable frame rate in the test setup, 1000 Hz, resulted in a latency of 2.81 ms on average. In contrast, the lowest measured frame rate was 128 Hz and resulted in a latency of 7 ms. According to Teather et al., an NDI Polaris tracking system has a latency of approximately 75 ms [106]. Wu and Taylor state that electro-magnetic tracking systems have an even higher latency [107]. Considering these tracking latencies an additional latency of 7 ms is acceptable.

The fact that the latency is decreasing with increasing frame rates is due to the implemented buffers that cause a big part of the total latency. This means that the faster the buffers are polled, the lower the latency will be. Therefore, the latency can be decreased by running the "consuming" pipeline with a higher frame rate than the transmission, e.g. the transmission runs with 128 Hz and the pipeline with 512 Hz. Another way to improve this behavior could be to couple the message reception with the pipeline by triggering the pipeline update once a message is received.

According to [81], around 32 Hz are sufficient for real-time US imaging. The implementation measures up to 512 Hz with enabled rendering and a median latency of 14 ms. HD grayscale images were processed with 128 Hz and a latency of 66 ms. Theoretically, HD RGB images could be sent with up to 43 Hz ($128/3 \approx 43$), which is still more than the recommended 32 Hz. Therefore, the presented implementation is able to cover most applications utilizing image messages.

Enabling the rendering of transmitted images only showed differences in Experiment 2 but not in Experiment 3. In Experiment 2, US image data was transmitted with up to 512 Hz and a difference occurred for frame rates higher than 128 Hz. In Experiment 3, HD image data was transmitted with up to 128 Hz. It is assumed that the PCs are able to transmit and process images up to 128 Hz, independent of the image size, but they are partly overloaded for higher frame rates. This is based on the fact that the increase in processing time does not correlate with the increase in image size when comparing US with HD images. In MITK the handling of US and HD images is exactly the same, since the management differentiating between the image sizes for rendering purposes is running on the GPU and does not influence the measurement.

A direct comparison between the presented results and the previously published experiments of Clarkson et al. [87] and Tokuda et al. [81] is not possible since they concentrated on the network performance and their OpenIGTLink implementation. The presented analysis, on the contrary, covers the whole pipeline, from the data conversion in MITK to the rendering of the data in the other MITK instance. Clarkson and Tokuda state a latency of around 0.3 ms or 0.36 ms, respectively, for a tracking data transfer with 128 Hz, whereas the presented results show a latency of 7 ms. [87] and [81] measure the time from creating an OpenIGTLink message at the sender host until the end of the deserialization at the receiver host. These measurements are very interesting concerning the OpenIGTLink interface but do not give information about the performance of an application. They do not include visualization nor management of messages. In the presented tests the application-specific latency is measured: generation of real data (as MITK data types), conversion into messages, transmission and vice versa on the receiving side. Moreover, buffers are implemented to easily integrate OpenIGTLink into the pipelined structure of MITK. The most time-consuming component in the tests by [87] and [81] is the networking. In the 128 Hz tracking data test, an average network latency of 0.19 ms was reached. Creation, serialization and deserialization can be considered as less time consuming as the networking, which means that the implementation performs similarly to [87] and [81].

For image data transfers with frame rates higher than 512 Hz the network load was so high that the PTPd synchronization packages arrived delayed. In this scenario, two separate network connections might be necessary, one for the data and one for the synchronization.

This chapter described how OrthoCAD can utilize arbitrary input devices and how the data inside OrthoCAD can be used in external applications (e.g. for testing and verification). The communication between these environments and devices is based on OpenIGTLink. Therefore, a new software module was integrated into MITK, which represents the base of OrthoCAD. Performance tests were carried out and the usage scenarios in OrthoCAD were explained. MITK-OpenIGTLink was released as open source together with the MITK toolkit release 2016-03. MITK and OrthoCAD can now be combined with other toolkits in a plug-and-play manner.

CHAPTER 6

Intraoperative Calibration of Navigated Instruments

Contents

CAOS systems often utilize navigation systems and tracked surgical instruments. These can be simple pointing devices as well as tracked burrs or saws (active instruments). As shown in Chapter 2 such tools are used for bone resections in orthopedic surgery. A pointing device can be used to define resection areas, which are removed by an active and tracked instrument. To ensure that the active instrument only removes the defined areas, a calibration is required that not only includes the pose of the instrument tip but also its surface. The following chapter concentrates on medical applications, however, it can also be applied in other fields.

Many active instruments allow using different tool tips such as drill bits, burrs and blades. Every time the tip is changed the tool has to be recalibrated. Other works calibrate their tracked tools by touching previously measured registration pins [14] or by pivoting the instrument [74]. Commercial products often utilize dedicated calibration jigs that allow a fast and accurate calibration. The fact that all these methods only work for a limited amount of tips emphasizes the importance of a flexible and generic intraoperative calibration technique.

The final goal is to reconstruct the 3D surface of the instrument tip in the coordinate system of the integrated or attached tool tracker (see Figure 6.1). By rotating the instrument in front of one or more cameras, which are calibrated in the coordinate system of an attached tracker, the instrument surface is reconstructed. In contrast to pivoting, the proposed technique is able to calibrate arbitrary objects as long as they do not contain cavities. A first version of this technique was previously published in [108].

Chapter 6.1 summarizes the different coordinate systems of the hardware components. Before the (tracked) camera can be used to determine the 3D surface of the instrument tip, it has to be calibrated once with respect to the attached tracker (see Chapter 6.2). The instrument calibration is described in Chapter 6.3. Subsequently, the accuracy analysis is described in Chapter 6.4 and the results are provided in Chapter 6.5. Chapter 6.6 concludes the presented calibration approach.

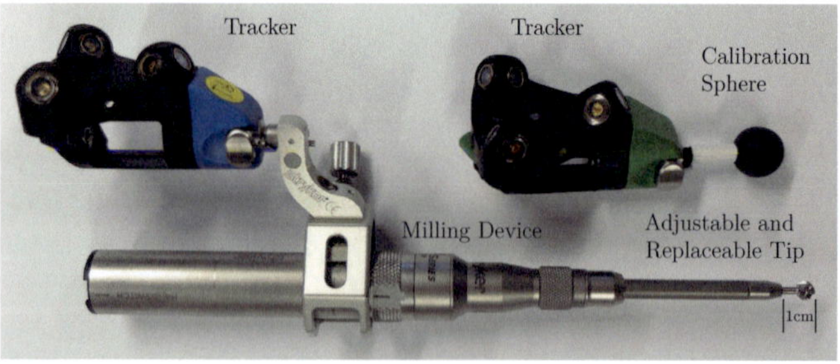

Figure 6.1.: The tracked calibration sphere and a milling device with adjustable and interchangeable instrument tip.

6.1 Setup

The calibration setup is shown in Figure 6.2. An instrument, in this case a simplified drill, with an attached tracker is held in front of a tracked camera. Both trackers are tracked by the navigation system defining the world coordinate system. In order to improve the contrast of the camera scene, a lighted white background is used. This background is rigidly attached to the camera. For simplification the setup only shows one camera, however the algorithms also work with two or more. The following coordinate systems are used:

C	...	coordinate system in which the camera was calibrated (in mm)
A	...	coordinate system of the tracker attached to the camera(s) (in mm)
G	...	coordinate system of the voxel grid (in voxel indices)
S	...	coordinate system of the scaled voxel grid (in mm)
N	...	coordinate system of the tracker attached to the tool (in mm)
W	...	coordinate system of the navigation system (in mm)
I	...	coordinate system of the camera image (in pixel indices)

For the accuracy analysis a USB3 industry camera MQ013MG-ON (XIMEA, Germany) with 1.3 megapixel and a lens with a focal length of 10 mm was used. The navigation system was an FP6000 (Stryker, USA) using trackers with active LEDs.

6.2 Tracked Camera Calibration

Before the tracked camera can be used to calibrate the instrument, the transformation F_{AC} from the camera calibration coordinate system C to the coordinate system A of the attached tracker has to be determined. The camera was calibrated with the approach of Hoppe et al. [101], which calibrates every single pixel individually without using a parametric model. See Chapter 4.4 for a more detailed description. This calibration provides straight lines given by two points $\vec{a}_{near,C}(u,v)$ and $\vec{a}_{far,C}(u,v)$

for each single camera pixel (u, v). The calibration pattern as used in a standard pinhole-model calibration [68], [109] is replaced by a monitor showing a horizontal and vertical cosine pattern, which is shifted by one period. The resulting camera images are used to calculate monitor positions $\vec{a}_{i,C}(u, v)$ resulting in a regression line for each camera pixel (u, v). $\vec{a}_{near,C}(u, v)$ indicates the beginning of the calibrated region and $\vec{a}_{far,C}(u, v)$ its end. In case of the setup used in the analysis section, the near points are approximately 70 mm, the far points 130 mm in front of the camera.

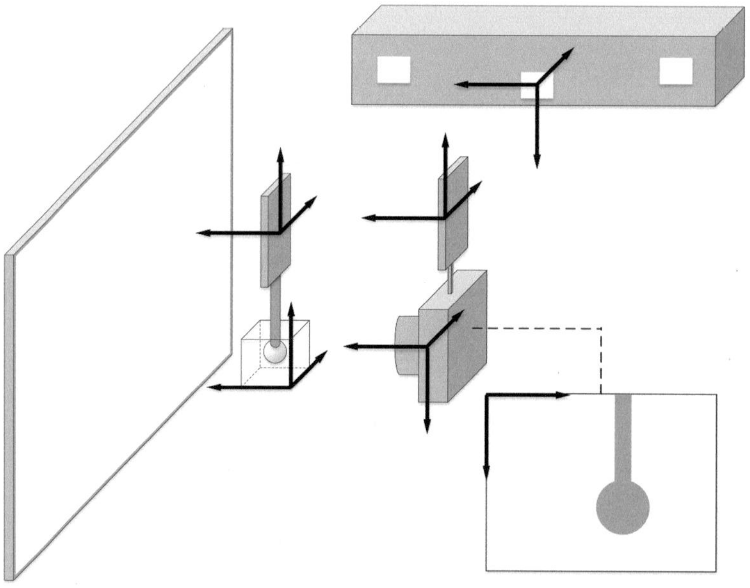

Figure 6.2.: Overview showing the hardware (navigation system, tracked instrument, tracked camera, illuminated background) and its coordinate systems.

In order to find the rigid transformation F_{AC}, a tracked calibration sphere is moved in front of the camera. The center of the calibration sphere $\vec{p}_N$ was previously determined by pivoting. With every frame $\{F_{AW}$, F_{NW}, Image$\}$ two transformations and one image are recorded. The two transformations F_{AW} and F_{NW} are the transformations from the navigation system W to the trackers A and N and are used to transform $\vec{p}_N$ into coordinate system A by applying $\vec{p}_A = F_{AW} \cdot F_{NW}^{-1} \cdot \vec{p}_N$. The camera image shows the calibration sphere (similar to Figure 6.3a). It is used to determine the center of the sphere in image coordinates $\vec{p}_I$. The corresponding line l_C in camera calibration coordinates C is given by the camera calibration. Thus, given a set of M lines $\{l_{Ci}\}$ and M sphere centers $\{\vec{p}_{Ai}\}$ the transformation F_{AC} is calculated using an iterative closest point algorithm:

1. Transform the original points $\vec{p}_{Ai}$ into camera coordinates C using the previous estimation $F_{CA} \Rightarrow \vec{p}_{Ci}$. In the first iteration the identity transform is used.
2. Calculate their closest points $\vec{q}_{Ci}$ on the according lines.
3. Calculate the transformation F_{CA} by matching the two point clouds $\vec{p}_{Ai}$ and $\vec{q}_{Ci}$ in a least square sense.
4. Repeat steps 1. to 3. until convergence.

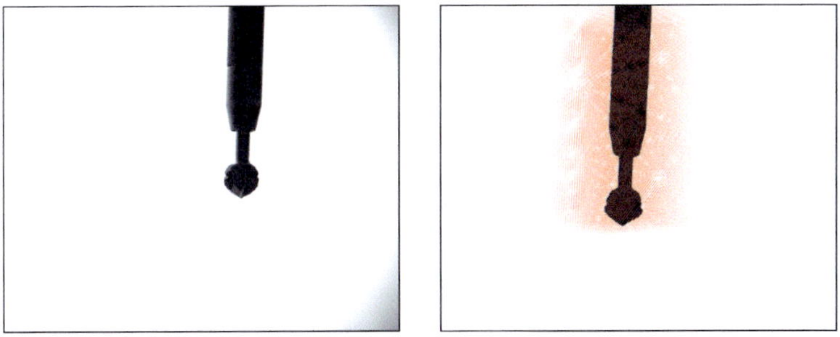

(a) Example camera image **(b)** Projected centers of grid voxels

Figure 6.3.: Example camera image and projected centers of grid voxels.

6.3 Tracked Instrument Calibration

The goal of this calibration is to find the 3D surface of the tracked instrument given in coordinate system N of the integrated or attached tracker. The algorithm can be split into the following parts:

1. Record image/transformation pairs.
2. Binarize the recorded images.
3. Determine a 3D voxel grid, which contains the instrument tip, and the transformation F_{NG} from grid to tracker coordinates.
4. Calculate the voxel-based visual hull of the instrument tip.
5. Calculate its 3D surface.
6. Optionally, fit a user-selected geometry (e.g. a sphere) into the surface.

First, the tracked instrument is rotated in front of the tracked camera. With every frame $\{F_{NA}, \text{Image}\}$, a camera image (see Figure 6.3a) and a transformation F_{NA} from coordinate system A of the camera tracker to coordinate system N of the tracked instrument is recorded.

Second, binarize the input images using an Otsu [110] calculated threshold. The background pixels have the value 1 and the instrument tip 0.

Third, a 3D voxel grid has to be determined that contains the bounding box of the instrument tip with an additional margin. The coordinate systems G and N of the grid and the tracker are not rotated with respect to each other but only scaled and translated. Therefore, the transformation F_{NG} is defined as:

$$F_{NG} = F_{NS} \cdot F_{SG} = \begin{pmatrix} 1 & 0 & 0 & \\ 0 & 1 & 0 & \vec{t}_{NS} \\ 0 & 0 & 1 & \\ 0 & 0 & 0 & 1 \end{pmatrix} \cdot \begin{pmatrix} s_x & 0 & 0 & 0 \\ 0 & s_y & 0 & 0 \\ 0 & 0 & s_z & 0 \\ 0 & 0 & 0 & 1 \end{pmatrix} \tag{6.1}$$

The scaling factors s_x, s_y and s_z are chosen by the user and define the resolution of the reconstruction, which has a major influence on the final accuracy. The extents of the grid are calculated by a series of geometric steps: In the images the bounding boxes of the instrument tip are calculated. The corners of these bounding boxes are transformed into the coordinates of the instrument tracker N (see Figure 6.4). The extents of the grid are defined as the bounding box including all the transformed corner points plus an additional margin. The transformation $\vec{t}_{NS}$ represents the center of the grid. For a detailed description of this algorithm see [108].

Forth, now the 3D voxel grid is defined such that it contains the instrument tip. The next goal is to find all grid voxels that belong to it (visual hull). The algorithm is a voxel-based version of the one described by Martin

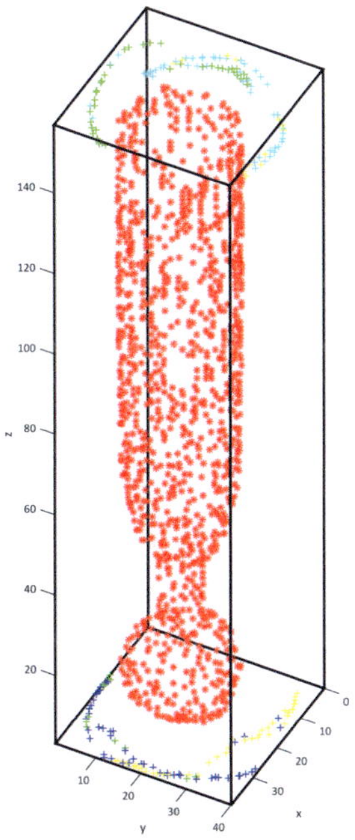

Figure 6.4.: The reconstructed tool inside the calculated bounding box given in coordinate system G with $s_x = s_y = s_z = 0.25$. Surface points ($*$) and the transformed bounding box corner points ($+$) are depicted.

and Aggarwal [111]. In all M binary images the instrument tip is shown as black and the background as white pixels (see Figure 6.3). By using the camera calibration the white background pixels can be converted into a set of lines. Each of these lines intersects with voxels in the grid and removes a part of it. With every new image there are more lines that remove parts of the grid until only the visual hull is left. However, this version implies that every pixel in all images from all viewpoints has to be checked, which is not performing well. Thus, the inverse approach is implemented. Instead of intersecting the pixel lines with the grid, the grid voxels are projected back into the images. The pixel value at the projected voxel position is added to the voxel's value. This process is shown in Figure 6.5.

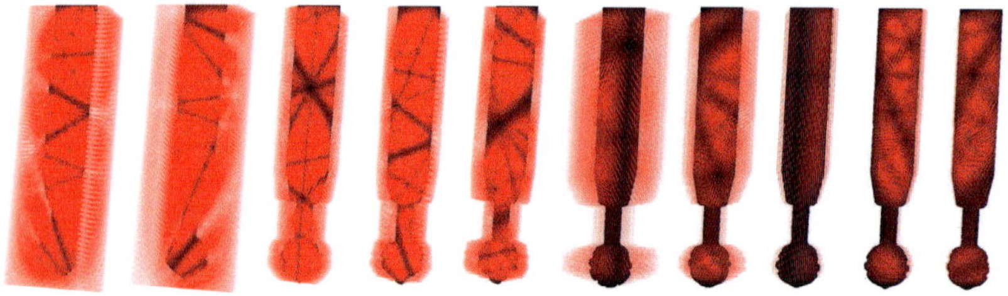

Figure 6.5.: The visual hull adaptation process of the instrument tip, in this case a burr. Only voxels with values smaller or equal to 1 are backprojected.

A voxel value of 0 means that this voxel belongs to the instrument, whereas a maximum value of M, where M is the number of collected images, means that it is part of the background. Values between 0 and 1 can be added to the voxel since the backprojection of the voxels is done with subpixel accuracy and, therefore, an interpolation is necessary. The basic procedure can be summarized as follows:

1. Transform each voxel position $\vec{v}_{Gi}$ into coordinate system N

$$\vec{v}_{Ni} = F_{NG} \cdot \vec{v}_{Gi} \text{ with } i = 0, ..., H-1 \tag{6.2}$$

   where H is the number of voxels in the grid.

2. For each image/transformation pair j and each voxel i

a) Transform each voxel position $\vec{v}_{Ni}$ into camera coordinates

$$\vec{v}_{Cij} = F_{CA} \cdot F_{ANj} \cdot \vec{v}_{Ni} \tag{6.3}$$

b) Use the camera calibration to find the pixel position $\vec{v}_{Iij}$ corresponding to the calculated $\vec{v}_{Cij}$. Figure 6.3b shows these backprojected pixels for one specific image.

c) Since $\vec{v}_{Iij}$ are given with subpixel accuracy their gray values are interpolated. These values are added to the corresponding grid voxels.

Fifth, a marching cubes algorithm as described in [112], which takes a threshold as input parameter, is used to calculate the surface of the tool.

Sixth, optionally CAD models or geometries (e.g. a sphere) can be fitted into this 3D surface in order to have a simplified representation that reduces computation time in certain applications.

6.4 Accuracy Analysis

Different tests were carried out to determine the accuracy of the proposed calibrations:

1. The previously described calibration sphere was pivoted several times to find its sphere center. This position was used as ground truth.

2. The tracked camera calibration (TCC) was performed using the calibration sphere and compared to the pivoting average of the first test. The position of the sphere was found by calculating the intersection point of the lines $\{l_C\}$ passing through the circle centers shown on the recorded images.

3. The tracked instrument calibration (TIC) was performed using the calibration sphere and compared to the pivoting average of the first test. To find the sphere center and radius, a sphere was matched into the calculated 3D surface.

4. A spherical burr instrument was pivoted in order to find its position.
5. The TIC was carried out for the spherical burr instrument. To find the burr center and radius, a sphere was matched into the calculated 3D surface.

Figure 6.6 shows the hardware setup used for these tests. Note that only one of the two cameras was used for the analysis.

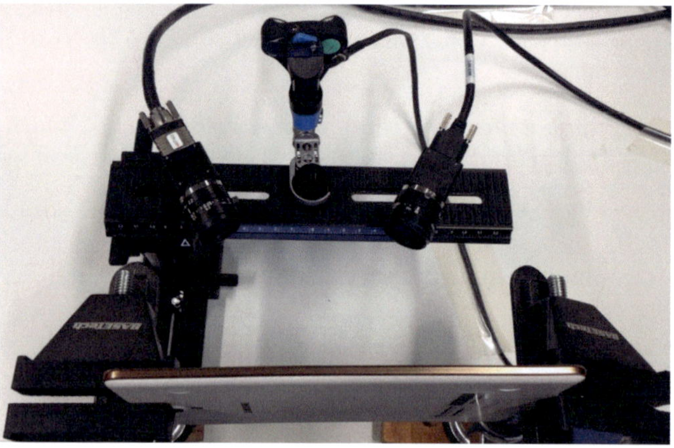

Figure 6.6.: Hardware setup.

6.5 Results

Tables 6.1 to 6.3 show the results of the five tests. The deviations of the position shown in Table 6.1 prove that the proposed TCC is as accurate as the one of pivoting. The distance between the average pivoting center and the average center resulting from the TCC is only 0.035 mm and therefore in the same magnitude as the deviations.

In Table 6.2 the TIC of the calibration sphere is compared to pivoting. The RMS deviations of the sphere centers calibrated using TIC are four times higher than those of the pivoting. The absolute difference between the pivoting centers and the TIC centers is 0.31 mm. However, the radius was reconstructed with an RMS error of 0.015 mm and the absolute difference to the measured one is only 0.0091 mm.

Test	Calibration	Number of calibration	Position deviation RMS	max	Δ_{Pos}
1	Pivoting	10	0.039	0.068	-
2	TCC	5	0.044	0.069	0.035

Table 6.1.: The results of test 1 and 2: The position deviations for the pivoting and the TCC using the calibration sphere. Δ_{Pos} is the absolute distance between the two average positions. All values are given in mm.

Test	Calibration	Number of calibration	Position dev. RMS	max	Radius dev. RMS	max	Δ_{Pos}	Δ_R
1	Pivoting	10	0.039	0.068	-	-	-	-
3	TIC	5	0.164	0.299	0.015	0.025	0.31	0.0091

Table 6.2.: The results of test 1 and 3: The position and radius deviations for the pivoting and the TIC using the calibration sphere. Δ_{Pos} is the absolute distance between the two average positions and Δ_R the difference of the reconstructed radius to the measured one. All values are given in mm.

The position errors in Table 6.3 show that for an instrument tip that is not perfectly spherical the TIC computes positions with smaller RMS values than the pivoting. The error distribution of the radius reconstruction was, by magnitude of 10, smaller than the position reconstruction. In the last column the radius was compared to the measured one (caliper). Since the tip has a fluted surface, the measured radius is the maximal radius of the burr edges and not the average. Therefore, the reconstructed radius differs from the measured one.

The marching cubes algorithm needs a threshold. Ideally, this threshold should be chosen to be 0.5 in the middle between 0 (black, part of the instrument tip) and 1 (white, part of the background). Empirical tests showed that a threshold of 0.1 yields the most accurate results. Figure 6.7 shows the original instrument tip and the result of the marching cubes algorithm for a burr and a saw.

Test	Calibration	Number of calibrations	Position dev.		Radius dev.		Δ_{Pos}	Δ_R
			RMS	max	RMS	max		
4	Pivoting	10	0.31	0.43	-	-	-	-
5	TIC	5	0.18	0.25	0.013	0.023	0.80	0.19

Table 6.3.: The results of test 4 and 5: The position and radius deviations for the pivoting and the TIC using a burr. Δ_{Pos} is the absolute distance between the two average positions and Δ_R the difference of the reconstructed radius to the measured one. All values are given in mm.

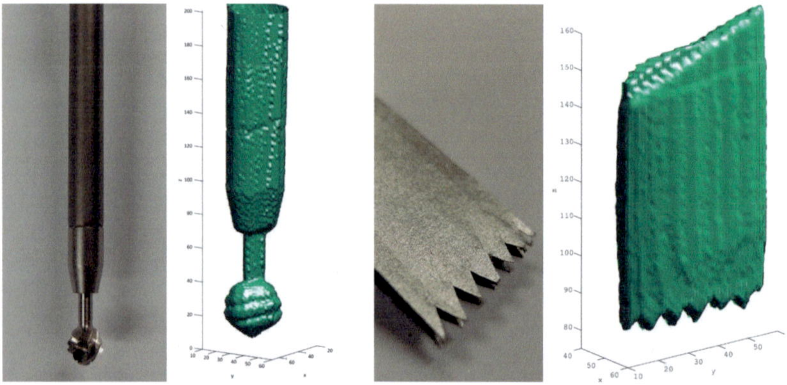

(a) Original burr with a diameter of 6 mm **(b)** Reconstructed burr given in coordinate system G, $s = \frac{1}{6} \frac{\text{mm}}{\text{pixel}}$ **(c)** Original saw with a width of 25 mm and a thickness of 2.5 mm **(d)** Reconstructed saw given in coordinate system G, $s = \frac{1}{2} \frac{\text{mm}}{\text{pixel}}$

Figure 6.7.: Images of the original burr and saw and their reconstructed surfaces. In both examples the scaling factors were the same in all directions $s_x = s_y = s_z = s$.

6.6 Conclusion

Whereas rigid instruments can be calibrated preoperatively, instruments with an interchangeable instrument tip must be calibrated intraoperatively, inside the OR and every time the tip is interchanged or adjusted. Therefore, it is important that the calibration is intuitive and time-efficient. The procedure as described in this chapter utilizes a Cartesian voxel grid to reconstruct the instrument tip. Regions of interest as well as uninteresting regions (background) have the same resolution. Hence, the processing of the background also consumes time. This means that the current time consumption depends on the grid size and the grid resolution, which in turn depends on the scaling factor s (see Equation 6.1). The calibration of the sphere-shaped burr as shown in Figure 6.7b approximately takes 40 s with previously recorded transformation/image pairs. Future work will integrate an octree-based image processing, which is more time-efficient due to the fact that regions of interest are processed with high resolution, whereas uninteresting regions are sampled with low resolutions.

In this chapter, three different kinds of instrument tips were reconstructed: a simple sphere-shaped burr, a fluted sphere-shaped burr and a saw blade. The first two were chosen since they can also be calibrated using the pivoting calibration. The third one proofs that non-sphere-shaped tips can be reconstructed. In general, the presented procedure is only able to calibrate tips that do not contain cavities but — to the author's knowledge — tips with cavities are of little avail.

The used navigation system, is an active system utilizing infrared LEDs. A single LED can be tracked with a standard deviation of 0.07 mm. However, the tracking of the instrument tip center depends on the LED configuration, on how many LEDs are visible and on the distance of the instrument tip to the LEDs. Assuming the following case:

- a symmetrical configuration with three times three LEDs
- in average four LEDs are visible

- the center of the instrument tip is located at a distance of 178 mm from the center of the LEDs

In this case the center of the instrument tip can be tracked with an accuracy of approx. 0.42 mm RMS. The exemplary instrument with attached tracker shown in Figure 6.1 has such a configuration. The presented calibration technique is able to determine the center of the instrument tip with an RMS deviation of 0.18 mm.

By using only one camera the tracked instrument has to be rotated by 180°. This is a limitation for instruments whose trackers do not have a 180° visibility. In order to eliminate this drawback two or more cameras can be used. This also contributes to speeding up the calibration process since the user has to rotate the instrument less.

In case the calibration is performed intraoperatively in the OR, it is important that the calibration station can be kept sterile. This can be achieved by placing the setup under a transparent and sterile cover such that the camera(s) look through a transparent panel of known thickness and refraction index, which can be accounted for in the camera calibration process.

A camera-based calibration method for tracked instruments was presented. The presented approach works generically and precisely. The accuracy was demonstrated in several tests and by comparing it to a pivot calibration. Moreover, the surface reconstruction of two completely different tools was shown, a burr and a saw blade. Hence, the presented method is also able to calibrate non-spherical instrument tips. This emphasizes the advantage over the pivoting technique that is only able to calibrate spherical instrument tips.

CHAPTER
7

Control System for Handheld Robotic Devices with 3-DoF

Contents

Since the first orthopedic intervention was performed with ROBODOC 20 years ago [113], robotic systems became an integral part of many orthopedic interventions. Stationary robots improve the accuracy but also require adapted surgical workflows. Handheld robotic devices (see Figure 7.1), however, are easily integrated into existing workflows and represent a more economical solution. Their limited range of motion is compensated by the dexterity of the surgeon.

This chapter presents a robot control system for HHRDs with multiple degrees of freedom. The RCS implements the concept of virtual fixtures by protecting pre- and intraoperatively constrained regions from being penetrated by the end effector (e.g. a burr). In order to evade these constrained regions, the joints as well as the device's power is controlled. There are two ways to react in case that the end effector collides with one of the constraints: First and as long as possible, the end effector retreats in order not to intersect the constraint (see Figure 7.2). Second and in case this is not possible anymore, the end effector's power is turned off to put it into a safe state. By using the degrees of freedom of the HHRD the frequency of the on/off switching of the device's power is decreased and almost eliminated. The milling task is more intuitive since the end effector position is corrected automatically by the control system. Moreover, the system is based on the control of the device's position rather than the applied force.

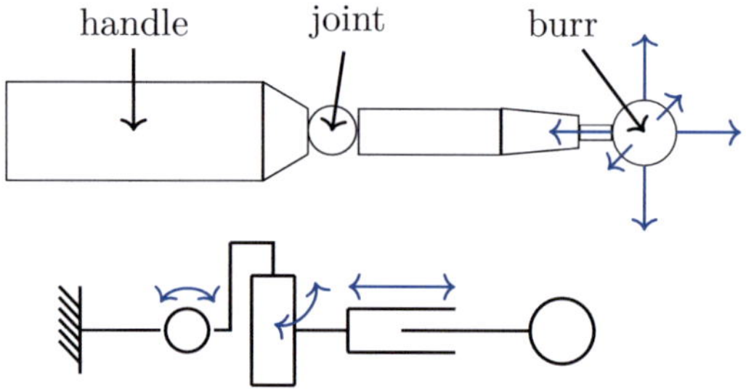

Figure 7.1.: A handheld robotic device with three degrees of freedom and a milling end effector.

The presented control system can process arbitrarily shaped constraints (planes, wedges, triangle meshes in general). These constraints are non-closed surfaces that do not represent closed volumes as used in other works. These constraints are defined using OrthoCAD (see Chapter 3).

The following section shows an overview of the system and the software architecture of the robot control system. Chapter 7.2 describes and illustrates different control modes. Chapter 7.3 to 7.5 explain the collision detection, the position control algorithm and the speed control algorithm in further detail, since they play a major role in this system. The analysis of the system is conducted using a table-top robotic milling device (see Chapter 7.7 and 7.8). Finally, the results are shown, discussed and concluded in Chapter 7.9 and 7.10.

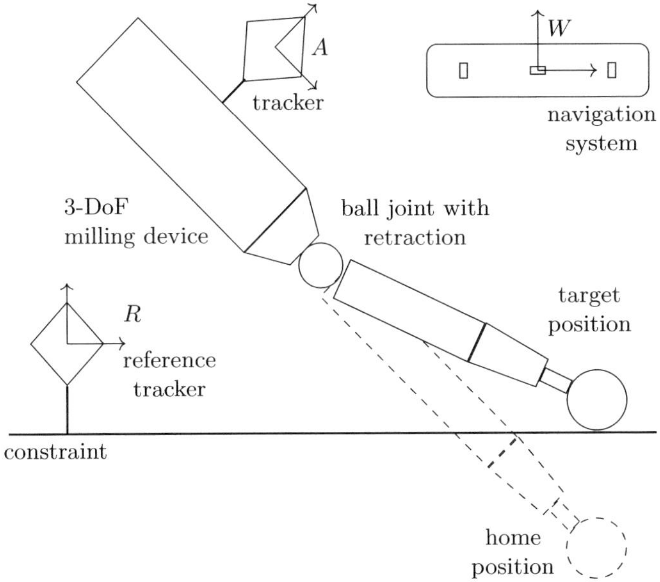

Figure 7.2.: A 3-DoF milling device evading a constraint by adjusting the end effector position accordingly. The home position is the position in which the tool is located when there are no intersecting constraints. The target position is the corrected position that does not intersect the constraints.

7.1 Architecture

The RCS consists of several components that are responsible for controlling the HHRD (see Figure 7.3): the path, the behavior, the kinematic and the motor controller. Additional to the controllers there are two components for reading input data and providing data to components outside the RCS. The path controller receives the planning data and the current transformations as well as the calibrated home position. According to a predefined path, an offset is added to the home position. The behavior controller receives this adapted position and computes the target position as well as the end effector speed (see Chapter 7.4 and 7.5) These parameters are passed to the kinematic controller, which calculates the joint parameters according to a kinematic model (inverse kinematics). These joint parameters are sent to the motor controller that communicates with the motors. Besides this forwarding pipeline, there is also one for feedback. The motor controller reads the current joint parameters and passes them to the kinematic controller, which then computes the current position (forward kinematics) and passes it to the behavior controller.

The path and the behavior controller are completely independent from the hardware and can be applied to tools with any degrees of freedom. The position control algorithm performs a collision detection (see Chapter 7.3) to find a valid position in which the tool does not intersect any constraint. The kinematic model of the kinematic controller must be adapted to the hardware. Additional to the forward and the inverse kinematics, it must also perform plausibility checks for the reachability of a given position. It simply ensures that the computed parameters are within a range that the hardware can reach. In case that these parameters are outside the reachable range, the motor controller turns off the end effector.

The subsequent sections refer to the following coordinate systems:

- A ... coordinate system of the tracker attached to the HHRD (in mm)
- R ... coordinate system of the reference tracker attached to the patient's bone (in mm)
- W ... coordinate system of the navigation system (in mm)

The RCS currently expects spherical burrs, however, differently shaped burrs can also be used after adapting the collision detection algorithm.

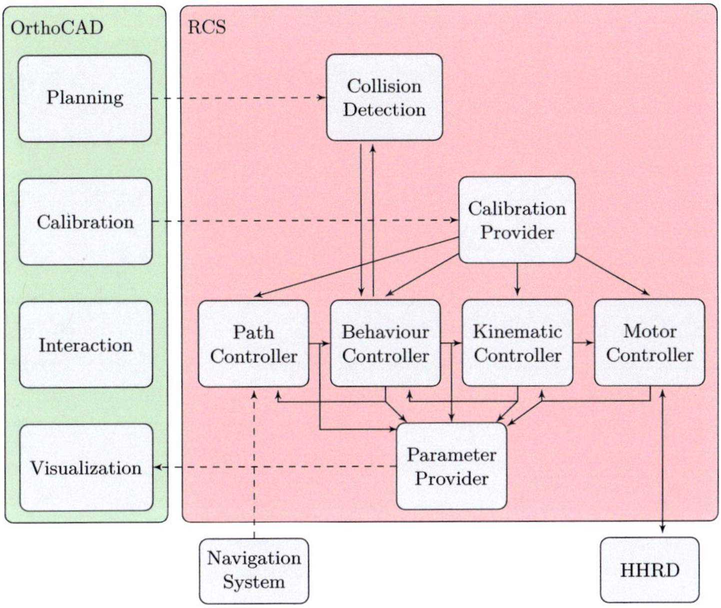

Figure 7.3.: Overview of the software components of the RCS and OrthoCAD. The path controller receives the planning data from OrthoCAD and the current position from the navigation system. It adapts the home position according to the predefined path and passes it to the behavior controller. The behavior controller computes the speed and target position. The kinematic controller calculates the joint parameters and passes them to the motor controller. The motor controller updates the HHRD and reads the current joint parameters. The calibration provider imports the calibrations and updates the controllers. The parameter provider collects calculated parameters and supplies them to the visualization on request.

7.2 Control Modes

The RCS can run in three different modes depending on the available robot and the surgeon's selection. The most basic mode is the power-controlled mode (PCM) in which only the end effector's speed of rotation is controlled. The position of the end effector stays rigid. This implies that the end effector stops running as soon as the target position differs from the home position (see Figure 7.4a). This mode can also be used for rigid tools (0-DoF). In the evasive mode (EM), the end effector's position is controlled. As explained in the previous sections, the end effector deflects in order to avoid penetrating a constraint (see Figure 7.4b). As soon as the end effector reaches its maximal deflection, the power of the end effector is turned off. This stops the milling process and therefore protects the patient. The smoothing mode (SM) is similar to the evasive mode with the difference that the end effector moves along a predefined path (see Figure 7.4c). In the standard case this is a circular path lying in the xy-plane of the end effector's coordinate system. Due to this movement, smoother surfaces are milled.

The controllers are set up depending on the control mode. The path controller is inactive in the power-controlled and evasive mode but modifies the home position in the smoothing mode. The behavior controller is running independently of the mode. The kinematic model inside the kinematic controller has to be adapted to the hardware and the mode. In the case of the power-controlled mode, a kinematic model with 0-DoF has to be set. Therefore, the only difference between the power-controlled and the evasive mode is the kinematic model. The motor controller depends only on the hardware and not on the mode.

7.3 Collision Detection Algorithm

The collision detection component finds any collision between the end effector movement and the defined constraints. A constraint is a surface consisting of one or more triangles. A typical discrete approach (a posteriori) finds a collision after it occurred. A continuous approach (a priori) predicts the movement of the objects and finds a collision before it occurs. In the presented setup, a continuous approach cannot be applied, since there are two movements: the movement of the human hand and the movement of the end effector (caused by the joints). Whereas the movement of the end effector is controlled, the human movement is difficult to predict, since there is only an optical navigation system without additional sensors (tremor prediction normally uses high-speed 6-DoF gyroscopes, see for example [41]). Therefore, a discrete approach that calculates the collision for a given sphere movement (spherical end effector) is used.

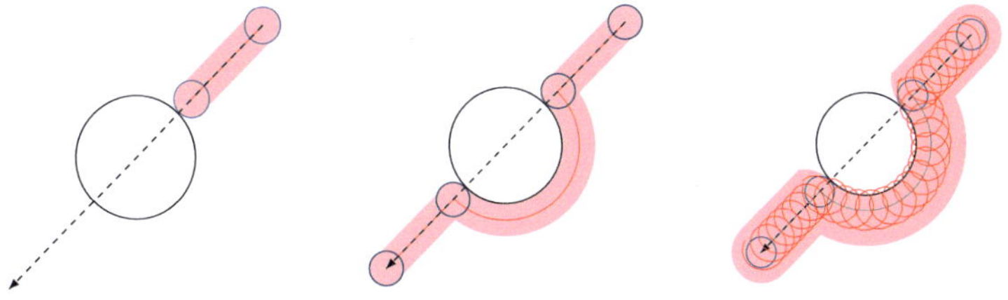

(a) Power-controlled **(b)** Evasive **(c)** Smoothing

Figure 7.4.: Behavior of control modes. The dashed line represents a slow movement of the robotic device by the surgeon. The big sphere represents a constraint. The smaller sphere represents a spherical end effector. The pink area indicates the milling area. In the case of the power-controlled mode, the end effector stops as soon as the constraint is touched. By using the evasive mode, the end effector is able to move around the constraint. While using the smoothing mode, the end effector moves around in circles.

The convex hull of a linear sphere movement trajectory is a capsule. Therefore, the presented algorithms are optimized for finding collisions of capsules with given triangle meshes. For simplicity and optimization this collision detection is performed in the triangle's base coordinate system T. In this coordinate system, the first triangle corner coincides with the origin, the second one lies on the positive x-axis and the third one lies in the xy-plane with a positive y-coordinate (see Figure 7.5).

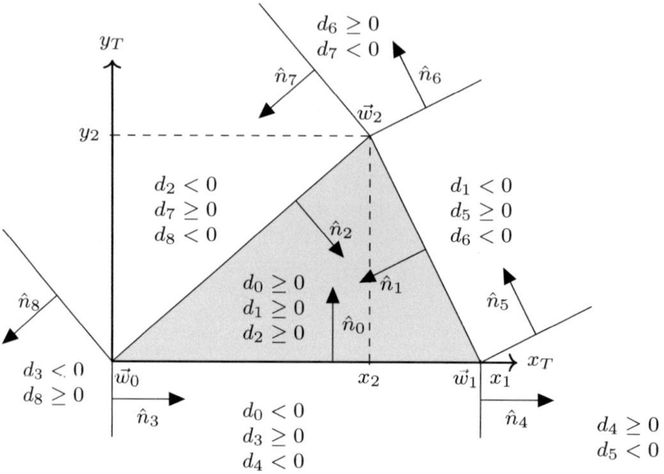

Figure 7.5.: Optimized base coordinate system of the capsule triangle collision algorithm. The z-coordinate is always 0, $\vec{w}_0$ and $\vec{w}_1$ lie on the x-axis and $\vec{w}_0$ is located in the origin of the coordinate system. The plane in which a triangle lies is split into seven regions by nine line segments. The lines are defined by their normals $\hat{n}_0$ to $\hat{n}_8$. The region in which a projected point $\vec{u}$ lies is indicated by the sign of the distances to the lines. If a point lies inside the triangle, the distance to line 0, 1 and 2 is positive. If a point lies beneath line 0, the distance to line 0 and 4 is negative and the one to line 3 is positive.

The sphere movement is defined by the start position $\vec{p}$ and the target position $\vec{q}$ of the sphere center (see Figure 7.6). The algorithm returns a factor s that indicates how far the sphere can move from $\vec{p}$ to $\vec{q}$ until it collides with the triangle. The factor s is given in percent: 0.0 means that the sphere at position $\vec{p}$ already collides with the triangle whereas 1.0 means that the sphere can move from $\vec{p}$ to $\vec{q}$ without intersecting the triangle. A complete overview of all parameters is shown in Figure 7.7. These parameters are:

- $\vec{m}$: The move vector from $\vec{p}$ to $\vec{q}$, $\vec{m} = \vec{q} - \vec{p}$
- $\vec{n}$: The normal vector of the triangle
- $\vec{i}$: The point of contact of the sphere on the triangle

$\vec{b}$: The "best guess" position is the position of the sphere center where it touches the triangle

$\vec{c}$: The nearest point to $\vec{p}$ on the triangle (independent of $\vec{q}$)

$\vec{a}$: The "away vector" from $\vec{c}$ to $\vec{p}$, $\vec{a} = \vec{p} - \vec{c}$. $\vec{a}$ is only parallel to $\vec{n}$ if $\vec{c}$ lies inside the triangle. This vector is independent from the movement and only depends on the initial position $\vec{p}$

$\vec{\eta}$: The vector from $\vec{i}$ to $\vec{b}$ that is called "move plane normal". It defines the plane in which the sphere can move without intersecting the triangle. $\vec{\eta}$ only equals the triangle normal $\vec{n}$ in certain cases. The move plane normal depends on the movement of the sphere

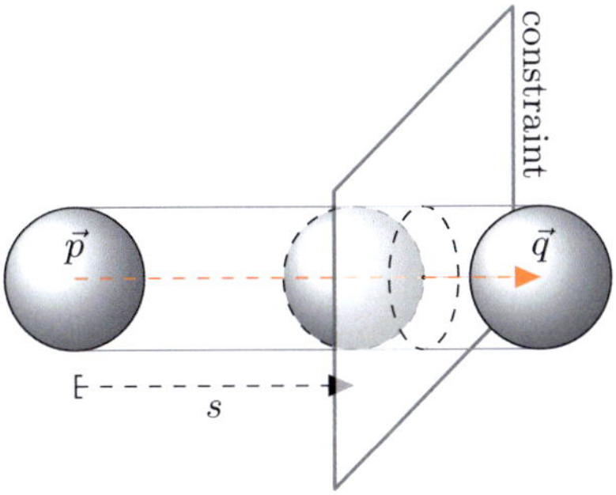

Figure 7.6.: The sphere movement (capsule) from $\vec{p}$ to $\vec{q}$ and the factor s indicating how far the sphere can move.

The collision detection algorithm consists of two parts. First, the nearest point on the triangle $\vec{c}$ is calculated in order to know if the movement $\vec{m}$ points towards the triangle. This is the case if $\vec{a}^T \cdot \vec{m} < 0$. In case the movement points towards the triangle, the second part of the algorithm is executed to find $s_{\min}$ and $\vec{\eta}$. Figure 7.8 shows a flowchart of the collision detection algorithm.

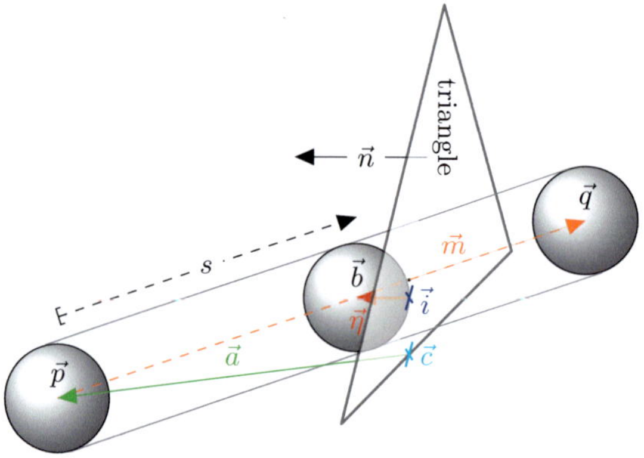

(a) Example 1: Collision inside the triangle

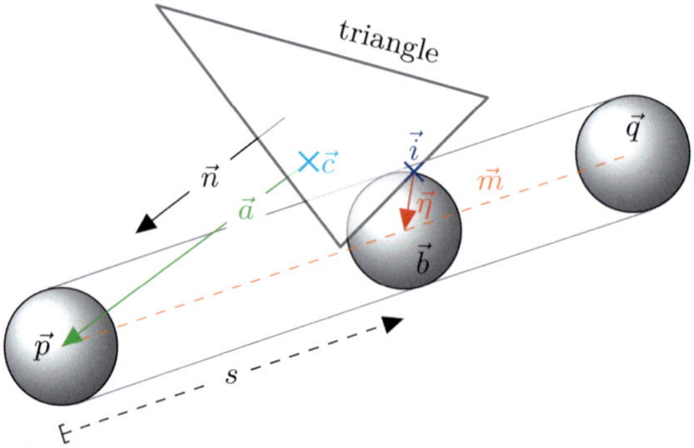

(b) Example 2: Collision on the edge of the triangle

Figure 7.7.: Two examples of a sphere movement colliding with a triangle. All parameters calculated in the collision detection are shown. Note the difference between the vectors $\vec{\eta}$, $\vec{n}$ and $\vec{a}$ as well as the points $\vec{i}$ and $\vec{c}$.

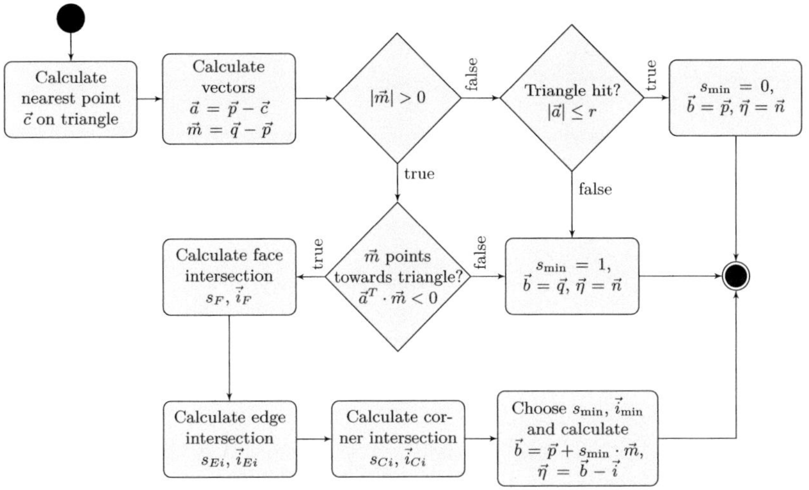

Figure 7.8.: The collision detection algorithm calculating the collision between a capsule and a triangle. For simplicity reasons invalid cases are not shown.

7.3.1 Nearest Point on Triangle Algorithm

In order to calculate the nearest point $\vec{c}$ to the sphere center $\vec{p}$ on the triangle, the center $\vec{p}$ is transformed into base coordinates $(u_x, u_y, u_z)^T$ and dropped into the xy-plane $(u_x, u_y)^T$. This point may lie in one of seven possible regions: inside the triangle, perpendicular above or below one of the triangle sides or such that one of the triangle corners is nearest. These seven regions are defined by nine straight lines (see Figure 7.5). The combination of oriented distances to these lines

$$d_i = \hat{n}_i^T \cdot \vec{x} - c_i \tag{7.1}$$

where $\hat{n}_i$ is the unit normal vector of the line, c_i the corresponding Hesse constant and $\vec{x}$ an arbitrary point in the xy-plane, can be used to distinguish the seven regions. In coordinates T, this results in

$$\begin{aligned}
d_0 &= && y \\
d_1 &= n_{1x} \cdot (x - x_1) + && n_{1y} \cdot y \\
d_2 &= n_{2x} \cdot x + && n_{2y} \cdot y \\
d_3 &= x && \\
d_4 &= x - x_1 && \\
d_5 &= n_{1y} \cdot (x - x_1) - && n_{1x} \cdot y \\
d_6 &= n_{1y} \cdot (x - x_2) - && n_{1x} \cdot (y - y_2) \\
d_7 &= n_{2y} \cdot (x - x_2) - && n_{2x} \cdot (y - y_2) \\
d_8 &= n_{2y} \cdot x - && n_{2x} \cdot y
\end{aligned} \tag{7.2}$$

Figure 7.5 shows the regions and the corresponding signs of the oriented distances. Depending on the determined region, the nearest point $\vec{c}$ on the triangle is calculated:

$$\begin{aligned}
d_0 \geq 0,\ d_1 \geq 0,\ d_2 \geq 0 &\rightarrow \vec{c} = && (u_x, u_y, 0)^T \\
d_0 < 0,\ d_3 \geq 0,\ d_4 < 0 &\rightarrow \vec{c} = && (u_x, 0, 0)^T \\
d_4 \geq 0,\ d_5 < 0 &\rightarrow \vec{c} = && (x_1, 0, 0)^T \\
d_1 < 0,\ d_5 \geq 0,\ d_6 < 0 &\rightarrow \vec{c} = && (u_x - d_1 n_{1x}, u_y - d_1 n_{1y}, 0)^T \\
d_6 \geq 0,\ d_7 < 0 &\rightarrow \vec{c} = && (x_2, y_2, 0)^T \\
d_2 < 0,\ d_7 \geq 0,\ d_8 < 0 &\rightarrow \vec{c} = && (u_x - d_2 n_{2x}, u_y - d_2 n_{2y}, 0)^T \\
d_3 < 0,\ d_8 \geq 0 &\rightarrow \vec{c} = && (0, 0, 0)^T
\end{aligned} \tag{7.3}$$

7.3.2 Triangle Intersection Algorithm

The goal of this algorithm is to calculate how far the sphere can move from $\vec{p}$ to $\vec{q}$ without intersecting the constraints. The best guess position in which the sphere touches a constraint is defined as $\vec{b} = \vec{p} + s_{\min} \cdot \vec{m}$ with $\vec{m} = \vec{q} - \vec{p}$. Additional to these parameters, the move plane normal $\vec{\eta}$ is determined.

Surface Intersection Intersecting the line from $\vec{p}$ to $\vec{q}$ with the plane $z = r'$ (with $r' = r$ for $m_z < 0$ and $r' = -r$ otherwise) results in $s_F = \frac{r'-p_z}{m_z}$, $\vec{b}_F = \vec{p} + s_F \cdot \vec{m}$ and $\vec{i}_F = (b_{Fx}, b_{Fy}, 0)^T$.

Edge Intersection Let $\vec{w}_i$ and $\vec{w}_j$ be the start and end position of the currently considered triangle edge. Then the edge itself is described by $\vec{w}_i + t \cdot \vec{d}$ with $\vec{d} = \vec{w}_j - \vec{w}_i$ and $0 \leq t \leq 1$. In case the sphere touches the edge, the distance of a point $\vec{p} + s_E \cdot \vec{m}$ to the edge equals r:

$$\frac{\left|\left((\vec{p} + s_E \cdot \vec{m}) - \vec{w}\right) \times \vec{d}\right|}{|\vec{d}|} = r \tag{7.4}$$

With $\vec{h}_1 = (\vec{p} - \vec{w}) \times \vec{d}$ and $\vec{h}_2 = \vec{m} \times \vec{d}$ this results in

$$s_{E1,2} = \frac{-b \pm \sqrt{D}}{a} \text{ with } D = b^2 - a \cdot c,\ a = \vec{h}_2^T \cdot \vec{h}_2,\ b = \vec{h}_1^T \cdot \vec{h}_2 \text{ and}$$
$$c = \vec{h}_1^T \cdot \vec{h}_1 - r^2 \cdot |\vec{d}|^2 \tag{7.5}$$

The best guess position $\vec{b}_{E1,2} = \vec{p} + s_{E1,2} \cdot \vec{m}$ projected onto the edge $\vec{w}_i + t \cdot \vec{d}$ results in the point of contact $\vec{i}_{E1,2} = \vec{w}_i + t_{L1,2} \cdot \vec{d}$ with

$$t_{L1,2} = \frac{\vec{d}^T \cdot (\vec{b}_{E1,2} - \vec{w}_i)}{\vec{d}^T \cdot \vec{d}} \tag{7.6}$$

Corner Intersection The distance of a corner $\vec{w}$ to a point on the line $\vec{p} + s_C \cdot \vec{m}$ is $d = |\vec{p} + s_C \cdot \vec{m} - \vec{w}|$. In case the sphere touches the corner, this distance equals r and therefore $|\vec{p} + s_C \cdot \vec{m} - \vec{w}| = r$.

With $\vec{h} = \vec{p} - \vec{w}$ this results in

$$s_{C1,2} = \frac{-b \pm \sqrt{D}}{a} \text{ with } D = b^2 - a \cdot c,\ a = \vec{m}^T \cdot \vec{m},\ b = \vec{m}^T \cdot \vec{h} \text{ and}$$
$$c = \vec{h}^T \cdot \vec{h} - r^2 \tag{7.7}$$

The best guess is $\vec{b}_{C1,2} = \vec{p} + s_{C1,2} \cdot \vec{m}$ and the point of contact coincides with the corner point $\vec{i}_C = \vec{w}$.

Selection of the Applicable Case From all possible and valid factors s the smallest one has to be determined:

$$\begin{aligned} s_{\min} = \min\{&\{s_F \mid 0 \leq s_F \leq 1\} \cup \\ &\{s_E \mid 0 \leq s_E \leq 1 \wedge 0 \leq t_L \leq 1\} \cup \\ &\{s_C \mid 0 \leq s_C \leq 1\}\} \end{aligned} \tag{7.8}$$

The corresponding best guess and point of contact are chosen and the move plane normal is $\vec{\eta} = \vec{b} - \vec{\imath}$.

7.4 Position Control Algorithm

Finding and correcting the end effector position such that the constraints stay untouched is the elementary task of this component. As long as there is no constraint close to the end effector, the target position $\vec{t}$ and the home position coincide. If the user holds the HHRD in such a way that the home position collides with the constraint, the target position must be adapted. The distance between target and home position is minimized without intersecting any constraint. The calculated target position is saved and used as the last valid position $\vec{l}$ in the next iteration. In order to prevent the end effector from sticking on the constraint, the end effector slides along the constraint until the distance between the home position $\vec{r}$ and the last valid position $\vec{l}$ is minimized.

Figure 7.9a shows an example of a movement $\vec{l} \rightarrow \vec{r}$ that collides with the constraint after a certain distance. In this case, the algorithm moves the sphere until it touches the constraint and finishes.

Consider the example in Figure 7.9b. The last valid position $\vec{l}$ touches one of the constraints. Therefore, $\vec{r}$ is projected onto the touched constraint. The projected point is called projected target position $\vec{\tau}_1$ where the subscript identifies the phase number k with $0 \leq k \leq 2$. Due to the fact that the new movement $\vec{l} \rightarrow \vec{\tau}_1$ could intersect other constraints, another collision detection has to be performed. Given that $s_{\min} > 0$ for this new movement, the movement can be executed partially. The target position is calculated by $\vec{t} = \vec{l} + s_{\min} \cdot (\vec{\tau}_1 - \vec{l})$.

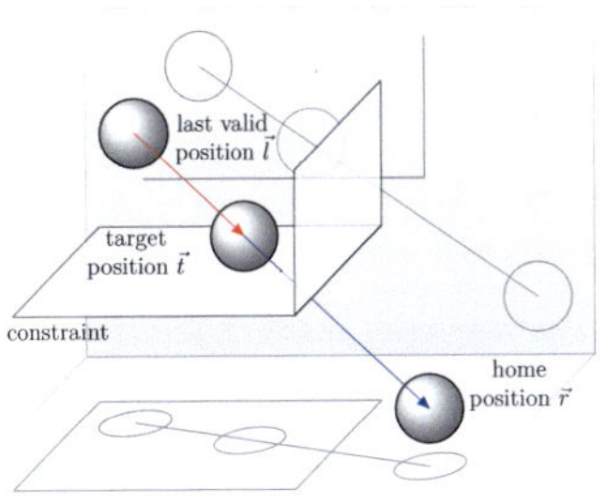

(a) Iteration with one phase

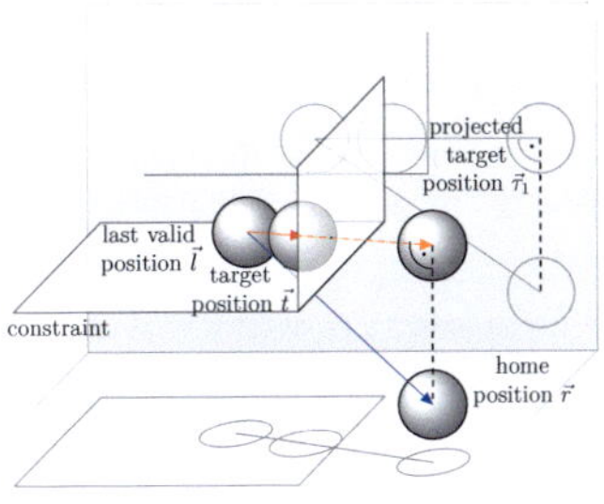

(b) Iteration with two phases

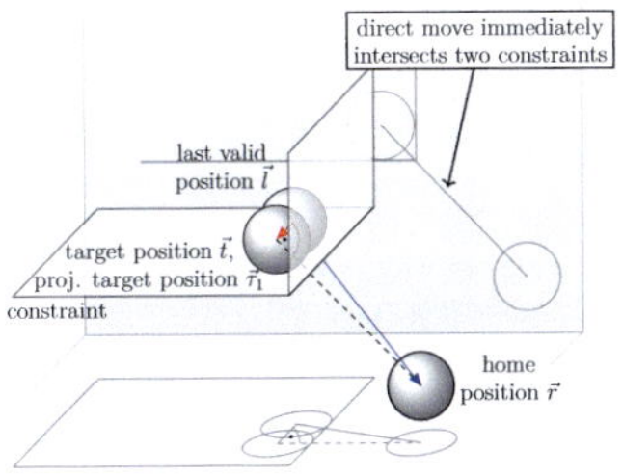

(c) Iteration with two phases

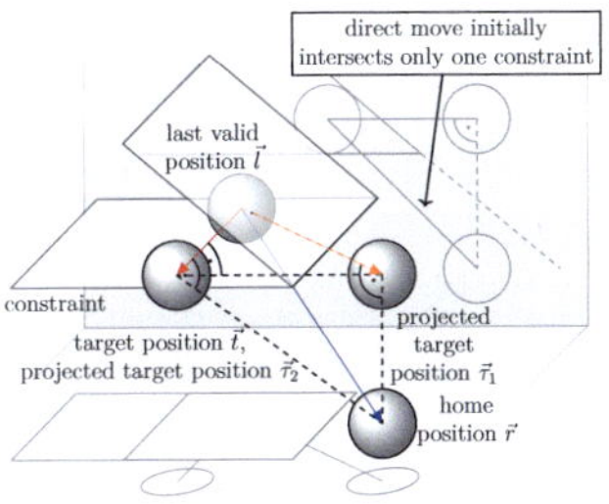

(d) Iteration with three phases

Figure 7.9.: Four individual sphere movements $\vec{l} \to \vec{r}$ and how the position control algorithm finds the target position $\vec{t}$. The blue movement $(\vec{l} \to \vec{r})$ would be the optimum without considering constraints. The red one $(\vec{l} \to \vec{t})$ is the final movement of the end effector. The dashed orange ones $(\vec{l} \to \vec{\tau})$ are theoretical intermediate movements. In (a) the end effector can move partially and on a direct way towards the home position. In (b) a direct movement is not possible. A collision is detected and a second phase is started. In the second phase, the movement is projected and the end effector can move partially until it hits the second constraint. In (c) a direct movement is not possible, since the direct movement intersects both constraints. In the second phase, the movement is projected onto the line defined by the two constraints and the end effector can move. In (d) a direct movement is not possible. A collision with the lower constraint is detected and a second phase is started. In the second phase, the movement is projected onto the constraint. The resulting projection causes another collision and a third phase is started. In the third phase, the movement is projected onto the line defined by both constraints and the end effector can move.

Since the projected movement could intersect other constraints (or the same constraint in other points), the collision detection has to be performed once in each phase. Performing a collision detection up to three times in one iteration guarantees that the HHRD does not execute a movement that is not previously checked against all constraints. This multi-phased architecture is attributed to the special nature of an HHRD. In each iteration, the home position and the last valid position have to be considered, since they are moving relative to each other.

This iterative position control algorithm can be summarized in the following steps (see Figure 7.10):

1. Calculate the projected target position $\vec{\tau}_k$ according to the intersected triangles from the previous phases and the movement from $\vec{l}$ to $\vec{r}$. In the first phase, $\vec{\tau}$ equals $\vec{r}$.
2. In case the projected target position $\vec{\tau}_k$ equals the last valid position $\vec{l}$, the algorithm terminates.
3. Otherwise, a collision detection for the sphere movement from the last valid position to the projected target position $\vec{l} \rightarrow \vec{\tau}_k$ is performed.
4. The smallest allowed movement is determined (triangles from previous phases are ignored).
5. If there is a possible movement ($s_{\min} > 0$), the target position is set and the algorithm terminates.
6. Otherwise, the next phase is started with step 1.

7.4.1 Move Plane Normal versus Triangle Normal

Every touched triangle defines a move plane normal $\vec{\eta}$ and a factor s indicating how far the end effector can move from $\vec{l}$ to $\vec{\tau}_k$. The move plane normal defines the plane in which the end effector is allowed to move relative to the triangle without intersecting it. Every move plane normal restricts the space in which the end effector can move. If there are two different move plan normals with $s = 0$, the space is restricted to the direction of the intersection line of the two planes. In this case, the end effector could subsequently move in this direction. This case occurs in Figure 7.9c and 7.9d. In case there are three different move plane normals (all with $s = 0$), they intersect each other in one point, which means that the end effector is completely restricted. In this case, the projected target $\vec{\tau}_k$ equals the last valid position $\vec{l}$. One example would be a movement through the tip of a tetrahedron while touching the three faces of the tip.

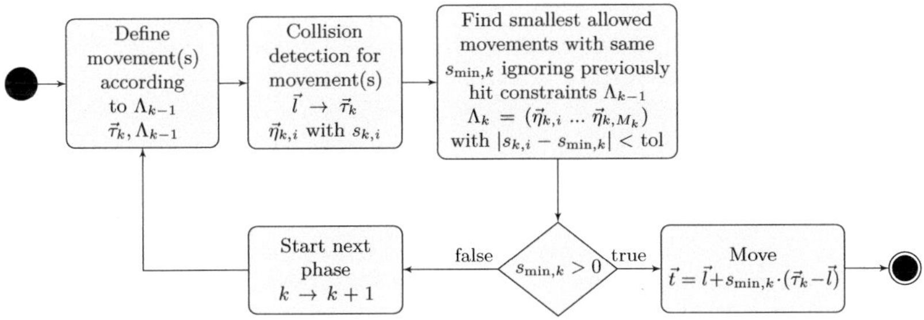

Figure 7.10.: The position control algorithm. Inputs are the home position $\vec{r}$ and the last valid position $\vec{l}$. The output is the target position $\vec{t}$. Every collision of the current movement from $\vec{l}$ to the projected target position $\vec{\tau}_k$ produces one pair of $\vec{\eta}_{k,i}$ with corresponding $s_{k,i}$. After the smallest allowed movement is found, only the move plane normals with an s of $s_{\min,k}$ are stored in Λ_k.

The position control algorithm uses the move plane normal to compute in which direction the end effector is allowed to move. The move plane normal $\vec{\eta}$ is the vector from the contact point $\vec{i}$ to the sphere center $\vec{b}$. Therefore, it is parallel to the triangle's normal when the point of contact $\vec{i}$ lies inside the triangle and differs if $\vec{i}$ lies on one of the triangle's edges or corners. Figure 7.11 describes the importance of using the move plane normal instead of the triangle normal. Using the move plane normal, the sphere slides around the edge of the triangle. This behavior produces smoother movements around corners and edges.

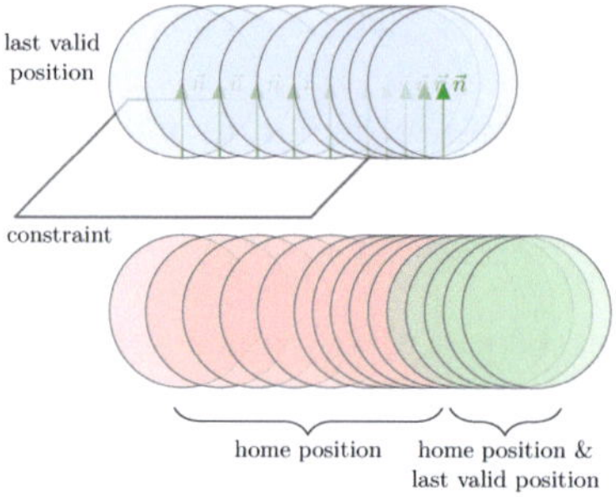

(a) Sphere movement using the triangle's normal

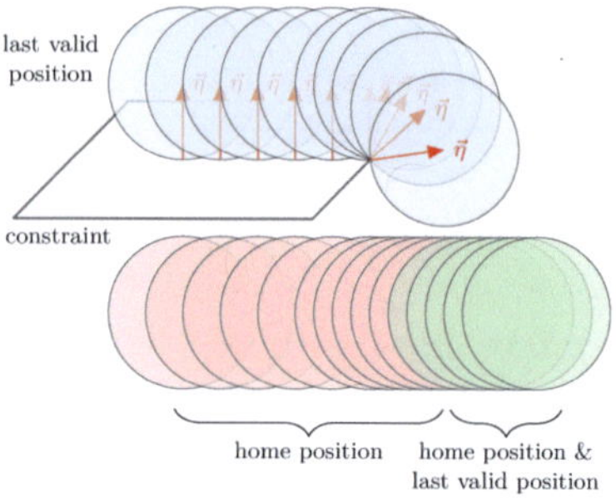

(b) Sphere movement using the move plane normal

Figure 7.11.: Difference between using the triangle normal $\vec{n}$ (left) and the triangle's move plane normal $\vec{\eta}$ (right). At the beginning both approaches show the same results. They differ as soon as the sphere passes the edge of the triangle. $\vec{\eta}$ is the vector from the nearest point on the triangle to the sphere center. This vector defines a plane in which the sphere is allowed to move. The triangle's normal is constant. Therefore, by using the move plane normal the sphere moves around the edge, whereas in case of the normal it continues straight until it can pass the triangle without collision.

7.4.2 Finding the Smallest Allowed Movement

The collision detection algorithm returns a move plane normal $\vec{\eta}_{k,i}$ with corresponding factor $s_{k,i}$ for every collision (with $0 \leq i < C_k$). Different triangles can be intersected at different distances. Since only the closest collisions matter, the move plane normals corresponding to the smallest allowed movement defined by $s_{\min,k}$ are searched. It is possible that several triangles can be intersected at the same distance. Hence, the result of this search is a matrix

$$\Lambda_k = (\vec{\eta}_{k,0} \ \ldots \ \vec{\eta}_{k,M_k-1}) \text{ with } M_k \leq C_k \tag{7.9}$$

containing the move plane normals corresponding to $s_{\min,k}$.

Moreover, it is important that the hit triangles from the previous phase, represented by Λ_{k-1}, are ignored, since they are implicitly included in the projected movement (the projection was calculated according to the previous triangles). In the first phase, there are no previous triangles.

Eventually the case occurs that $\vec{l} \rightarrow \vec{\tau}_k$ collides with a constraint. If $s_{\min} > 0$ the algorithm calculates the target position $\vec{t} = \vec{l} + s_{\min} \cdot (\vec{\tau}_k - \vec{l})$ and finishes the iteration (see Figure 7.9a). If $s_{\min} = 0$ the end effector cannot move on the given movement direction and the next phase is started.

7.4.3 Defining the Movement According to Detected Constraints

Depending on the found constraints, the current move vector $\vec{l} \rightarrow \vec{r}$ is projected onto planes, lines, or points. Figure 7.12 shows a flowchart of the projection algorithm (Section 7.4.4 explains the outlined cases).

Before calculating the projection it has to be determined how restricted the space already is. This determination depends on the current phase. **In the first phase** ($k = 0$) the space is not yet restricted, and therefore no projection is necessary:

$$\vec{\tau}_k = \vec{r} \tag{7.10}$$

In the second phase ($k = 1$) the space is restricted by the move plane normals found in the first phase $\Lambda_0 = (\vec{\eta}_{0,0} \, ... \, \vec{\eta}_{0,M_0-1})$. In order to find the vector space defined by the move plane normals, a singular value decomposition (SVD) is applied:

$$\mathrm{SVD}(\Lambda_0^T) = U_0 \Sigma_0 V_0^T \tag{7.11}$$

$$\Sigma_0 = \begin{pmatrix} \sigma_{0,0} & 0 & 0 \\ 0 & \sigma_{0,1} & 0 \\ 0 & 0 & \sigma_{0,2} \\ 0 & 0 & 0 \\ \vdots & \vdots & \vdots \\ 0 & 0 & 0 \end{pmatrix} \tag{7.12}$$

$$V_0 = (\vec{v}_{0,0}\ \vec{v}_{0,1}\ \vec{v}_{0,2}) \tag{7.13}$$

The interesting part of the decomposition is matrix V_0 which is a 3×3 matrix whose column vectors are the right-singular vectors of Λ_0. Each right-singular vector $\vec{v}_{0,i}$ corresponds to one singular value $\sigma_{0,i}$, $i = 0, 1, 2$. The vectors belonging to non-zero singular values define how the movement is restricted. They are stored in matrix $N_0 = (\vec{v}_{0,0} \ldots \vec{v}_{0,W_0-1})$ with W_0 being the number of non-zero singular values $\sigma_{0,i}$.

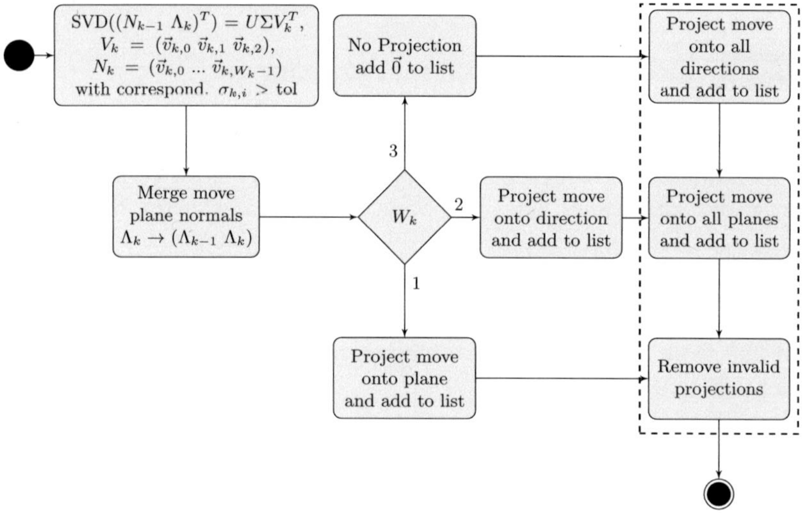

Figure 7.12.: The algorithm that defines the movements according to the given restrictions. To provide greater clarity the indices are incremented by 1. Inputs are the right-singular vectors N_{k-1} and the move plane normals Λ_k as well as the movement from the last valid position $\vec{l}$ to the home position $\vec{r}$. The output is a list of possible projected target positions $\{\vec{\tau}_{k+1,\gamma}\}$ with corresponding move plane normals $\Lambda_{k,\gamma}$. The outlined parts are executed when the special cases are considered.

The vectors of N_0 can form three different restrictions with three different projections (with $\vec{m} = \vec{r} - \vec{l}$):

1. There is one right-singular vector $\vec{v}_{0,0}$ with $\sigma_{0,0} > 0$ ($W_0 = 1$) that defines a plane onto which the move vector is projected (see Figure 7.9b).

$$\vec{r}_1 = \vec{l} + \frac{\vec{m}^T \cdot \vec{v}_{0,0}}{\vec{v}_{0,0}^T \cdot \vec{v}_{0,0}} \cdot \vec{v}_{0,0} \tag{7.14}$$

2. There are two right-singular vectors $\vec{v}_{0,0}$ and $\vec{v}_{0,1}$ with $\sigma_{0,i} > 0$ ($W_0 = 2$) that define a line onto which the move vector is projected (see Figure 7.9c).

$$\vec{r}_1 = \vec{l} + \frac{\vec{m}^T \cdot \vec{d}}{\vec{d}^T \cdot \vec{d}} \cdot \vec{d} \text{ with } \vec{d} = \vec{v}_{0,0} \times \vec{v}_{0,1} \tag{7.15}$$

3. There are three right-singular vectors with $\sigma_{0,i} > 0$ that define a point, the move vector is $\vec{0}$.

$$\vec{r}_1 = \vec{l} \tag{7.16}$$

The third phase ($k = 2$) is similar to the second one. Additional to the move plane normals from the second phase $\Lambda_1 = (\vec{\eta}_{1,0} \ldots \vec{\eta}_{1,M_1-1})$, the right-singular vectors from the first phase N_0 are used as inputs for the SVD:

$$\text{SVD}((\vec{\eta}_{1,0} \ldots \vec{\eta}_{1,M_1-1}\ \vec{v}_{0,0} \ldots \vec{v}_{0,W_0-1})^T) = U_1 \Sigma_1 V_1^T \tag{7.17}$$

Since the vectors belonging to non-zero singular values N_1 are the result of the singular value decomposition of matrix ($N_0\ \Lambda_1$), they implicitly contain the vectors of matrix Λ_1. Therefore, the vectors of N_1 can only form two different restrictions with two different projections (with $\vec{m} = \vec{r} - \vec{l}$):

1. There are two right-singular vectors $\vec{v}_{1,0}$ and $\vec{v}_{1,1}$ with $\sigma_{1,i} > 0$ that define a line onto which the move vector is projected (see Figure 7.9d).

$$\vec{r}_2 = \vec{l} + \frac{\vec{m}^T \cdot \vec{d}}{\vec{d}^T \cdot \vec{d}} \cdot \vec{d} \text{ with } \vec{d} = \vec{v}_{1,0} \times \vec{v}_{1,1} \tag{7.18}$$

2. There are three right-singular vectors with $\sigma_{1,i} > 0$ that define a point, the move vector is $\vec{0}$.

$$\vec{\tau}_2 = \vec{l} \tag{7.19}$$

An example shall further clarify this algorithm. In the first phase, there are no restrictions from previous phases. Therefore, the movement $\vec{l} \rightarrow \vec{\tau}_0$ with $\vec{\tau}_0 = \vec{r}$ is checked in the collision detection. It is assumed that four collisions with $s_{\min} = 0$ and the following move plane normals are found:

$$\vec{\eta}_{00} = \begin{pmatrix} 0.267 \\ 0.535 \\ 0.802 \end{pmatrix}, \vec{\eta}_{01} = \begin{pmatrix} 0.402 \\ 0.723 \\ 0.562 \end{pmatrix}, \vec{\eta}_{02} = \begin{pmatrix} 0.402 \\ 0.723 \\ 0.562 \end{pmatrix}, \vec{\eta}_{03} = \begin{pmatrix} 0.248 \\ 0.287 \\ -0.925 \end{pmatrix} \tag{7.20}$$

In the second phase, an SVD is performed in order to calculate the restriction following out of the move plane normals. The results are

$$\Sigma = \begin{pmatrix} 1.753 & 0 & 0 \\ 0 & 0.964 & 0 \\ 0 & 0 & 0.000 \end{pmatrix}, V_0 = \begin{pmatrix} -0.304 & -0.431 & 0.850 \\ -0.587 & -0.618 & -0.523 \\ -0.751 & 0.658 & 0.065 \end{pmatrix} \tag{7.21}$$

The singular values show that the movement is restricted in two directions, which are the first two columns $\vec{v}_{0,0}$ and $\vec{v}_{0,1}$ of V_0. Therefore, the new projected target position $\vec{\tau}_1$ is calculated according to Equation 7.15. It is assumed that the collision detection checks the movement from $\vec{l} \rightarrow \vec{\tau}_1$ and finds another collision with a move plane normal $\vec{\eta}_{1,0}$ and corresponding $s_{\min} = 0$.

In the third phase, another SVD is calculated considering the following inputs:

$$\vec{\eta}_{1,0} = \begin{pmatrix} 0.640 \\ 0.768 \\ 0 \end{pmatrix}, \vec{v}_{0,0} = \begin{pmatrix} -0.304 \\ -0.587 \\ -0.751 \end{pmatrix}, \vec{v}_{0,1} = \begin{pmatrix} -0.431 \\ -0.618 \\ 0.658 \end{pmatrix} \tag{7.22}$$

Note that the previous constraints $\vec{\eta}_{0,0}$, $\vec{\eta}_{0,1}$, $\vec{\eta}_{0,2}$ and $\vec{\eta}_{0,3}$ are ignored, since they are implicitly included in $\vec{v}_{0,0}$ and $\vec{v}_{0,1}$. The SVD results in

$$\Sigma = \begin{pmatrix} 1.411 & 0 & 0 \\ 0 & 1.000 & 0 \\ 0 & 0 & 0.101 \end{pmatrix}, \; V_1 = \begin{pmatrix} 0.584 & 0.051 & 0.810 \\ 0.812 & -0.042 & -0.582 \\ -0.005 & -0.998 & 0.066 \end{pmatrix} \tag{7.23}$$

All three singular values are unequal 0 meaning that the movement is completely restricted ($\vec{m} = \vec{0}$). Therefore, the projected target position $\vec{\tau}_2$ equals the last valid position $\vec{l}$.

7.4.4 Special Projection Cases

The assumptions from the previous section generate valid move vectors, however, the performed projections do not allow a natural interaction. There are certain cases where it is not sufficient to check projections defined by the right-singular vectors of the constraints. Valid and more optimal projections exist that are calculated by using the move plane normals. The example in Figure 7.13 shows two planes defining a projection onto a line. It is obvious that certain home positions cause different projections. The movement $\vec{l} \to \vec{r}^B$ has to be handled differently than the movement $\vec{l} \to \vec{r}^A$ since the end effector would stick on the line even when the user movement indicates that he wants to slide the end effector along the constraint. Hence, it might be better to project the movement onto one of the two planes instead of projecting it onto the line.

As explained above, the number of right-singular vectors in N_{k-1} indicates how to project. Additional to the standard cases from the previous section (see Figure 7.12), different movement projections are calculated and added to a list of possible projections:

1. If there are two right-singular vectors, the movement can be projected onto the constraints themselves (the move plane normals $\vec{\eta}$ of the constraints are retrieved from Λ_{k-1}).

2. If there are three right-singular vectors, the movement $\vec{l} \rightarrow \vec{r}$ is projected onto all possible lines calculated by combining the move plane normals $\vec{\eta}$ in Λ_{k-1}. As in the previous case, the movement is also projected onto all constraints.

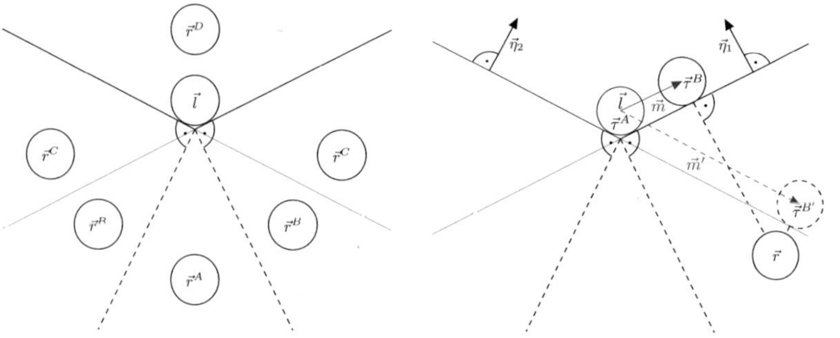

(a) All possibilities

(b) Example: $\vec{r}^A$ is $\vec{r}$ projected onto the line, $\vec{r}^B$ is $\vec{r}$ projected onto plane 1 (valid), $\vec{r}^{B'}$ is $\vec{r}$ projected onto plane 2 (invalid). Prefer $\vec{r}^B$ to $\vec{r}^A$

Figure 7.13.: Different projection cases. Two constraints are touched by the end effector (see (a)). The shown home positions $\vec{r}^A, \vec{r}^B, \vec{r}^C, \vec{r}^D$ result in different projections. $\vec{l} \rightarrow \vec{r}^D$ represents a movement away from the constraints, therefore, no projection is necessary. $\vec{l} \rightarrow \vec{r}^C$ intersects only with one of the two constraints and the movement is projected onto the plane defined by the constraint. $\vec{l} \rightarrow \vec{r}^A$ intersects both constraints, which is why it has to be projected onto the intersection line defined by the constraints. Even $\vec{l} \rightarrow \vec{r}^B$ also causes a collision with both constraints, the movement can be projected onto one of the two constraints and the resulting move vector does not collide with any of the two (see example in (b)). Therefore, it is important to also check the projections onto the individual constraints even when two different constraints are intersected.

Now there is a list of possible projections that have to be tested against all move plane normals in Λ_{k-1}. Invalid ones are removed from the list. A projection is invalid if the angle between the move plane normal and the projected movement is greater than 90°. An angle of 90° is a parallel movement to the plane defined by the move plane normal. An angle smaller than 90° indicates that the movement points away from the plane defined by the move plane normal. For the example shown in Figure 7.13b, the following angles apply:

$$\sphericalangle(\vec{m}, \vec{\eta}_1) = 90°,\ \sphericalangle(\vec{m}, \vec{\eta}_2) < 90°,\ \sphericalangle(\vec{m}', \vec{\eta}_1) > 90°,\ \sphericalangle(\vec{m}', \vec{\eta}_2) = 90° \tag{7.24}$$

Therefore, $\vec{\tau}^B$ is valid but $\vec{\tau}^{B'}$ is invalid, since it lies behind the first plane. This is only a fast check and does not replace the collision detection. Finally, the projection with the longest allowed movement is chosen.

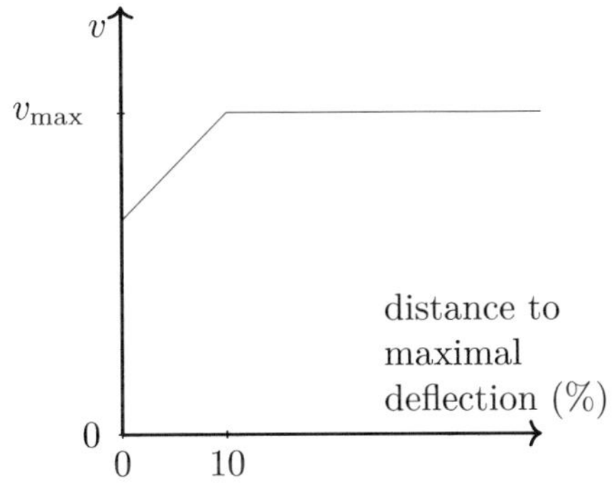

Figure 7.14.: The speed of the end effector depending on the deflection.

7.5 Speed Control Algorithm

The speed controller determines the speed of the end effector depending on the deflection of the tool, which is calculated by the kinematic controller (see Figure 7.14). As long as the HHRD can deflect, the maximal speed is set. As soon as one of the joints approximates its maximal deflection, the speed is decreased. If its maximum deflection is reached, the speed is set to 0. The deceleration of the speed is audible and gives the surgeon an additional feedback. Subsequently, he can reposition the HHRD to recover the maximal speed.

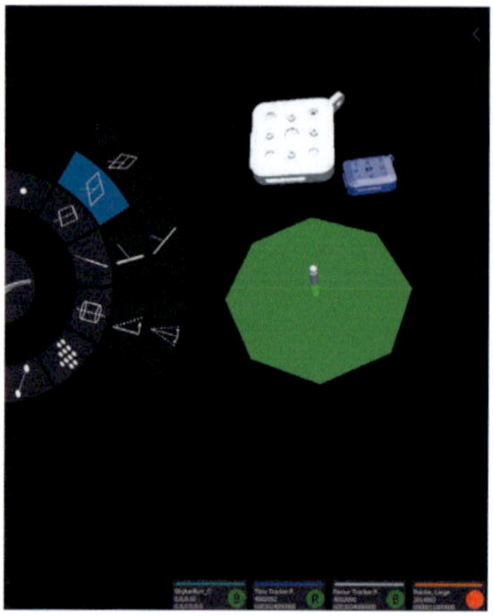

(a) OrthoCAD

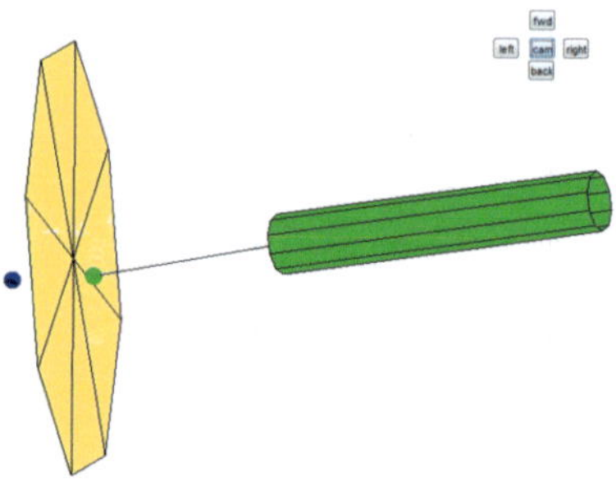

(b) MATLAB simulation front-end

Figure 7.15.: OrthoCAD and MATLAB environment showing the same scene. The blue and the green sphere represent the home position and the last valid position. The plane as well as the tracking data is transmitted via OpenIGTLink.

7.6 Test and Simulation Environment

In order to guarantee a correct behavior in extreme cases, a multitude of configurations is checked in unit tests and by using a simulation environment. Unit tests are implemented for the most important components such as the collision detection and the controllers. A simulation environment is implemented in MATLAB allowing to compare the behavior of the robot with the predefined simulation (see Figure 7.15). This environment receives positions and transformations as well as the constraints from OrthoCAD. During the runtime of the RCS, parameters inside the simulation environment can be adapted. By using this environment, misbehaviors can be found faster than in the control system.

7.7 Table-Top Prototype

Since the actual HHRD was not yet available, a robot consisting of an xyz-linear stage was used for the tests. This prototype (see Figure 7.16) is composed of four linear stages (CCM Rails, China), which are driven by three intelligent NEMA23 motors (Technosoft Motion, Switzerland), and an orthopedic milling device (Stryker, USA). The communication between the motors and the PC is implemented via CAN. The CAN bus uses the maximal baud rate of 1 Mbps. The attached milling device allows the surgeon to easily exchange the end effector. The linear stages have a pitch of 75 mm per revolution. The motors can run with up to 11.7 revolutions per second, which allow speeds of up to 877 mm per second. Although the working volume of the robot could be much larger, it is restricted (by software) to a cube with an edge length of 25 mm. This cube resembles the working volume of the target device.

The calibration of the translational table-top prototype consists of three steps:

1. Homing the translation stages
2. Calibration of the transformation F_{CA} from tracker coordinates A to linear stages coordinates C
3. Pivoting of the end effector to find the home position $\vec{r}_A$

The homing of the device finds its maximum deflection and its center position (home position). Since the tracker coordinates A do not coincide with the axes orientation of the prototype, the transformation F_{CA} from coordinate system A to C has to be found. For this purpose the reference tracker is rigidly attached to the tool shaft, whereas the tool tracker stays untouched. The tool shaft is moved to the maximum deflection in all three directions while recording the poses of the trackers (F_{WR}, F_{WA}). This results in $3N$ transformations where N is the number of recorded transformation per axes. The transformation from the reference tracker to the tool tracker is calculated by $F_{AR} = F_{WA}^{-1} \cdot F_{WR}$. The origin is extracted from these transformations. For all three records the extracted origins are used to calculate a regression line. The three calculated directions are part of the transformation matrix from A to C. The translation is zero. Finally, the end effector is pivoted to find the home position $\vec{r}_A$. During the pivoting calibration, the end effector's tip is placed in a tracked mould. The user rotates the tool while keeping the end effector in the mould. After the calibration, the end effector position can be calculated from the recorded transformations. As a last step its radius has to be specified manually. In order to calibrate the radius (or the shape) of the end effector, an optical calibration, as described in Chapter 6, is used.

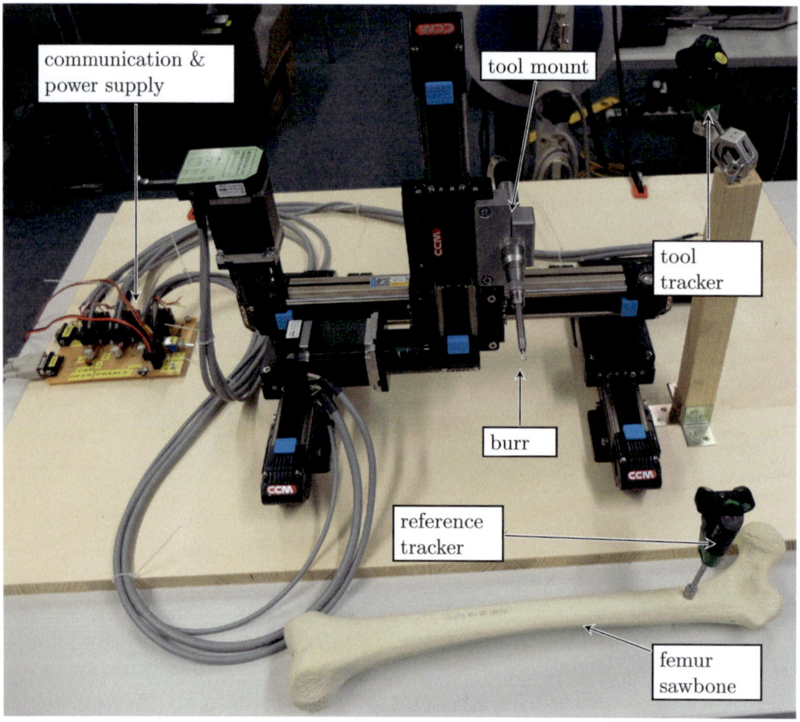

Figure 7.16.: A prototype consisting of four translation stages driven by three motors.

7.8 Accuracy Tests

Two different geometries, used in different surgical interventions, are milled and evaluated. Both geometries are milled utilizing the power-controlled, the evasive and the smoothing mode. The geometries are loaded as CAD files to guarantee the reproducibility of test results. Polyurethane hard foam blocks ($240\,\mathrm{kg/m^3}$) are used as milling medium, since its characteristics are comparable to those of bones. A burr with a radius of 2.5 mm is used.

First, a cuboid of $30\,\mathrm{mm}\times 30\,\mathrm{mm}\times 15\,\mathrm{mm}$ is removed from the test block. Such a bone removal could be used to deepen the bone surface in order to place an implant. Second, a half sphere with a radius of 15 mm is milled. Such an intervention is used in hip arthroplasties (hip replacement surgery) where the diameter of the acetabulum has to be increased in order to place an implant.

The milled geometries are sampled using the previously mentioned navigation system FP6000 by Stryker with the corresponding pointing device. The pointer tip can be localized with a standard deviation of 0.15 mm.

For the first test, the cuboid bottom plane is recorded. Its regression plane is calculated and analyzed. For the second test, a sphere with the given radius of 15 mm is matched into the point cloud of the half sphere.

7.9 Results

Figure 7.17 shows the difference between a cuboid milled with the power-controlled, the evasive and the smoothing mode. Whereas the power-controlled mode produced ragged edges and cratered surfaces, the evasive mode produced clearer edges and smoother surfaces. The smoothest surfaces are milled using the smoothing mode.

Table 7.1 and 7.2 show the error measures for the cuboid and the half sphere tests. The corresponding boxplots are shown in Figure 7.18 and 7.19. For each test, between 900 and 3500 points were digitized.

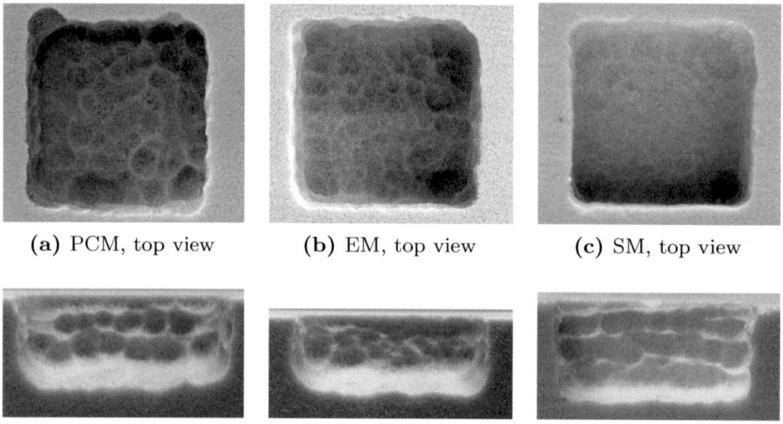

(a) PCM, top view (b) EM, top view (c) SM, top view

(d) PCM, cross-sect. view (e) EM, cross-sect. view (f) SM, cross-sect. view

Figure 7.17.: Cuboids milled with a 5 mm burr and different modes. (a) and (d) show the result using the power-controlled mode, whereas (b) and (e) were milled with the evasive mode. (c) and (f) represent the smoothing mode. Note that the smoothing mode produces smoother surfaces than the other two modes. It is also visible that the smoothing and the evasive mode show sharper edges.

The results show that all three modes produce RMS errors of less than 0.6 mm. The deviations and their variances show that the smoothing mode produces the best results and that the evasive mode is more accurate than the power-controlled mode. The improvement is most visible in the minimal and the maximal deviation. In the cuboid tests, the smoothing mode produces much smoother surfaces than the evasive mode. However, in the half sphere tests, this difference is not so clear anymore. In one test, the RMS error using the smoothing mode is even worse than using the evasive mode. This is probably caused by the fact that the end effector oscillates around its shaft and that the shaft, in case of the cuboid tests, points perpendicular to the surface, whereas in case of the half sphere tests it does not. Therefore, it can be assumed that the smoothing mode only produces smoother surfaces when the shaft points perpendicular to the surface.

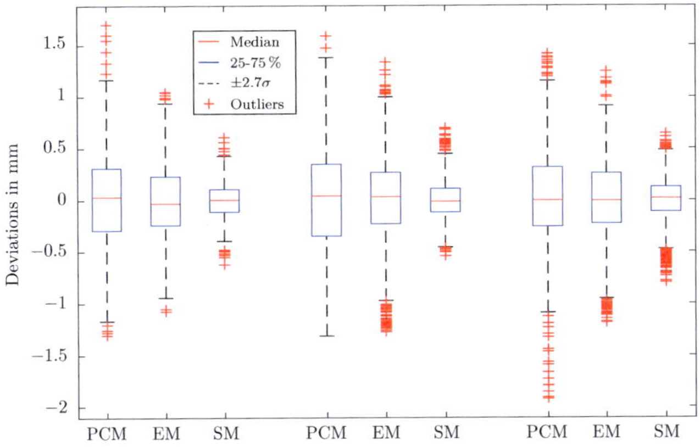

Figure 7.18.: Deviations to regression plane of different trials and different modes. PCM stands for power-controlled mode, EM for the evasive mode and SM for the smoothing mode.

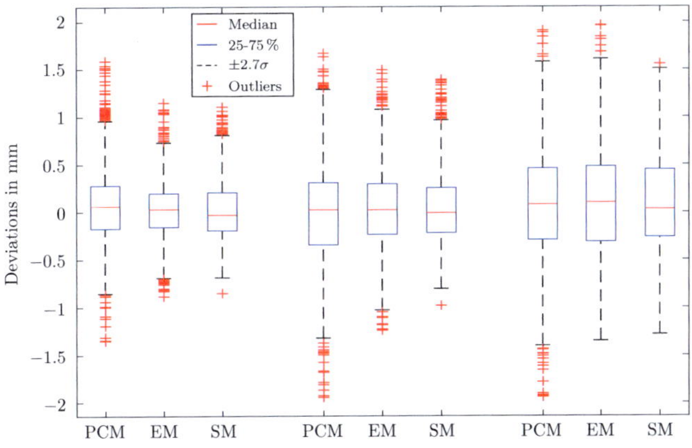

Figure 7.19.: Deviations to sphere-fit of different trials and different modes, radius was given (from CAD file), center was fitted. PCM stands for power-controlled mode, EM for the evasive mode and SM for the smoothing mode.

Trial	Mode	Number of points	δ_{rms} [mm]	δ_{var} [mm^2]	δ_{max} [mm]	δ_{min} [mm]
1	PCM	2010	0.44	0.20	-1.31	1.70
1	EM	1411	0.36	0.13	-1.08	1.05
1	SM	1567	0.16	0.03	-0.62	0.61
2	PCM	1294	0.49	0.24	-1.92	1.42
2	EM	1596	0.41	0.17	-1.19	1.24
2	SM	2657	0.21	0.04	-0.80	0.64
3	PCM	2366	0.49	0.24	-1.31	1.59
3	EM	2640	0.39	0.15	-1.28	1.34
3	SM	2367	0.18	0.03	-0.54	0.70

Table 7.1.: Deviations to regression plane of different trials and different modes. EM stands for the evasive mode, PCM for power-controlled mode and SM for the smoothing mode.

Trial	Mode	Number of points	δ_{rms} [mm]	δ_{var} [mm^2]	δ_{max} [mm]	δ_{min} [mm]
1	PCM	2077	0.40	0.16	-1.35	1.59
1	EM	3444	0.29	0.08	-0.88	1.15
1	SM	941	0.32	0.11	-0.85	1.11
2	PCM	1778	0.54	0.29	-1.95	1.67
2	EM	1489	0.43	0.19	-1.24	1.49
2	SM	1648	0.37	0.14	-0.98	1.39
3	PCM	2455	0.60	0.36	-1.94	1.91
3	EM	2175	0.58	0.34	-1.35	1.96
3	SM	1466	0.51	0.26	-1.28	1.56

Table 7.2.: Deviations to sphere-fit of different trials and different modes, radius was given (from CAD file), center was fitted. EM stands for the evasive mode, PCM for power-controlled mode and SM for the smoothing mode.

7.10 Conclusion

This chapter described a robot control system for HHRDs used in orthopedic surgery. This system protects previously defined regions from being penetrated by the HHRD. Different modes can be used depending on the hardware and the current task. A power-controlled mode simply turns off the device's speed when penetrating a constraint, whereas the evasive mode adapts the end effector's position to evade the constraint. A smoothing mode, similar to the evasive mode, oscillates the end effector around its home position. Constraints can be arbitrarily shaped (convex, concave) and do not have to form a closed volume. As a prototype, a table-top robotic milling device is utilized. The accuracy analysis shows that the presented control algorithms work robustly and accurately and that the quality of the milled objects depends on the used mode. The smoothing mode produces the best results, whereas the power-controlled mode has the biggest deviations.

The experiments show that the RMS deviations, while using the evasive mode, are less than 0.6 mm. The minimal and maximal deviations range between -1.4 mm and 2.0 mm. One source for the high range of deviations is the latency of the prototype and the navigation camera. A future prototype will improve these latencies. The smoothing mode further decreased these deviations to a range of -0.8 mm to 0.7 mm. The results of the evasive mode are comparable to the ones presented by Brisson et al. [14]. They state the minimal and maximal deviation with -1.7 mm and 1.2 mm. Xia et al. [45] use a cooperative stationary robot for skull base surgery. They perform accuracy tests on a cadaver with penetration errors of 1-2 mm and maximal errors of up to 3 mm. They further state that previous tests on foam blocks produced better results.

Additionally, the tests have shown that the milling speed of the device has a strong influence on the accuracy of the power-controlled mode. The higher the speed was, the better the results became. The presented tests were executed with a milling speed of 50000 rounds per minute. When the burr starts turning while touching the bone, it might happen that the burr gets caught in the bone. With a lower speed, the starting burr causes a movement of the whole tool whereas a higher speed is able to remove the material.

A semi-automatic mode could further improve the usage and handling of such devices. The HHRD automatically removes material inside its workspace (restricted by the individual kinematics) while the user simply holds the device close to the to-be-milled structures. As soon as the material is removed, the user has to move the HHRD to the next part.

The simulation of an HHRD with a table-top robotic tool works for testing the algorithms, however, it is difficult for the operator to see the possible range of motion of the tool. In case of HHRDs held by the operator, the range of motion is directly visible. In case of the table-top robotic tool, the theoretical range of motion is much bigger and is only limited by software bounds. Another prototype will improve this by placing the robot in such a way that the milling device points towards the table surface.

CHAPTER 8

Evaluation

Contents

Before the evaluation of the overall system is described and discussed, the evaluations from the previous chapters are summarized:

OrthoCAD, as an intraoperative, image-free, and generic planning application for orthopedic surgery, was evaluated by means of a planning of a femoral neck osteotomy. The individual planning steps are depicted and illustrate the functionality and capacity of OrthoCAD (see Chapter 3.13).

For the pixel-wise OSTG calibration two experiments were carried out (see Chapter 4.9 and 4.10). The first experiment tested the pixel triangulation approach on two different OSTG. The second experiment included a series of tests to calculate the accuracy of overlays using the presented pixel-wise calibration. The former experiment showed that the triangulation approach works well on OSTG with simple optics, such as the STAR 1200XLD, but fails on OSTG with more complex optics, such as the BT-200. In the latter experiment a series of tests with different camera/eye positions were carried out. The tests showed that the presented calibration allows overlays with a maximal error of 1.4 pixel or 2.26 arcmin, which translates to 0.33 mm at a distance of 500 mm. Compared to other works it is by a factor of two more accurate. However, this result has to be considered with care since all compared works used different devices.

In order to evaluate the intraoperative instrument calibration with its two calibration steps, different objects were calibrated and compared to each other (see Chapter 6.4 and 6.5). For the tracked camera calibration a sphere was calibrated using the presented technique and by pivoting. The results show almost identical accuracies. In a second step the sphere's surface was reconstructed and used to calculate the sphere's center position. In this test the presented approach is four to five times more inaccurate than pivoting. However, pivoting is not able to determine the sphere's surface. The same was repeated for a burr. In this case the presented approach is by a factor of 1.7 more accurate than pivoting since the burr is not completely spherical.

The OpenIGTLink implementation was evaluated according to its latency and frame rate in different scenarios (see Chapter 5.3 and 5.4.2). Tracking data (16 channels) can be transferred with a frame rate of 1000 Hz and a latency of 2.81 ms, US streams with 512 Hz and 14 ms latency and HD grayscale US streams with 128 Hz and 66 ms. These values were measured in real application scenarios meaning that there was a data producer and a data consumer, e.g. a navigation system and a visualization.

Milling tests with simple geometries in hard foam blocks show the accuracy and quality of the table-top robotic prototype and its control algorithms (see Chapter 7.8 and 7.9). Cuboids and half spheres were milled and compared to their CAD model. A power-controlled mode with rigid burr was compared to an evasive mode with position controlled burr (3-DoF). Additionally, a smoothing mode was tested. The results show that all three modes produce RMS errors of less than 0.6 mm. However, the variances show that the smoothing mode produces the best results and therefore smoother surfaces. All three modes produce surfaces that are accurate enough for orthopedic interventions and much better than manually milled surfaces.

Whereas these quantitative evaluations focused on individual algorithms and processes, this chapter describes the evaluation of the overall system and the collaboration of their components. Even though most of the following evaluations do not determine accuracies, they demonstrate that the complete system from the planning over the visualization to the execution works without any problems. To demonstrate that OrthoCAD works with different kind of robots, a table-top and a hand-held one are used.

Clinical tests were not performed yet. However, the whole system was developed under a collaboration with the Medical University of Innsbruck. Therefore, the system was used, evaluated and improved by surgeons. The feedback was positive throughout.

Chapter 8.1 describes the evaluation of the augmented in-situ view in collaboration with OrthoCAD and the table-top robot TTR. In Chapter 8.2, a femur neck osteotomy and a tibia wedge osteotomy are carried out using the TTR and a proprietary HHRD. Subsequently, in Chapter 8.3, the accuracies of the two robots are compared on the basis of milling tests performed on foam blocks. Chapter 8.4 contains an expert review of the presented system, which states the system's importance and opportunities. Finally, in Chapter 8.5, the evaluation results are summarized.

8.1 Augmented In-Situ View

Figure 8.1 shows an augmented in-situ view visualizing the surgical plan directly on the bone of the patient. The figures visualize a femoral neck osteotomy before and after the milling process. For these experiments, an Epson Moverio BT-200 was used and connected to the PC as described in Chapter 4.3. The figures also illustrate that only the most important objects are visualized on the OSTG (osteotomy planes, femur axis, landmarks and measurements between them). Menus and trackers are not visualized since menus cannot be used in this view and trackers already exist in the real scene. Occlusion effects are not applied and it remains a point of discussion if they are beneficial (important measurements or structures could be hidden).

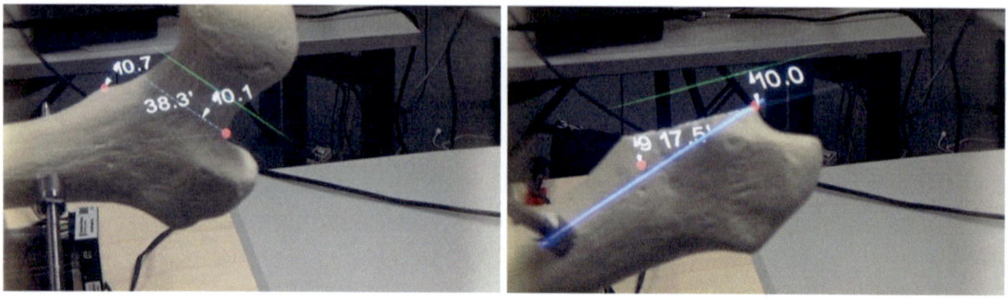

(a) Plan before execution (b) Plan after execution

Figure 8.1.: Augmented in-situ view of femoral neck osteotomy using OrthoCAD and the presented OSTG. Note that the images are taken from different trials.

After the planning phase the TTR is used to resect parts of the bone (see Figure 8.2). The augmented in-situ view visualizes a virtual end effector superimposing the real one. The home position of the end effector is visualized in white whereas the current position is visualized in red. This helps the surgeon to see how far the end effector is deflected. This might be a redundant information in case of an HHRD since the surgeon sees the deflection directly, however, in case of a bigger robot where the deflection is not directly visible, e.g. the presented TTR, this information is important. In this example, the surgeon defined a planar constraint perpendicular to the femoral neck. The shown scene is recorded after the surgeon has already removed the femoral head. It is visible how the constraint caused the robot to deflect.

8.2 Exemplary Interventions

The previous section evaluated the system consisting of OrthoCAD, OSTG and TTR according to how well the plan shown on the OSTG overlays the patient's bone. The goal of the following sections is to evaluate OrthoCAD in collaboration with two different robots. For this purpose, tests on bone imitations were performed. These imitations consist of hard foam comparable to the consistency of real bones. Figures showing the plans, the execution and the results illustrate the advantage and flexibility of the system.

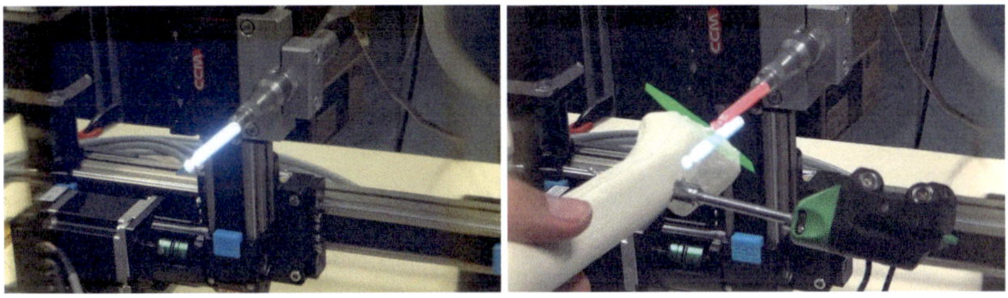

(a) Superimposed end effector (b) Evasive movement of end effector

Figure 8.2.: Augmented in-situ view of robot execution. The home position of the end effector is superimposed in white whereas the current position is shown in red.

8.2.1 Execution with Table-Top Robot

In a first stage, OrthoCAD was evaluated using the presented TTR prototype with 3-DoF as described in Chapter 7.7. This prototype consists of three translational joints. Even though the working volume could be much bigger, it is restricted (by software) to a cube with an edge length of 25 mm. This cube represents a working volume as it is used for HHRDs. This prototype was used in conjunction with the control system presented in Chapter 7.

Femoral Neck Osteotomy

In order to show the functionality of OrthoCAD together with the developed control system, a femoral neck osteotomy is performed. This procedure represents a preparation for a hip arthroplasty (hip replacement) in which the femur's head is completely replaced by an implant. Before the implant can be inserted into the femur, the head and the

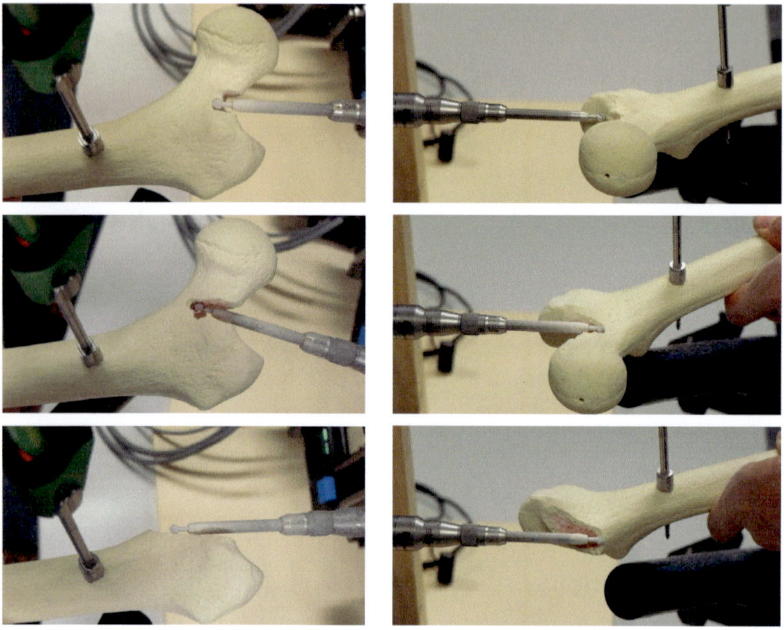

(a) First trial (b) Second trial

Figure 8.3.: Milling procedure of femoral neck osteotomy in several steps using TTR.

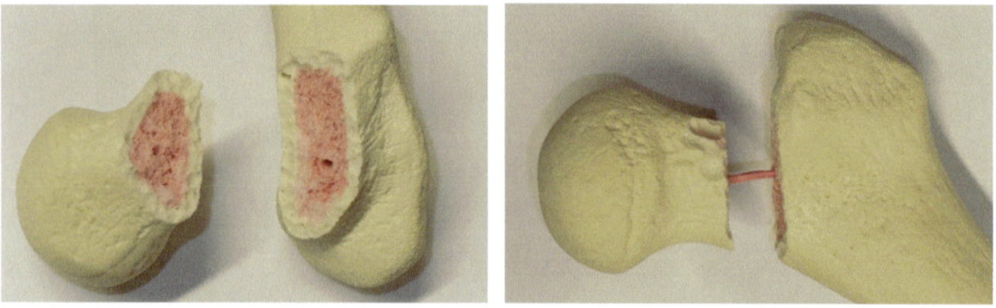

(a) First trial (b) Second trial

Figure 8.4.: The results of the femoral neck osteotomy using TTR.

neck have to be removed. This resection is performed by removing an approximately 1 cm thick cut from the femur neck. The cut of 1 cm is necessary to make space to remove the femur head from the acetabulum. Since the femur head is disposed after surgery, only one tracker is required. See Chapter 3.13 for the detailed explanation of this intervention as well as the planning data.

Figure 8.3 shows the milling procedure in several steps. This image sequence illustrates how the instrument tip evades from the defined constraints. Figure 8.4 shows the results of the intervention.

Wedge Osteotomy on Tibia with Malunion

A wedge osteotomy is performed on a tibia with a midshaft malunion. Malunions are bone fractures that healed in an unacceptable way, thus causing impairment and pain. This includes several misalignments like twists, bents, shortages of the bone or several of these. From a certain level on, malunions have to be corrected in a surgery. In case a larger part of the malunion has to be removed, filling material has to be inserted to guarantee the correct length of the bone.

In the following case, a midshaft malunion of a tibia caused a bent of approximately 27° (see Figure 8.5a). The first step to correct the tibia pose is to remove the biggest parts of the malunion. In the following example the surgeon decided to cut out a wedge that comprises the malunion. The wedge is chosen such that the two planes of the wedge are perpendicular to the axes of the two tibia parts (see Figure 8.5b). Since the resulting bone is too short, filling material must be inserted.

Figure 8.6 shows the milling procedure in several steps. This image sequence illustrates how the instrument tip evades from the defined constraints. In a real surgery two trackers would be required guaranteeing that both sides of the bone are milled with the maximal accuracy. However, in these tests only one tracker was attached. Figure 8.7 shows the results of the intervention.

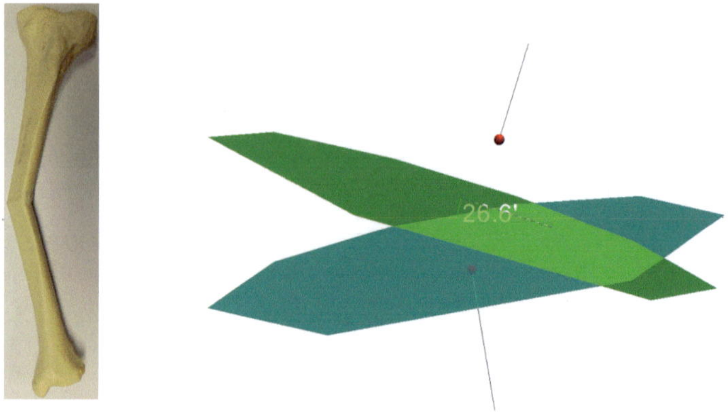

(a) Tibia with midshaft malunion **(b)** OrthoCAD plan: the two lines ending at the points represent the axes of the two tibia parts

Figure 8.5.: A tibia with midshaft malunion and the planned wedge osteotomy.

8.2.2 Execution with a Proprietary HHRD

In a second stage, OrthoCAD was evaluated using a proprietary HHRD prototype with 3-DoF. In contrast to the previous translational prototype, the proprietary one consists of two rotational and only one translation joint (similar to the one shown in Figure 7.1). The working volume of this device is specified by a cube with an edge length of approximately 25 mm. The rear part of the device is used to hold it and is rigid. The rotational joints are located at the end of the handle. The front segment of the device can be translated along the device's axis.

This prototype was used in conjunction with the proprietary control system. Therefore, the plan was sent to the proprietary control system once it was completed. The planning procedure in OrthoCAD works as usual and for the user there is no visible difference.

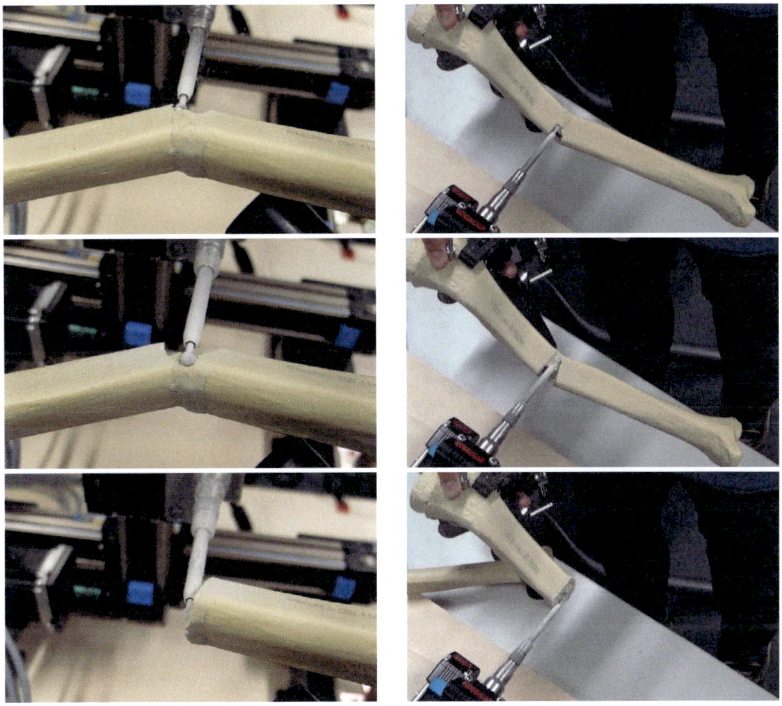

(a) First trial (b) Second trial

Figure 8.6.: Milling procedure of tibia wedge osteotomy in several steps using the TTR.

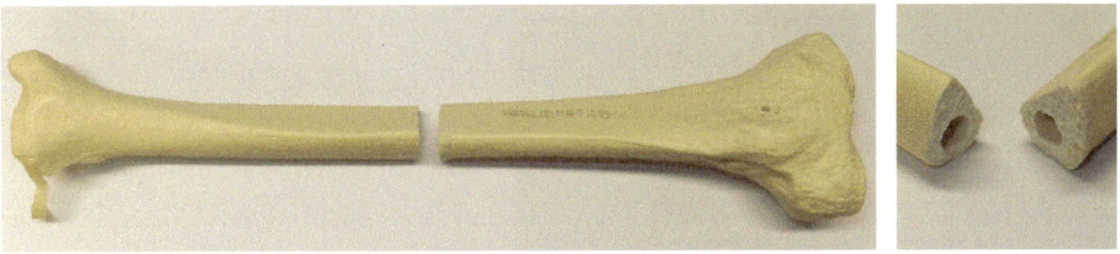

Figure 8.7.: The results of the tibia wedge osteotomy using the TTR.

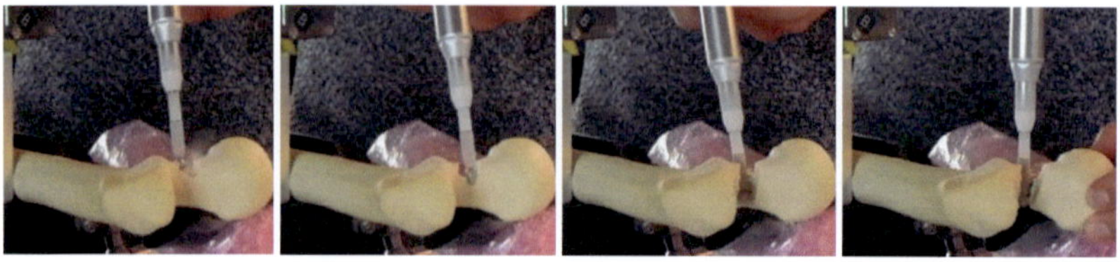

(a) First trial

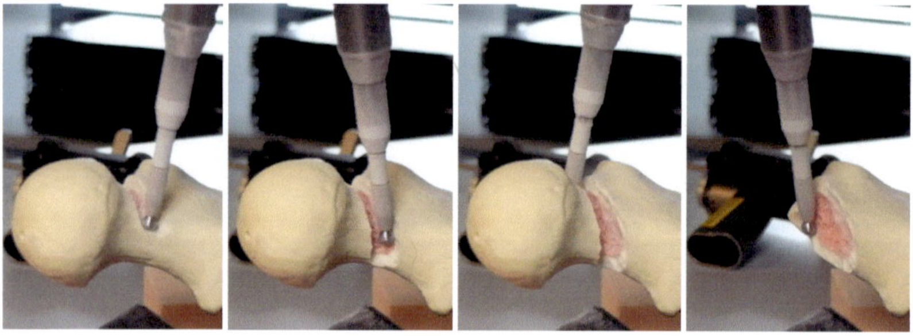

(b) Second trial

Figure 8.8.: Milling procedure of femoral neck osteotomy shown in several steps and from two different perspectives using the proprietary HHRD.

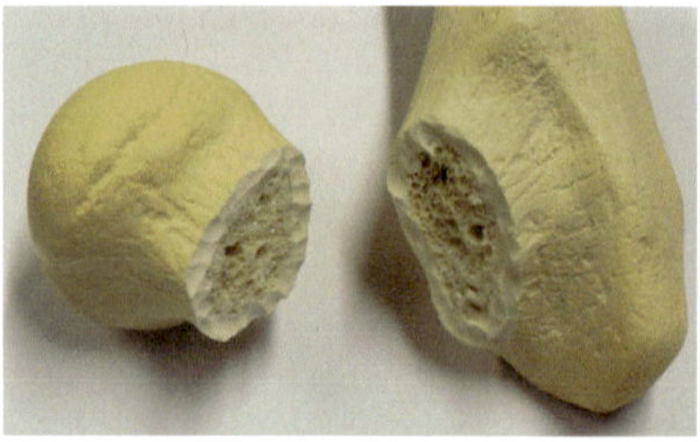

(a) First trial

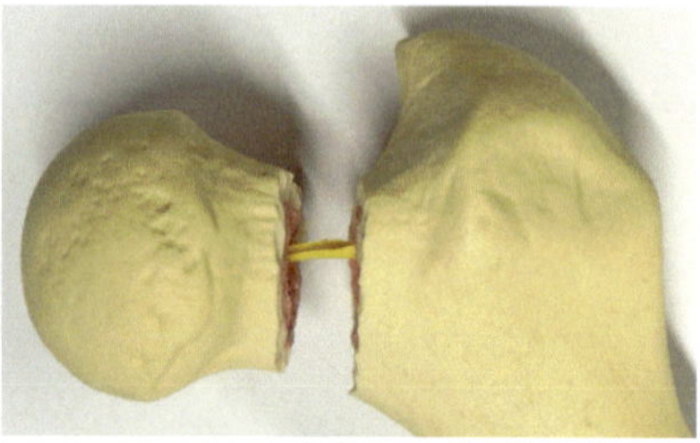

(b) Second trial

Figure 8.9.: The results of the femoral neck osteotomy using the proprietary HHRD.

Femoral Neck Osteotomy

As described in Chapter 8.2.1, a femoral neck osteotomy was performed. Figure 8.8 shows the milling procedure in several steps and from two different perspectives. These image sequences illustrate how the instrument tip evades from the defined constraints. Figure 8.9 shows the results of the intervention.

Wedge Osteotomy on Tibia with Malunion

As described in Chapter 8.2.1, a correction of a tibia with midshaft malunion was performed. Figure 8.10 shows the milling procedure in several steps. These image sequences illustrate how the instrument tip evades from the defined constraints. Figure 8.11 shows the results of the intervention.

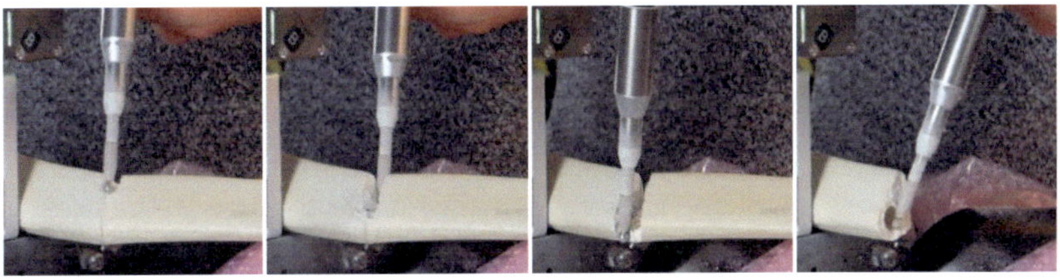

Figure 8.10.: Milling procedure of tibial wedge osteotomy in several steps using the proprietary HHRD.

8.3 Accuracy Comparison between TTR and HHRD

In order to compare the accuracy of the presented TTR with the proprietary HHRD the accuracy tests described in Chapter 7.8 were repeated using the HHRD. A cuboid as well as a half sphere were removed from a test block. In both cases the evasive mode was used. Figure 8.12 and

8.13 show the accuracies of the bottom plane of the milled cuboid and the surface of the milled half sphere, respectively. In general, the HHRD produces smoother surfaces and has less outliers. However, the difference in accuracy is stronger in the cuboid tests than in the half sphere tests. One reason that explains the accuracy improvement using an HHRD is the higher update rate of its control system. Whereas OrthoCAD and the presented control system run on the same computer under Windows, the HHRD control system runs on a separate computer using a real-time operating system.

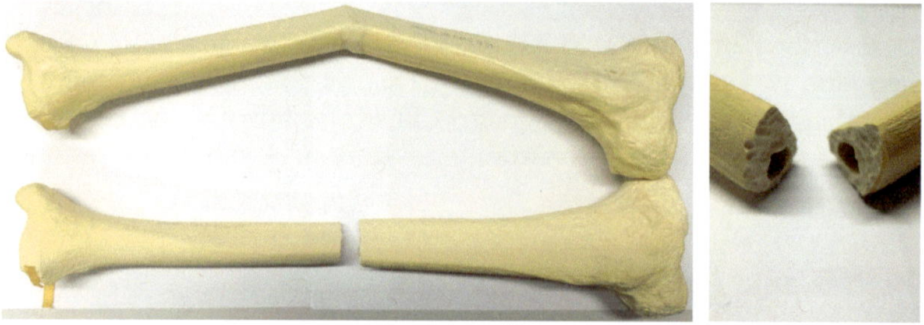

Figure 8.11.: The results of the tibial wedge osteotomy using the proprietary HHRD. An identical tibia is shown as reference.

8.4 Expert Review

To conclude this chapter, an expert review of one of the clinical partners is presented. As mentioned previously, OrthoCAD was developed in cooperation with the department for experimental orthopedics of the Medical University of Innsbruck. Prof. Dr. Michael Nogler is the head of this department and the main medical advisor of OrthoCAD. His complete review can be found in Appendix A.

Nogler describes that orthopedic surgery can be split into two parts: osteotomy and osteosynthesis. The former separates the bone into two or more parts whereas the latter combines the pieces again. In between,

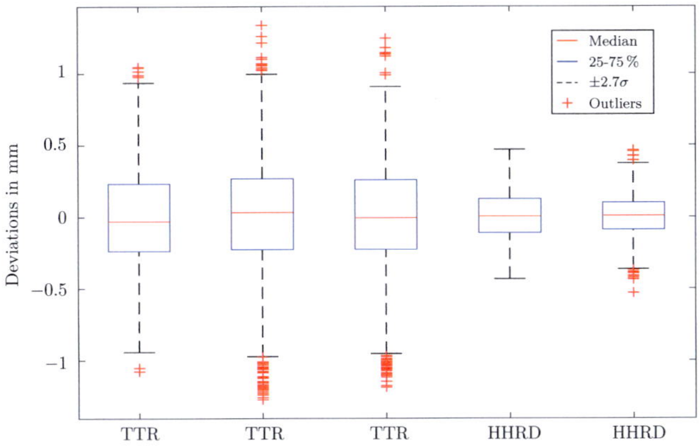

Figure 8.12.: Deviations to regression plane of milled cuboid using the evasive mode running on a TTR and an HHRD.

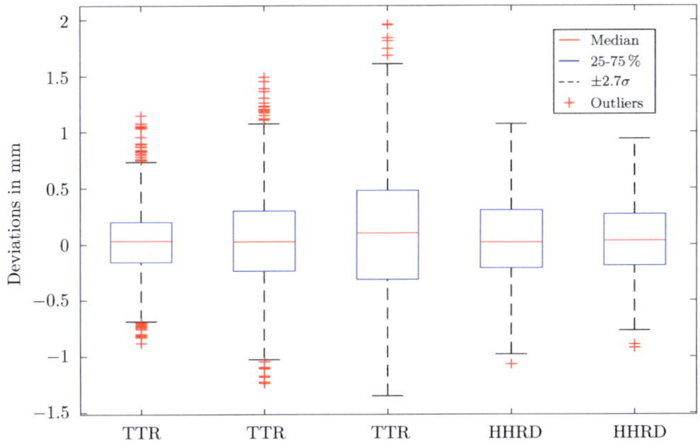

Figure 8.13.: Deviations to fitted sphere of milled half sphere. The radius was read from the CAD file and the center was fitted. In all cases the evasive mode was used.

the biomechanical situation of the bone is adapted by placing the bone parts accordingly. This principle resembles procedures known from wood or metal processing. In these sectors the material is processed using computer-assisted technologies. In the orthopedic sector, however, manual interventions are still standard. In the last years such systems improved and will probably be used more frequently in the future. The drawback of all these systems is that they are limited to one or two procedures. A computer-assisted planning and execution application for arbitrary interventions was missing so far.

OrthoCAD represents such a system and is the first approach to formulate a general platform for orthopedic surgery. It represents a change of paradigm in the operational actions of orthopedic surgery. For the first time a surgeon can use a CAD system in the sterile environment. With a robot the execution of the plan is possible. This causes a severe improvement in accuracy and precision compared to conventional manual systems.

8.5 Conclusion

This chapter presented the evaluation of the intraoperative planning and execution environment that can be employed in arbitrary orthopedic interventions. The first part summarized the evaluations of all individual components whereas the second part described different evaluations concerning the overall system:

- The augmented in-situ view is evaluated by planning and executing a femoral neck osteotomy using the OSTG and the table-top robot. It is shown that accurate overlays are guaranteed and that the visualization is only showing the most important information. Occlusion effects are not applied and it remains a point of discussion if they are beneficial.

- Two exemplary osteotomies, the first one on the femoral neck and the second one on a tibia with malunion, were planned in OrthoCAD and executed using the TTR and a proprietary HHRD. All tests were successful and demonstrate that the presented system does not depend on a specific robot.
- Milling tests on foam blocks with both robots were carried out in order to compare their results. Both robots produce results that are more accurate than conventional methods. The HHRD produces smoother surfaces than the TTR, which is explainable by a more optimized and faster processing (Microsoft Windows vs. real-time operating system).

Furthermore, an expert opinion emphasizes the importance and the opportunities of this new system. The review results from the collaboration with the Medical University of Innsbruck. The feedback of all other involved surgeons was positive throughout.

CHAPTER 9

Conclusion

Contents

The presented system for an intraoperative planning and execution of arbitrary interventions contributes to several different fields of science and engineering: computer science; robotics; electrical, control and mechanical engineering; and medicine. Thus, it is characterized by its interdisciplinarity. The level of contribution varies per field. The main contributions are in the field of computer science and medicine and can be summarized as computer-assisted surgery. Concerning computer science, the following domains are involved: image processing, photogrammetry, machine vision, computer graphic and augmented reality. In the field of medicine, this work mainly addresses orthopedic surgery but also traumatology and neurosurgery.

This chapter summarizes the essential aspects of the presented work. The results are discussed and future work shows how the proposed system can further be improved.

9.1 Summary

Although CAOS systems have been available for at least two decades, most interventions are still carried out in a conventional manual way. Several possible reasons explaining this fact were identified, which include the costs of these systems, the missing flexibility, the additional training and in case of a robotic execution, an increased radioactive exposure due to additional CT scans needed for a detailed planning. Therefore, surgeons and clinics regard this topic with a certain amount of skepticism.

In order to improve these drawbacks, a new system called OrthoCAD is proposed that improves several of these disadvantages. The presented system allows the surgeon to plan and execute arbitrary orthopedic interventions. The planning is performed intraoperatively without the requirement of additional imaging. Known concepts from commercial CAD-applications influenced the design of the planning software. Since normal input devices (keyboard and mouse) are not applicable in the OR (not sterilizable), new interaction concepts were presented. For this purpose, a touch screen as well as a navigated pointing device are used. In order to evaluate the functionality of OrthoCAD, a planning of a femoral neck osteotomy was performed.

In addition to the pointing device and the touch screen, arbitrary input devices can be connected to OrthoCAD via the OpenIGTLink protocol. This is demonstrated by an ultrasound workstation that, first, extracts the bone's surface from an US scan and, second, transmits it to OrthoCAD. A performance analysis shows the latency and frame rate of this protocol in real application scenarios.

Another important requirement was the development of a system that visualizes the planning data directly on the situs in order to prevent a continuous change of perspective from the patient to the monitor and vice versa. Therefore, an augmented in-situ view based on OSTG and a corresponding calibration technique were developed. The presented method calibrates display pixels individually without utilizing a model. The procedure is camera-based and runs completely automatic. Two approaches were discussed and evaluated. It is demonstrated that the first approach, which triangulates the display pixels, works well for OSTG with simple optics but fails for more complex ones. The second approach using the viewing rays of the display pixels works well for all tested OSTG and produces better accuracies than existing works. The evaluation together with OrthoCAD shows that this calibration allows an accurate overlay helping the surgeon to perform the intervention.

Subsequent to the planning procedure, the plan can be safely executed using different robots. For this purpose, a robot control system was developed. It guarantees that defined regions are not penetrated by the end effector. The surgeon can choose between different modes with distinct characteristics. In the evasive mode, the end effector evades the planned regions as long as the kinematics allow it. If the maximal deflection is reached, the power of the device is turned off. The smoothing mode resembles the evasive mode with the difference that the end effector oscillates around its axis. This results in milled surfaces with a higher smoothness. This control system was evaluated by milling different geometries inside a foam block. The results show that the evasive mode produces more accurate results than a rigid milling device and that the smoothing mode improves the surface quality even more.

Initial tests were conducted using a navigated milling device. Since the HHRD was not yet available, a first robot prototype with an attached milling device had to be developed. Finally, just shortly before the end of this research work, the HHRD was available for tests. Due to this reason, some of the methods were evaluated only with the self-developed prototype whereas some others were tested with both. The evaluation shows that devices running with the robot control system as well as the HHRD produce accurate results. Among all tested devices the HHRD produces slightly better results.

In contrast to existing specialized CAOS applications, the described generic and intraoperative planning and execution system for arbitrary orthopedic interventions provides the following benefits:

- lower price, due to the fact that only one generic application is used instead of several specialized ones and that the mechanics of an HHRD are simpler than the ones of a stationary robot with 6-DoF

- higher flexibility, due to the generic approach and the possibility to switch between planning and execution
- lower training time, since personal is only trained on one application instead of several ones and an HHRD is similar to a standard milling device that is already available in many ORs
- lower radioactive exposure, due to image-free planning

By improving these points it might be easier for surgeons and clinics to switch from conventional manual methods to computer-assisted interventions. This is confirmed by the collaborating experts of the Medical University of Innsbruck. They further state that by migrating to this innovative approach the outcome of interventions is improved. It can be summarized that all requirements are met.

9.2 Future Work

In the near future, the presented system can offer surgeons an easier migration from conventional to computer-assisted surgery. The presented solution can be extended in a variety of ways and adapted to special conditions. One option would be to adapt the application in such a way that it can be used in other medical disciplines such as neuro- or oral and maxillofacial surgery. Prior to clinical use, a number of extensions and improvements are required. Hereby, the following aspects seem particularly promising and important:

Currently, the surgeon has to manually select which objects are annotated with measurement values. In a future version, measurements should be visualized automatically according to predefined criteria. This is not trivial, since the interest and focus of the surgeon have to be identified. If there are only a few measurements shown, the wanted one might be missing. In case there are too many, the surgeon might not find the important one.

It was shown that the augmented in-situ view is useful and beneficial for orthopedic interventions. However, OSTG still have disadvantages that will be improved by upcoming generations (weight, field of view, depth of focus, etc.). Therefore, the surgeon will be able to wear the OSTG during the complete intervention without disturbing him.

The calibration of OSTG is often split into two parts, a one-time system calibration and a continuous eye adaptation. The presented approaches were focusing on the system calibration. In order to guarantee an accurate overlay over a longer time, the patient's eye must be tracked and its location continuously updated.

A semi-automatic mode could further improve the usage and handling of HHRDs. The HHRD automatically removes material inside its workspace (defined by its kinematics) while the user simply holds the device close to the structures that have to be removed. As soon as the material is removed the user continues moving the HHRD.

The proprietary control system and HHRD produces slightly better results than the presented control system together with the table-top robot. An improved control system should further decrease the inaccuracy of the presented system. For this purpose, the control system should be moved to a real-time operating system. Additionally, the optical navigation should be extended with additional sensors (e.g. gyroscopes) to increase the tracking frame rate.

As described before, this work concentrates on the control system and not the robot's hardware. Currently, HHRDs are still a matter of research with almost no commercial products available. Besides others, the key challenges are to further miniaturize the devices and to find a way for autoclaving.

APPENDIX A

Review Dr. Nogler

Univ. Prof. Mag. Dr. Michael Nogler MSc.
Experimentelle Orthopädie
Universität Innsbruck
Innrain 36
A-6020 Innsbruck
Michael.nogler@i-med.ac.at

Innsbruck, am 13.01.2017

Betrifft: **Beurteilung des OrthoCAD Systems aus orthopädisch chirurgischer Sicht**

Die Orthopädie beschäftigt sich in ihrem chirurgischen Teil mit der Bearbeitung von Knochen. Hierbei müssen Knochen mit unterschiedlichen Verfahren getrennt (**Osteotomie**) und nach Positionskorrektur wieder verbunden werden (**Osteosynthese**). Ziel dieser Verfahren ist es in der Regel, die biomechanische Situation zu verändern. Hierzu werden Achsen korrigiert, d.h. der getrennte Knochen wird in seiner Position verändert und in dieser veränderten Position wieder zusammengefügt.

Grundsätzlich gleichen diese Verfahren denen in der Mechanik bzw. im Handwerk wie etwa der Holz- oder Metallbearbeitung. In diesen Bereichen wird schon seit vielen Jahren nicht mehr freihändig, sondern auf der Basis von computerunterstützten Plänen, Material automatisiert bearbeitet. Eine solche CNC Technologie hat sich in der Orthopädie noch nicht durchgesetzt, alle Arbeiten erfolgen rein manuell. Allerdings gibt es in den letzten Jahren sehr vielversprechende Ansätze, computergesteuerte Frässysteme auch in der Knochenbearbeitung zu etablieren. Dabei sind zahlreiche technische Hürden zu nehmen. Insbesondere die Tatsache, dass es unmöglich ist, das Werkstück (den Knochen) einzuspannen zu fixieren ist eine große Schwierigkeit. Computerbasierten Navigationssysteme, die den Knochen in seiner Position präzise verfolgen können, erreichen aber mittlerweile eine Genauigkeit und Brauchbarkeit, die auf ihren intraoperativen Einsatz in größeren Zahlen hoffen lässt.

Alle bisher vorgestellten und eingeführten Systeme kranken aber daran, dass sie eine sehr enge Fokussierung auf meist nur eine oder zwei Prozeduren haben. Was in der Orthopädie fehlt, ist ein generelles Modell zum Einsatz von computerbasierten Planung und Umsetzung dieser Planungen operative Verfahrensschritte.

Das System **OrthoCAD** ist der erste bekannte Versuch eine allgemeine Plattform zu formulieren, in der es möglich ist, intraoperativ computerbasierten Operationsschritte zu planen. Das System basiert auf intraoperativen Positionsbestimmungen von relevanten Knochen-Landmarken. Diese Landmarken werden zu einer komplexen Darstellung des Knochens im Raum kombiniert und erlauben mit einem auf den Chirurgen als User zugeschnittenem User Interface die intraoperative Konstruktion der geplanten Osteotomie in Echtzeit. Das System stellt einen kompletten Paradigmenwechsel im operativen Vorgehen in der Orthopädie dar. Zum ersten Mal ist es dem Chirurgen möglich während der Operation im sterilen Umfeld ein CAD – System zu verwenden. Und mit einem intraoperativen Stresssystem ist dann die korrekte Umsetzung der Planung möglich. Dies bedeutet eine massive Erhöhung der Präzision und Wiederholgenauigkeit in der Orthopädie im Vergleich zu den bisherigen rein Hand geführten Systemen.

Michael Nogler

List of Figures

List of Tables

Acronyms

AR	Augmented Reality
CAD	Computer-Aided Design
CAOS	Computer-Assisted Orthopedic Surgery
CAS	Computer-Assisted Surgery
CT	Computer Tomography
DoF	Degree of Freedom
EM	Evasive Mode
GPGPU	General Purpose Graphical Processing Unit
GUI	Graphical User Interface
HHRD	Handheld Robotic Device
ITK	Insight Toolkit
MBARS	Mini Bone-Attached Robotic System
MITK	Medical Imaging Interaction Toolkit
MP	Measurement Point
MR	Magnetic Resonance
MRI	Magnetic Resonance Imaging
OpenIGTLink	Open Image-Guided Therapy Link
OR	Operating Room
OSTG	Optical See-Through Glasses
PCM	Power-Controlled Mode

PTPd	Precision Time Protocol daemon
RCS	Robot Control System
RMS	Root Mean Square
SDK	Software Development Kit
SM	Smoothing Mode
SVD	Singular Value Decomposition
TCC	Tracked Camera Calibration
TIC	Tracked Instrument Calibration
TTR	Table-Top Robot
US	Ultrasound
VTK	Visualization Toolkit

Bibliography

[1] B. Jaramaz, M. A. Hafez, and A. M. DiGioia, "Computer-assisted orthopaedic surgery", *Proceedings of the IEEE*, vol. 94, no. 9, pp. 1689–1695, 2006. DOI: 10.1109/JPROC.2006.880675.

[2] L. Joskowicz and E. J. Hazan, "Computer Aided Orthopaedic Surgery: Incremental shift or paradigm change?", *Medical Image Analysis*, vol. 33, pp. 84–90, 2016. DOI: 10.1016/j.media.2016.06.036.

[3] D. Putzer, J. L. Moctezuma, and M. Nogler, "Computer aided planning of orthopaedic surgeries: the definition of generic planning steps for bone removal procedures", *International Orthopaedics*, vol. 41, no. 11, pp. 2221–2227, 2017. DOI: 10.1007/s00264-017-3626-8.

[4] N. Andry de Bois-Regard, *Orthopaedia: Or, the Art of Correcting and Preventing Deformities in Children.* London: A. Millar, 1743.

[5] R. Takeuchi, Y. Umemoto, M. Aratake, H. Bito, I. Saito, K. Kumagai, Y. Sasaki, Y. Akamatsu, H. Ishikawa, T. Koshino, and T. Saito, "A mid term comparison of open wedge high tibial osteotomy vs unicompartmental knee arthroplasty for medial compartment osteoarthritis of the knee", *Journal of Orthopaedic Surgery and Research*, vol. 5, no. 65, pp. 1–8, 2010. DOI: 10.1186/1749-799X-5-65.

[6] F. Picard, J. E. Moody, A. M. DiGioia III, and B. Jaramaz, "Clinical classifications of CAOS systems", *Computer and Robotic Assisted Hip and Knee Surgery*, pp. 43–48, 2004.

[7] W. L. Bargar, A. Bauer, and M. Börner, "Primary and Revision Total Hip Replacement Using the Robodoc System", *Clinical orthopaedics and related research*, vol. 354, pp. 82–91, 1998.

[8] J. Raczkowsky, S. Däuber, D. Engel, H. Hoppe, W. Korb, O. Schorr, S. Hassfeld, and H. Wörn, "Karlsruhe Surgical Robotics Research", in *ACRA 2003 conference*, 2003, pp. 1–3.

[9] P. Knappe, I. Gross, S. Pieck, J. Wahrburg, S. Kuenzler, and F. Kerschbaumer, "Position control of a surgical robot by a navigation system", *Proceedings 2003 IEEE/RSJ International Conference on Intelligent Robots and Systems (IROS 2003) (Cat. No.03CH37453)*, vol. 3, no. October, pp. 3350–3354, 2003. DOI: 10.1109/IROS.2003.1249673.

[10] A. Wolf and B. Jaramaz, "MBARS: Mini bone attached robotic system for joint arthroplasty", *Proceedings of the First IEEE/RAS-EMBS International Conference on Biomedical Robotics and Biomechatronics, 2006, BioRob 2006*, vol. 2006, pp. 1053–1058, 2006. DOI: 10.1109/BIOROB.2006.1639231.

[11] S. Song, A. Mor, and B. Jaramaz, "HyBAR: Hybrid bone-attached robot for joint arthroplasty", *International Journal of Medical Robotics and Computer Assisted Surgery*, vol. 5, no. 2, pp. 223–231, 2009. DOI: 10.1002/rcs.254.

[12] J. Petermann, R. Kober, R. Heinze, J. J. Frölich, P. F. Heeckt, and L. Gotzen, "Computer-assisted planning and robot-assisted surgery in anterior cruciate ligament reconstruction", *Operative Techniques in Orthopaedics*, vol. 10, no. 1, pp. 50–55, 2000. DOI: 10.1016/S1048-6666(00)80042-7.

[13] S. J. Harris, M Jakopec, J Cobb, and B. L. Davies, "Intra-operative Application of a Robotic Knee Surgery System", *Medical Image Computing and Computer-Assisted Intervention: MICCAI 1999*, pp. 1116–1124, 1999. DOI: 10.1007/10704282_121.

[14] G. Brisson, T. Kanade, A. Digioia, and B. Jaramaz, "Precision Freehand Sculpting of Bone", *Medical Image Computing and Computer-Assisted Intervention*, pp. 105–112, 2004. DOI: 10.1007/978-3-540-30136-3_14.

[15] M. Kneissler, A. Hein, M. Mätzig, U. W. Thomale, T. C. Lueth, and C. Woiciechowsky, "Concept and clinical evaluation of navigated control in spine surgery", in *IEEE/ASME International Conference on Advanced Intelligent Mechatronics, AIM*, vol. 2, 2003, pp. 1084–1089. DOI: 10.1109/AIM.2003.1225493.

[16] G. Kane, G. Eggers, R. Boesecke, J. Raczkowsky, H. Wörn, R. Marmulla, and J. Mühling, "System Design of a Hand-Held Mobile Robot for Craniotomy", in *Medical Image Computing and Computer-Assisted Intervention – MICCAI 2009*, Springer Berlin Heidelberg, 2009, pp. 402–409. DOI: 10.1007/978-3-642-04268-3_50.

[17] B. Hagag, R. Abovitz, H. Kang, B. Schmitz, M. Conditt, and S. Robotics, "RIO: Robotic-Arm Interactive Orthopedic System MAKOplasty: User Interactive Haptic Orthopedic Robotics", in *Surgical Robotics: Systems Applications and Visions*, J. Rosen, B. Hannaford, and R. M. Satava, Eds., Boston, MA: Springer US, 2011, pp. 219–246. DOI: 10.1007/978-1-4419-1126-1_10.

[18] J. H. Lonner, "Robotically Assisted Unicompartmental Knee Arthroplasty with a Handheld Image-Free Sculpting Tool", *Orthopedic Clinics of North America*, vol. 47, no. 1, pp. 29–40, 2016. DOI: 10.1016/j.ocl.2015.08.024.

[19] K. C. Wong, S. M. Kumta, K. S. Leung, K. W. Ng, E. W. K. Ng, and K. S. Lee, "Integration of CAD/CAM planning into computer assisted orthopaedic surgery.", *Computer Aided Surgery*, vol. 15, no. 4-6, pp. 65–74, 2010. DOI: 10.3109/10929088.2010.514131.

[20] H. Haider, O. A. Barrera, and K. L. Garvin, "Minimally Invasive Total Knee Arthroplasty Surgery Through Navigated Freehand Bone Cutting. Winner of the 2005 "HAP" PAUL AWARD", *Journal of Arthroplasty*, vol. 22, no. 4, pp. 535–542, 2007. DOI: 10.1016/j.arth.2007.01.010.

[21] G. Wang, G. Zheng, P. Keppler, F. Gebhard, A. Staubli, U. Mueller, D. Schmucki, S. Fluetsch, and L. P. Nolte, "Implementation, accuracy evaluation, and preliminary clinical trial of a CT-free

navigation system for high tibial opening wedge osteotomy", *Computer aided surgery : official journal of the International Society for Computer Aided Surgery*, vol. 10, no. 2, pp. 73–85, 2005. DOI: 10.3109/10929080500228837.

[22] C. Plaskos, P. Cinquin, S. Lavallée, and A. J. Hodgson, "Praxiteles: a miniature bone-mounted robot for minimal access total knee arthroplasty", *The International Journal of Medical Robotics and Computer Assisted Surgery*, vol. 1, no. 4, pp. 67–79, 2005. DOI: 10.1002/rcs.59.

[23] D. Koulalis, P. F. O'Loughlin, C. Plaskos, D. Kendoff, M. B. Cross, and A. D. Pearle, "Sequential versus automated cutting guides in computer-assisted total knee arthroplasty", *The Knee*, vol. 18, no. 6, pp. 436–442, 2011. DOI: 10.1016/j.knee.2010.08.007.

[24] G. Brandt, K. Radermacher, A. Zimolong, G. Rau, P. Merloz, T. Klos, J. Robb, and H.-W. Staudte, "CRIGOS – Entwicklung eines Kompaktrobotersystems für die bildgeführte orthopädische Chirurgie", *Der Orthopäde*, vol. 29, no. 7, pp. 645–649, 2000. DOI: 10.1007/PL00003751.

[25] M. Sati, H.-U. Stäubli, Y. Bourquin, M. Kunz, and L.-P. Nolte, "Real-time computerized in situ guidance system for ACL graft placement", *Computer Aided Surgery*, vol. 7, no. 1, pp. 25–40, 2002. DOI: 10.1002/igs.10028.

[26] H. Handels, J. Ehrhardt, W. Plötz, and S. J. Pöppl, "Virtual planning of hip operations and individual adaption of endoprostheses in orthopaedic surgery", *International Journal of Medical Informatics*, vol. 58-59, pp. 21–28, 2000. DOI: 10.1016/S1386-5056(00)00072-1.

[27] D. J. Jacofsky and M. Allen, "Robotics in Arthroplasty: A Comprehensive Review", *Journal of Arthroplasty*, vol. 31, no. 10, pp. 2353–2363, 2016. DOI: 10.1016/j.arth.2016.05.026.

[28] M. Yamamura, N. Nakamura, H. Miki, T. Nishii, and N. Sugano, "Cement Removal from the Femur Using the ROBODOC System in Revision Total Hip Arthroplasty", *Advances in orthopedics*, vol. 2013, p. 5, 2013. DOI: 10.1155/2013/347358.

[29] H. Gottschling, M. Roth, A. Schweikard, and R. Burgkart, "Intraoperative, fluoroscopy-based planning for complex osteotomies of the proximal femur", *The international Journal of Medical Robotics and Computer Assisted Surgery (MRCAS)*, vol. 1, no. 3, pp. 67–73, 2005. DOI: 10.1002/rcs.29.

[30] S. T. Canale, *Campbell's Operative Orthopaedics*, 10th ed. Mosby, 2003, vol. 1-4. DOI: 10.1097/00006534-198903000-00043.

[31] J. E. Münchenberg, "Rechnergestützte Operationsplanung in der Mund-Kiefer-Gesichts-Chirurgie", PhD thesis, Universität Karlsruhe (TH), Herdecke, 2001, pp. 1–176.

[32] B. A. Klatt, N. Goyal, M. S. Austin, and W. J. Hozack, "Custom-Fit Total Knee Arthroplasty (OtisKnee) Results in Malalignment", *Journal of Arthroplasty*, vol. 23, no. 1, pp. 26–29, 2008. DOI: 10.1016/j.arth.2007.10.001.

[33] C. Scholes, V. Sahni, S. Lustig, D. A. Parker, and M. R. J. Coolican, "Patient-specific instrumentation for total knee arthroplasty does not match the pre-operative plan as assessed by intra-operative computer-assisted navigation", *Knee Surgery, Sports Traumatology, Arthroscopy*, vol. 22, no. 3, pp. 660–665, 2014. DOI: 10.1007/s00167-013-2670-1.

[34] N. Helmy, M. L. Dao Trong, and S. P. Kühnel, "Accuracy of Patient Specific Cutting Blocks in Total Knee Arthroplasty", *BioMed Research International*, vol. 2014, 2014. DOI: 10.1155/2014/562919.

[35] M. Shoham, I. H. Lieberman, E. C. Benzel, D. Togawa, E. Zehavi, B. Zilberstein, M. Roffman, A. Bruskin, A. Fridlander, L. Joskowicz, S. Brink-Danan, and N. Knoller, "Robotic assisted spinal surgery–from concept to clinical practice", *Computer Aided Surgery*, vol. 12, no. 2, pp. 105–115, 2007. DOI: 10.3109/10929080701243981.

[36] R. Elfring, M. De La Fuente, and K. Radermacher, "Assessment of optical localizer accuracy for computer aided surgery systems", *Computer Aided Surgery*, vol. 15, no. 1-3, pp. 1–12, 2010. DOI: 10.3109/10929081003647239.

[37] P.-L. Docquier, L. Paul, O. Cartiaux, C. Delloye, and X. Banse, "Computer-Assisted Resection and Reconstruction of Pelvic Tumor Sarcoma", *Sarcoma*, vol. 2010, p. 125 162, 2010. DOI: 10.1155/2010/125162.

[38] G. Brandt, A. Zimolong, L. Carrat, P. Merloz, H. W. Staudte, S. Lavallee, K. Radermacher, and G. Rau, "CRIGOS: a compact robot for image-guided orthopedic surgery", *IEEE Transactions on Information Technology in Biomedicine*, vol. 3, no. 4, pp. 252–260, 1999. DOI: 10.1109/4233.809169.

[39] Stryker. (2017). Mako: Robotic-Arm Assisted Surgery, [Online]. Available: https://www.stryker.com/us/en/portfolios/orthopaedics/joint-replacement/mako-robotic-arm-assisted-surgery.html (visited on 11/11/2017).

[40] C. N. Riviere, W. T. Ang, and P. K. Khosla, "Toward Active Tremor Canceling in Handheld Microsurgical Instruments", *IEEE Transactions on Robotics and Automation*, vol. 19, no. 5, pp. 793–800, 2003. DOI: 10.1109/TRA.2003.817506.

[41] B. C. Becker, S. Voros, R. a. Maclachlan, G. D. Hager, and C. N. Riviere, "Active Guidance of a Handheld Micromanipulator using Visual Servoing.", in *IEEE International Conference on Robotics and Automation (ICRA)*, vol. 2009, 2009, pp. 339–344. DOI: 10.1109/ROBOT.2009.5152632.

[42] L. Rosenberg, "Virtual fixtures: Perceptual tools for telerobotic manipulation", *Proceedings of IEEE Virtual Reality Annual International Symposium*, pp. 76–82, 1993. DOI: 10.1109/VRAIS.1993.380795.

[43] S. A. Bowyer, B. L. Davies, and F. Rodriguez Y Baena, "Active constraints/virtual fixtures: A survey", *IEEE Transactions on Robotics*, vol. 30, no. 1, pp. 138–157, 2014. DOI: 10.1109/TRO.2013.2283410.

[44] S. S. Park, R. D. Howe, and D. F. Torchiana, "Virtual fixtures for robot-assisted minimally-invasive cardiac surgery", *Proc. Medical Image Computing and Computer-Assisted Intervention (MICCAI)*, pp. 1419–1420, 2001.

[45] T. Xia, C. Baird, G. Jallo, K. Hayes, N. Nakajima, N. Hata, and P. Kazanzides, "An integrated system for planning, navigation and robotic assistance for skull base surgery", *International Journal of Medical Robotics and Computer Assisted Surgery*, vol. 4, no. 4, pp. 321–330, 2008. DOI: 10.1002/rcs.213.

[46] T. Haidegger, T. Xia, and P. Kazanzides, "Accuracy improvement of a neurosurgical robot system", *Proceedings of the 2nd Biennial IEEE/RAS-EMBS International Conference on Biomedical Robotics and Biomechatronics, BioRob 2008*, pp. 836–841, 2008. DOI: 10.1109/BIOROB.2008.4762912.

[47] A. Uneri, M. A. Balicki, J. Handa, P. Gehlbach, R. H. Taylor, and I. Iordachita, "New Steady-Hand Eye Robot with Micro-Force Sensing for Vitreoretinal Surgery", in *Biomedical Robotics and Biomechatronics (BioRob), 2010 3rd IEEE RAS and EMBS International Conference on*, 2010, pp. 814–819.

[48] L. B. Tabrizi and M. Mahvash, "Augmented reality–guided neurosurgery: accuracy and intraoperative application of an image projection technique", *Journal of Neurosurgery*, vol. 123, pp. 206–211, 2015. DOI: 10.3171/2014.9.JNS141001.Disclosure.

[49] X. Chen, L. Xu, Y. Wang, H. Wang, F. Wang, X. Zeng, Q. Wang, and J. Egger, "Development of a surgical navigation system based on augmented reality using an optical see-through head-mounted display", *Journal of Biomedical Informatics*, vol. 55, pp. 124–131, 2015. DOI: 10.1016/j.jbi.2015.04.003.

[50] H. Wang, F. Wang, A. P. Y. Leong, L. Xu, X. Chen, and Q. Wang, "Precision insertion of percutaneous sacroiliac screws using a novel augmented reality-based navigation system: a pilot study", *International Orthopaedics*, vol. 40, no. 9, pp. 1941–1947, 2016. DOI: 10.1007/s00264-015-3028-8.

[51] G. Badiali, V. Ferrari, F. Cutolo, C. Freschi, D. Caramella, A. Bianchi, and C. Marchetti, "Augmented reality as an aid in maxillofacial surgery: Validation of a wearable system allowing maxillary repositioning", *Journal of Cranio-Maxillofacial Surgery*, vol. 42, no. 8, pp. 1970–1976, 2014. DOI: 10.1016/j.jcms.2014.09.001.

[52] A. Elmi-Terander, H. Skulason, M. Söderman, J. Racadio, R. Homan, D. Babic, N. van der Vaart, and R. Nachabe, "Surgical Navigation Technology Based on Augmented Reality and Integrated 3D Intraoperative Imaging: A Spine Cadaveric Feasibility and Accuracy Study.", *Spine*, vol. 41, no. 21, E1303–E1311, 2016. DOI: 10.1097/BRS.0000000000001830.

[53] J. P. Rolland and H. Fuchs, "Optical Versus Video See-Through Head-Mounted Displays in Medical Visualization", *Presence: Teleoperators and Virtual Environments*, vol. 9, no. 3, pp. 287–309, 2000. DOI: 10.1162/105474600566808.

[54] H. Hoppe, "Projektorbasierte Erweiterte Realität in der rechnergestützten Chirurgie", PhD thesis, Universität Fridericiana zu Karlsruhe (TH), Herdecke, 2004, pp. 1–151.

[55] B. J. Dixon, M. J. Daly, H. Chan, A. D. Vescan, I. J. Witterick, and J. C. Irish, "Surgeons blinded by enhanced navigation: The effect of augmented reality on attention", *Surgical Endoscopy and Other Interventional Techniques*, vol. 27, no. 2, pp. 454–461, 2013. DOI: 10.1007/s00464-012-2457-3.

[56] N. Navab, J. Traub, T. Sielhorst, M. Feuerstein, and C. Bichlmeier, "Action- and workflow-driven augmented reality for computer-aided medical procedures", *IEEE Computer Graphics and Applications*, vol. 27, no. 5, pp. 10–14, 2007. DOI: 10.1109/MCG.2007.117.

[57] G. Kramida and A. Varshney, "Resolving the Vergence-Accommodation Conflict in Head Mounted Displays", *IEEE Transactions on Visualization and Computer Graphics*, vol. 22, no. 7, pp. 1–16, 2015. DOI: 10.1109/TVCG.2015.2473855.

[58] A. L. Janin, D. W. Mizell, and T. P. Caudell, "Calibration of head-mounted displays for augmented reality applications", in *Proceedings of IEEE Virtual Reality Annual International Symposium*, 1993, pp. 246 –255. DOI: 10.1109/VRAIS.1993.380772.

[59] R. Azuma and G. Bishop, "Improving static and dynamic registration in an optical see-through HMD", in *in Proceedings of the 21st Annual Conference on Computer Graphics and Interactive Techniques - SIGGRAPH '94*, 1994, pp. 197–204. DOI: 10.1145/192161.192199.

[60] A. Fuhrmann, D. Schmalstieg, and W. Purgathofer, "Fast calibration for augmented reality", in *Proceedings of the ACM symposium on Virtual reality software and technology - VRST '99*, 1999, pp. 166–167. DOI: 10.1145/323663.323692.

[61] E. McGarrity and M. Tuceryan, "A method for calibrating see-through head-mounted displays for AR", in *Proceedings 2nd IEEE and ACM International Workshop on Augmented Reality (IWAR'99)*, IEEE, 1999, pp. 75–84. DOI: 10.1109/IWAR.1999.803808.

[62] M. Tuceryan and N. Navab, "Single point active alignment method (SPAAM) for optical see-through HMD calibration for AR", in *Proceedings IEEE and ACM International Symposium on Augmented Reality (ISAR 2000)*, IEEE, IEEE, 2000, pp. 149–158. DOI: 10.1109/ISAR.2000.880938.

[63] Y. Genc, M. Tuceryan, A. Khamene, and N. Navab, "Optical see-through calibration with vision-based trackers: Propagation of projection matrices", in *Proceedings - IEEE and ACM International Symposium on Augmented Reality, ISAR 2001*, 2001, pp. 147–156. DOI: 10.1109/ISAR.2001.970524.

[64] Y. Genc, M. Tuceryan, and N. Navab, "Practical solutions for calibration of optical see-through devices", in *Proceedings - International Symposium on Mixed and Augmented Reality, ISMAR 2002*, 2002, pp. 169–175. DOI: 10.1109/ISMAR.2002.1115086.

[65] F. Kellner, B. Bolte, G. Bruder, U. Rautenberg, F. Steinicke, M. Lappe, and R. Koch, "Geometric calibration of head-mounted displays and its effects on distance estimation", *IEEE Transactions on Visualization and Computer Graphics*, vol. 18, no. 4, pp. 589–596, 2012. DOI: 10.1109/TVCG.2012.45.

[66] E. McGarrity, Y. Genc, M. Tuceryan, C. Owen, and N. Navab, "A new system for online quantitative evaluation of optical see-through augmentation", *Proceedings IEEE and ACM International Symposium on Augmented Reality*, pp. 157–166, 2001. DOI: 10.1109/ISAR.2001.970525.

[67] C. B. Owen, J. Zhou, A. Tang, and F. Xiao, "Display-relative calibration for optical see-through head-mounted displays", in *ISMAR 2004: Proceedings of the Third IEEE and ACM International Symposium on Mixed and Augmented Reality*, 2004, pp. 70–78. DOI: 10.1109/ISMAR.2004.28.

[68] R. Y. Tsai, "A Versatile Camera Calibration Technique for High-Accuracy 3D Machine Vision Metrology Using Off-the-Shelf TV Cameras and Lenses", *IEEE Journal on Robotics and Automation*, vol. 3, no. 4, pp. 323–344, 1987. DOI: 10.1109/JRA.1987.1087109.

[69] Y. Itoh and G. Klinker, "Interaction-free calibration for optical see-through head-mounted displays based on 3D Eye localization", *2014 IEEE Symposium on 3D User Interfaces (3DUI)*, pp. 75–82, 2014. DOI: 10.1109/3DUI.2014.6798846.

[70] K. Moser, Y. Itoh, K. Oshima, J. E. Swan II, G. Klinker, and C. Sandor, "Subjective Evaluation of a Semi-Automatic Optical See-Through Head-Mounted Display Calibration Technique", *IEEE Transactions on Visualization and Computer Graphics*, vol. 21, no. 4, pp. 491–500, 2015. DOI: 10.1109/TVCG.2015.2391856.

[71] S. Lee and H. Hua, "A robust camera-based method for optical distortion calibration of head-mounted displays", in *Virtual Reality (VR), 2013 IEEE*, vol. 1, 2013, pp. 27–30. DOI: 10.1109/VR.2013.6549353.

[72] Y. Itoh and G. Klinker, "Simultaneous Direct and Augmented View Distortion Calibration of Optical See-Through Head-Mounted Displays", *2015 IEEE International Symposium on Mixed and Augmented Reality*, pp. 43–48, 2015. DOI: 10.1109/ISMAR.2015.14.

[73] S. J. Gilson, A. W. Fitzgibbon, and A. Glennerster, "Spatial calibration of an optical see-through head-mounted display", *Journal of Neuroscience Methods*, vol. 173, no. 1, pp. 140–146, 2008. DOI: 10.1016/j.jneumeth.2008.05.015.

[74] L. C. L. Cao, Y. Z. Y. Zhang, J. W. J. Wei, Y. H. Y. Hu, and D. L. D. Liu, "Calibration and error analysis of surgical instrument based on stereo camera", in *Biomedical Engineering and Informatics (BMEI), 2010 3rd International Conference on*, vol. 4, 2010, pp. 1435–1439. DOI: 10.1109/BMEI.2010.5639405.

[75] A. De Leon-Cuevas, S. Tovar-Arriaga, E. Gorrostieta-Hurtado, L. Lopez-Vallejo, J. M. Ramos-Arreguin, and H.-M. Barragan-Campos, "Tool calibration with an optical tracker for skull milling", *2015 International Conference on Electronics, Communications and Computers (CONIELECOMP)*, pp. 149–154, 2015. DOI: 10.1109/CONIELECOMP.2015.7086942.

[76] K. D. Kim, J. P. Johnson, J. E. Masciopinto, O. Bloch, M. J. Saracen, and J. P. Villablanca, "Universal calibration of surgical instruments for spinal stereotaxy", *Neurosurgery*, vol. 44, no. 1, pp. 173–178, 1999. DOI: 10.1097/00006123-199901000-00105.

[77] J. B. West and C. R. Maurer, "Designing optically tracked instruments for image-guided surgery", *IEEE Transactions on Medical Imaging*, vol. 23, no. 5, pp. 533–545, 2004. DOI: 10.1109/TMI.2004.825614.

[78] H. K. Gumprecht, D. C. Widenka, and C. B. Lumenta, "First Experience with the BrainLab VectorVision Neuronavigation System", in *Minimally Invasive Techniques for Neurosurgery: Current Status and Future Perspectives*, D. Hellwig and B. L. Bauer, Eds. Berlin, Heidelberg: Springer Berlin Heidelberg, 1998, pp. 207–213. DOI: 10.1007/978-3-642-58731-3_36.

[79] O. Schorr, N. Hata, A. Bzostek, R. Kumar, C. Burghart, R. H. Taylor, and R. Kikinis, "Distributed Modular Computer-Integrated Surgical Robotic Systems: Architecture for Intelligent Object Distribution", in *Medical Image Computing and Computer-Assisted*

Intervention – MICCAI 2000: Third International Conference, vol. 3, 2000, pp. 979–987. DOI: 10.1007/978-3-540-40899-4_102.

[80] J. Von Spiczak, E. Samset, S. Dimaio, G. Reitmayr, D. Schmalstieg, C. Burghart, and R. Kikinis, "Device connectivity for image-guided medical applications", in *15th Annual Conference on Medicine Meets Virtual Reality, MMVR 2007*, vol. 125, 2007, pp. 482–484.

[81] J. Tokuda, G. S. Fischer, X. Papademetris, Z. Yaniv, L. Ibanez, P. Cheng, H. Liu, J. Blevins, J. Arata, A. J. Golby, T. Kapur, S. Pieper, E. C. Burdette, G. Fichtinger, C. M. Tempany, N. Hata, J Alexandra, T. Kapur, S. Pieper, E. C. Burdette, G. Fichtinger, M Clare, and N. Hata, "OpenIGTLink: an open network protocol for image-guided therapy environment", *International Journal of Medical Robotics and Computer Assisted Surgery*, vol. 5, no. 4, pp. 423–434, 2009. DOI: 10.1002/rcs.274.

[82] A. Fedorov, R. Beichel, J. Kalpathy-Cramer, J. Finet, J.-C. Fillion-Robin, S. Pujol, C. Bauer, D. Jennings, F. Fennessy, M. Sonka, J. Buatti, S. Aylward, J. V. Miller, S. Pieper, and R. Kikinis, "3D Slicer as an image computing platform for the Quantitative Imaging Network.", *Magnetic resonance imaging*, vol. 30, no. 9, pp. 1323–41, 2012. DOI: 10.1016/j.mri.2012.05.001.

[83] S. Ordas, Z. Yaniv, P. Cheng, J. Tokuda, H. Liu, N. Hata, and K. Cleary, "Interfacing proprietary hardware with the image-guided surgery toolkit (IGSTK): a case for the OpenIGTLink protocol", *Proceedings of SPIE*, vol. 7264, pp. 1–7, 2009. DOI: 10.1117/12.811667.

[84] H.-j. Kang, P. J. Stolka, and E. Boctor, "OpenIGTLinkMUSiiC : A Standard Communications Protocol for Advanced Ultrasound Research", *MIDAS Journal*, pp. 1–12, 2011.

[85] J. Egger, J. Tokuda, L. Chauvin, B. Freisleben, C. Nimsky, T. Kapur, and W. Wells, "Integration of the OpenIGTLink Network Protocol for image-guided therapy with the medical platform MeVisLab", *International Journal of Medical Robotics and Computer Assisted Surgery*, vol. 8, no. 3, pp. 282–290, 2012. DOI: 10.1002/rcs.1415.

[86] A. Lasso, T. Heffter, A. Rankin, C. Pinter, T. Ungi, and G. Fichtinger, "PLUS: open-source toolkit for ultrasound-guided intervention systems.", *IEEE transactions on bio-medical engineering*, pp. 1–11, 2014. DOI: 10.1109/TBME.2014.2322864.

[87] M. J. Clarkson, G. Zombori, S. Thompson, J. Totz, Y. Song, M. Espak, S. Johnsen, D. Hawkes, and S. Ourselin, "The NifTK software platform for image-guided interventions: platform overview and NiftyLink messaging", *International Journal of Computer Assisted Radiology and Surgery*, vol. 10, no. 3, pp. 301–316, 2014. DOI: 10.1007/s11548-014-1124-7.

[88] O. Zettinig, B. Fuerst, R. Kojcev, M. Esposito, M. Salehi, W. Wein, J. Rackerseder, B. Frisch, and N. Navab, "Toward Real-time 3D Ultrasound Image Registration-based Visual Servoing for Interventional Navigation", *2016 IEEE International Conference on Robotics and Automation (ICRA)*, pp. 945–950, 2016.

[89] S. Tauscher, J. Tokuda, G. Schreiber, T. Neff, N. Hata, and T. Ortmaier, "OpenIGTLink interface for state control and visualisation of a robot for image-guided therapy systems", *International Journal of Computer Assisted Radiology and Surgery*, vol. 10, no. 3, pp. 285–292, 2015. DOI: 10.1007/s11548-014-1081-1.

[90] A. Rasoulian, J. Osborn, S. Sojoudi, S. Nouranian, V. A. Lessoway, R. N. Rohling, and P. Abolmaesumi, "A System for Ultrasound-Guided Spinal Injections : A Feasibility Study", *International Conference on Information Processing in Computer-Assisted Interventions*, pp. 90–99, 2014.

[91] M. Nolden, S. Zelzer, A. Seitel, D. Wald, M. Müller, A. M. Franz, D. Maleike, M. Fangerau, M. Baumhauer, L. Maier-Hein, K. H. Maier-Hein, H. P. Meinzer, and I. Wolf, "The medical imaging interaction toolkit: Challenges and advances: 10 years of open-source development", *International Journal of Computer Assisted Radiology and Surgery*, vol. 8, no. 4, pp. 607–620, 2013. DOI: 10.1007/s11548-013-0840-8.

[92] H. J. Johnson, M. M. McCormick, and L. Ibanez, *The ITK Software Guide Book 2: Design and Functionality*, ITK 4.7. Kitware Inc., 2015, p. 520.

[93] W. Schroeder, K. Martin, and B. Lorensen, *The Visualization Toolkit*, 4th ed. Kitware Inc., 2006, p. 528.

[94] C. Sanderson and R. Curtin, "Armadillo: a template-based C++ library for linear algebra", *The Journal of Open Source Software*, vol. 1, no. 2, 2016. DOI: 10.21105/joss.00026.

[95] S. Jones, H. Al Hussainy, F. Ali, R. Betts, and M. Flowers, "Scarf osteotomy for hallux valgus", *The Journal of Bone and Joint Surgery*, vol. 86, no. 6, pp. 830–836, 2004. DOI: 10.1302/0301-620X.86B6.15000.

[96] H. Mukawa, K. Akutsu, I. Matsumura, S. Nakano, T. Yoshida, M. Kuwahara, and K. Aiki, "A full-color eyewear display using planar waveguides with reflection volume holograms", *Journal of the Society for Information Display*, vol. 17, no. 3, p. 185, 2009. DOI: 10.1889/JSID17.3.185.

[97] K. Sarayeddine, K. Mirza, P. Benoit, and X. Hugel, "Monolithic light guide optics enabling new user experience for see-through AR glasses", in *Proceedings of SPIE - The International Society for Optical Engineering*, vol. 9202, 2014. DOI: 10.1117/12.2064172.

[102] J. Salvi, S. Fernandez, T. Pribanic, and X. Llado, "A state of the art in structured light patterns for surface profilometry", *Pattern Recognition*, vol. 43, no. 8, pp. 2666–2680, 2010. DOI: 10.1016/j.patcog.2010.03.004.

[104] L. Ibanez, W. Schroeder, L. Ng, and J. Cates, "The ITK Software Guide", *The ITK Software Guide*, Updated for ITK version 2.4, vol. Second, no. May, p. 804, 2005.

[105] K. Correll, N. Barendt, and M. Branicky, "Design considerations for software only implementations of the IEEE 1588 precision time protocol", *Conference on IEEE*, vol. 1588, no. November, pp. 10–12, 2005. DOI: 10.1.1.67.4565.

[106] R. J. Teather, A. Pavlovych, W. Stuerzlinger, and I. S. MacKenzie, "Effects of tracking technology, latency, and spatial jitter on object movement", in *3DUI - IEEE Symposium on 3D User Interfaces 2009 - Proceedings*, 2009, pp. 43–50. DOI: 10.1109/3DUI.2009.4811204.

[107] X. Wu and R. H. Taylor, "A framework for calibration of electromagnetic surgical navigation systems", in *Proceedings 2003 IEEE/RSJ International Conference on Intelligent Robots and Systems (IROS 2003)*, vol. 1, 2003, pp. 547–552. DOI: 10.1109/IROS.2003.1250686.

[109] Z. Zhang, "A flexible new technique for camera calibration", *IEEE Transactions on Pattern Analysis and Machine Intelligence*, vol. 22, no. 11, pp. 1330–1334, 2000. DOI: 10.1109/34.888718.

[110] N. Otsu, "A Threshold Selection Method from Gray-Level Histograms", *IEEE Transactions on Systems, Man, and Cybernetics*, vol. 9, no. 1, pp. 62–66, 1979. DOI: 10.1109/TSMC.1979.4310076.

[111] W. N. Martin and J. K. Aggarwal, "Volumetric descriptions of objects from multiple views.", *IEEE transactions on pattern analysis and machine intelligence*, vol. 5, no. 2, pp. 150–8, 1983. DOI: 10.1109/TPAMI.1983.4767367.

[112] W. E. Lorensen and H. E. Cline, "Marching cubes: A high resolution 3D surface construction algorithm", *ACM SIGGRAPH Computer Graphics*, vol. 21, no. 4, pp. 163–169, 1987. DOI: 10.1145/37402.37422.

[113] P. Kazanzides, B. Mittelstadt, B. Musits, W. Bargar, J. Zuhars, B. Williamson, P. Cain, and E. Carbone, "An integrated system for cementless hip replacement", *IEEE Engineering in Medicine and Biology Magazine*, vol. 14, no. 3, pp. 307–313, 1995. DOI: 10.1109/51.391772.

Own Publications

[98] M. Klemm, H. Hoppe, and F. Seebacher, "[Poster] Non-parametric camera-based calibration of optical see-through glasses for augmented reality applications", in *Mixed and Augmented Reality (ISMAR), 2014 IEEE International Symposium on*, 2014, pp. 273–274. DOI: 10.1109/ISMAR.2014.6948446.

[99] M. Klemm, F. Seebacher, and H. Hoppe, "Non-Parametric Camera-Based Calibration of Optical See-Through Glasses for AR Applications", in *2016 International Conference on Cyberworlds (CW)*, 2016, pp. 33–40. DOI: 10.1109/CW.2016.13.

[100] M. Klemm, F. Seebacher, and H. Hoppe, "High accuracy pixel-wise spatial calibration of optical see-through glasses", *Computers & Graphics*, vol. 64, pp. 51–61, 2017. DOI: 10.1016/j.cag.2017.02.001.

[101] H. Hoppe, F. Seebacher, and M. Klemm, "Nicht modellbasierte Kalibration von Kameras mit Monitoren", in *Proc. Bildverarbeitung für die Medizin (BVM) 2016*, 2016, pp. 50–55. DOI: 10.1007/978-3-662-49465-3_11.

[103] M. Klemm, T. Kirchner, J. Gröhl, D. Cheray, M. Nolden, A. Seitel, H. Hoppe, L. Maier-Hein, and A. M. Franz, "MITK-OpenIGTLink for combining open-source toolkits in real-time computer-assisted interventions", *International Journal of Computer Assisted Radiology and Surgery*, vol. 12, no. 3, pp. 351–361, 2017. DOI: 10.1007/s11548-016-1488-y.

[108] M. Klemm, F. Seebacher, and H. Hoppe, "Flexible Three-dimensional Camera-based Reconstruction and Calibration of Tracked Instruments", in *2016 19th International Conference on Information Fusion (FUSION)*, 2016, pp. 861–867.

Karlsruhe Series on Intelligent Sensor-Actuator-Systems

Edited by Prof. Dr.-Ing. Uwe D. Hanebeck // ISSN 1867-3813

Band 1 **Oliver Schrempf**
Stochastische Behandlung von Unsicherheiten in kaskadierten dynamischen Systemen. 2008
ISBN 978-3-86644-287-0

Band 2 **Florian Weißel**
Stochastische modell-prädiktive Regelung nichtlinearer Systeme. 2009
ISBN 978-3-86644-348-8

Band 3 **Patrick Rößler**
Telepräsente Bewegung und haptische Interaktion in ausgedehnten entfernten Umgebungen. 2009
ISBN 978-3-86644-346-4

Band 4 **Kathrin Roberts**
Modellbasierte Herzbewegungsschätzung für robotergestützte Interventionen. 2009
ISBN 978-3-86644-353-2

Band 5 **Felix Sawo**
Nonlinear state and parameter estimation of spatially distributed systems. 2009
ISBN 978-3-86644-370-9

Band 6 **Gregor F. Schwarzenberg**
Untersuchung der Abbildungseigenschaften eines 3D-Ultraschall-Computertomographen zur Berechnung der 3D-Abbildungsfunktion und Herleitung einer optimierten Sensorgeometrie. 2009
ISBN 978-3-86644-393-8

Die Bände sind unter www.ksp.kit.edu als PDF frei verfügbar oder als Druckausgabe bestellbar.

Band 7 **Marco Huber**
Probabilistic Framework for Sensor Management. 2009
ISBN 978-3-86644-405-8

Band 8 **Frederik Beutler**
Probabilistische modellbasierte Signalverarbeitung zur instantanen Lageschätzung. 2010
ISBN 978-3-86644-442-3

Band 9 **Marc Peter Deisenroth**
Efficient Reinforcement Learning using Gaussian Processes. 2010
ISBN 978-3-86644-569-7

Band 10 **Evgeniya Ballmann**
Physics-Based Probabilistic Motion Compensation of Elastically Deformable Objects. 2012
ISBN 978-3-86644-862-9

Band 11 **Peter Krauthausen**
Learning Dynamic Systems for Intention Recognition in Human-Robot-Cooperation. 2013
ISBN 978-3-86644-952-7

Band 12 **Antonia Pérez Arias**
Haptic Guidance for Extended Range Telepresence. 2013
ISBN 978-3-7315-0035-3

Band 13 **Marcus Baum**
Simultaneous Tracking and Shape Estimation of Extended Objects. 2013
ISBN 978-3-7315-0078-0

Band 14 **Benjamin Noack**
State Estimation for Distributed Systems with Stochastic and Set-membership Uncertainties. 2014
ISBN 978-3-7315-0124-4

Band 15 **Jörg Fischer**
Optimal Sequence-Based Control of Networked Linear Systems. 2014
ISBN 978-3-7315-0305-7

Band 16 **Marc Reinhardt**
Linear Estimation in Interconnected Sensor Systems with Information Constraints. 2015
ISBN 978-3-7315-0342-2

Band 17 **Gerhard Kurz**
Directional Estimation for Robotic Beating Heart Surgery. 2015
ISBN 978-3-7315-0382-8

Band 18 **Igor Gilitschenski**
Deterministic Sampling for Nonlinear Dynamic State Estimation. 2016
ISBN 978-3-7315-0473-3

Band 19 **Florian Faion**
Tracking Extended Objects in Noisy Point Clouds with Application in Telepresence Systems. 2016
ISBN 978-3-7315-0517-4

Band 20 **Martin Klemm**
Intraoperative Planning and Execution of Arbitrary Orthopedic Interventions Using Handheld Robotics and Augmented Reality. 2018
ISBN 978-3-7315-0800-7
